AIMEE?   **MONTANA?**
PHYLICIA?   **ELIZABETH?**
JASON?   **ALEC?**   **JERMAINE?**
TYLER?

It's a good thing it takes nine months to have a baby. Sometimes it seems a new parent needs that much time to choose the perfect name!

With *The Very Best Book of Baby Names*, you can browse through thousands of names—from the traditional to the trendsetting, the popular to the unusual—and find the name that's just right!

THE VERY BEST BOOK OF

BABY NAMES

Berkley Books by Barbara Kay Turner

THE VERY BEST BOOK OF BABY NAMES
BABY NAMES FOR THE '90s
NAME THAT BABY

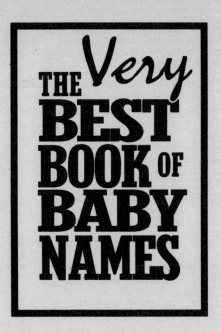

THE *Very*
BEST
BOOK OF
BABY
NAMES

Barbara Kay Turner

BERKLEY BOOKS, NEW YORK

THE VERY BEST BOOK OF BABY NAMES

A Berkley Book/published by arrangement with
the author

PRINTING HISTORY
Berkley edition/March 1994

ISBN: 0-425-14130-6

BERKLEY®
Berkley Books are published by The Berkley Publishing Group,
200 Madison Avenue, New York, New York 10016.
BERKLEY and the "B" design
are trademarks belonging to Berkley Publishing Corporation.

PRINTED IN THE UNITED STATES OF AMERICA

10 9 8 7 6

CONTENTS

INTRODUCTION

American Baby Names

When you choose a name for a baby born in America, you give three gifts—identity, heritage and potential.

At its simplest, the gift of identity is easy. Any name from the best to the worst will serve your child better than an anonymous "Hey, you!"

But how can you add heritage and potential to your choice of an identifying name?

You bestow heritage when the names you choose reflect a connection to your family history, ethnic or religious values, or anything that has special meaning to you, even just a sense of a name's "rightness."

The potential in a name is your third gift. Your choice will express your hope for your child's future.

The great thing about American baby names is the awesome number of choices. Some 10,000 are listed in *The Very Best Book of Baby Names*. You'll discover that all these names represent a truly rich international heritage. America is chiefly a nation of immigrants, past and present. Whatever your ancestral origins, your national heritage is sure to be represented somewhere in the vast name pool. But more than this, there are names that can reflect your interests—in nature or in places.

See what's in store for you in the pages that follow:

PART I describes the international origins of names, including names that are newcomers like Chiara and Sierra. It tells about some of the more amazing names parents have chosen for their children (and gives some cautions about this). For general interest and possible inspiration, it also lists some of the names celebrities have chosen for their children.

PART II helps with selection by type. What type of name best fits your desires for your child? Are you most interested in traditional and classic names, or do you want something more unusual? Would you like your daughter to have a very feminine name or a strong, dynamic name? Do you want a name with ethnic identity, perhaps a distinctively Irish or African name? If you'd like to try your hand at creating a new name, this section describes the basic techniques.

PART III is meant to be used as a tool kit. It contains a list of questions to help you clarify your name preferences, tips on avoiding misspellings and sample worksheets to help you compare and select your final choices.

PART IV the INDEX gives name origins, includes brief notes on historical, mythological and Biblical associations and provides a key to pronunciation. Contemporary names are listed, many of them grouped with the older names that inspired the modern-day versions. Just browsing through the index will give you a sense of history and the connection we all have to the past through the medium of names.

Whatever name you finally choose, remember this: Your child will stamp it with his or her personality.

Happy hunting!

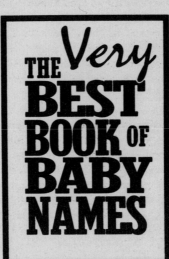

PART I

INFORMATION, PLEASE!

Where Do Names Come From?

From ancient times, parents from most language groups were guided in choosing names by such things as birthtime events, physical characteristics, hopes for future prosperity, wealth, fame or martial prowess, references to higher powers and ordinary vocabulary words. Name givers simply chose the word or phrase that conveyed the idea, and a name was created. This practice is the reason that meanings of many of the oldest names are still known to us, or at least can be guessed at, when only fragments of the original names remain.

A hundred or a thousand years from now, our descendants undoubtedly will examine and draw conclusions about our era from names like Dustin, Chevonne, Porsche, Elvis and Madonna. It seems only fitting that we should study our heritage to understand what we're now passing on to future generations.

Our Heritage From the Past

The story of how names came down to our time is a record that can be told in terms of people. In ancient days almost all peoples gave each of their children only one personal name, individually selected and tailored to fit a particular child. As population groups increased in number, it became necessary to expand the name pools. Instead of remaining unique to one person, names began to be reused for succeeding generations. "Son of" suffixes and prefixes came into use. Distinguishing nicknames became names in themselves.

Names began to travel, to be adopted and adapted by a variety of cultures and new peoples. Indo-European, Celtic and Teutonic branches reached outward, spreading their spheres of influence. Major descendants of these three branches all had a profound influence on names of Western civilization. These descendant influences include the Hebrews, Greeks, Romans, Scandinavians, Gaels, Anglo-Saxons and the French. Mythology and prominent religious groups (Christian, Jewish and Islamic) also had particular influence on names. In modern times, immigration increased enormously the list of names available to American parents. In capsule form, here are descriptions of these major influences.

THE HEBREWS. The Old Testament record is rich in names because of its focus on genealogical history and emphasis on the significance of name meanings. Because names were written down, and veneration for the Bible has helped preserve the ancient records, Hebrew names are among the oldest names that have survived. Names like David, Samuel and Sarah are now familiar around the world.

THE GREEKS. When Alexander the Great set forth to conquer the world, he also introduced the extensive pantheon of Greek mythology to many cultures. Names of gods and goddesses, nymphs and other mythical creatures became sources of inspiration. Helen and Diana are as well known today as Alexander.

THE ROMANS. The Latin-speaking Romans followed the Greeks in seizing world power and influence. The Romans had their own pantheon of gods and a multitude of family and clan names. Names like Marcus and Julius became familiar in many countries, including Britain. It became the fashion to Latinize (change the spelling of) names of every culture. The Greek Kynthia became Cynthia, for example.

THE SCANDINAVIANS. After the fall of the Roman Empire, men from the north pursued their own conquests. Danes, Swedes and Norwegians explored, raided, traded and settled in far-flung places—Russia, France, Spain, Germany and the British Isles. Scandinavian names and name fragments (many referring to Norse mythology) were adapted into all these cultures.

THE GAELS. Descendants of the Celts, the Gaels were fierce, independent men and women who populated much of England, Scotland, Ireland, Wales and the offshore islands of Britain. They opposed invaders from Scandinavia, and many names came into existence that pointed up the differences of "dark" and "fair" between the various peoples. Duncan and Duane are "dark" names, Gwen and Guinevere are "fair."

THE ANGLO-SAXONS. England's Anglo-Saxons were descendants of a fifth-century wave of Northern invasion via Germany, thus many old English names are Teutonic, or Norse/Germanic, in origin. Alfred and Edward are Anglo-Saxon names.

THE FRENCH. The ubiquitous Norsemen made incursions into northern France, finally settling permanently in what came to be called Normandy. Their descendants adopted the French language and customs, merging and adapting names as well. The Norse Ragnuald became the French Reynaud. Then, in the eleventh century, William, Duke of Normandy, laid claim to the throne of England and won.

The Norman conquest of England brought a wealth of French names into the British Isles. Names like Geoffrey and Henry soon became solidly entrenched as particularly English names. Other names were altered to English, Irish and Scottish forms; Renaud became Ronald.

THE CHRISTIANS. The great expansionary wave of missionary activity in the centuries following Christ's death also spread the names of Biblical heroes and personalities. Hebrew names like Jeremiah and Sarah and Greek names like Timothy and Eunice were Latinized and translated into a multitude of languages.

Saints' names began to play a distinctive role. As the number of converts grew in various countries, so did the roster of men and women revered as saints and martyrs. A great variety of names, many having origins in pagan mythology, came into common usage across national borders as parents named their children in honor of these saints.

THE JEWS. The Diaspora, the scattering of the Jews from their homeland in Palestine, began in the seventh century B.C. and lasted for some 2,500 years. Hebrew and uniquely Jewish names underwent changes as Jewish peoples were forced to migrate throughout Europe and Asia due to successive waves of persecution. Alternate spellings and substitution devices for Jewish names came into use, increasing the general stockpile of names as usage spread to still other peoples. Barak became Baruch, then Brock, for example.

THE MUSLIMS (Islam). In the Middle Ages, crusaders who returned to England and France from the Holy Lands in the near east brought back with them some of the Arabic and African influence in names. But it wasn't until the mid-1900s that Islamic/African names like Kareem and Ali rose to prominence in America through efforts of African-Americans seeking heritage links with their African past.

THE IMMIGRANTS. By the seventeenth and eighteenth centuries, when immigration to the colonies of America began, names that came to the New World included names influenced by all the sources described above. Through longtime usage, the majority of these names were generally perceived to be English.

Further immigration in the nineteenth and twentieth centuries expanded the American name pool to include the Baltic, Slavic, Oriental and Polynesian heritage of names. Today there are virtually no language groups of names unaccounted for in American society.

While some immigrants kept the native form of their names, many more respelled, shortened or otherwise altered the names to American preferences of an English look and sound. Where European spellings of familiar English names were retained, pronunciation indicators like accent marks and umlauts usually were dropped. Today a name like Krystyna may be thought of as a rather fanciful alternate spelling of Christina, when in fact it is a Polish form of the name.

Newcomers to the Name Pool

Through the centuries, new names have been created by poets, writers and parents. Often they have no specific meaning, unless they relate in some way to existing names. The best-liked of the literary and poetic names have survived due to continued publication that made them known to parents in succeeding generations. Jessica, Vanessa, Wendy, Pamela and Lorna are examples of literary creations.

New names tend to be created for girls. They can be totally original or they might be existing names that have almost been forgotten.

When new names come into prominence through literary characters or by singers, actors and other people in the news, parents find the names attractive and begin to consider them for naming their babies. Some names (Kayla is an example) become top choices almost immediately. Often the new names have such appeal that they stay popular long after the original name-bearer has dropped out of the limelight.

A prime consideration appears to be whether the new name has a fresh look and sound but relates in some ways (rhyming patterns, syllable structure) to existing names. Tiffany and Crystal are examples of new names that have proved their staying power over a period of years. Their similarity to traditional names like Stephanie, Bethany, Christa and Christine no doubt played a large part in their success. The acceptance of Hayley and Hailey as girls' names in the Sixties undoubtedly led to the acceptance of Bailey in the Eighties. Both names plus a number of spelling variants remain well up on the list of popular names for girls. Hayley probably owes its long-term acceptance to Holly and Hallie as much as to actress Hayley Mills.

Another source of new names can be found in alternate spellings of existing names. The index lists many of these alternates beneath each "parent" name. Other original new names are listed as main entries.

For further information on the types of created names,

as well as information on how to create your own new names, see page 43 in Part II.

Below is a sample list of names relatively new to baby name books. Some are inventions, others are surname forms or very obscure names rarely used as given names in the past.

Newcomer Names for Boys

Colton, Kolton	Houston	Taurean
Dakotah	Jamaine	Terran
Daylon	Jamar	Trevin
Destin	Jaron	Trevis
Ferron, Faron	Jerrell	Tyrell
Garron	Ryker	Zarek

Newcomer Names for Girls

Abriana	Deandra	Nichelle
Ashton, Ashten	Farren, Faryn	Payton, Peyton
Aviana	Jacey	Phylicia
Bailey	Jazlyn	Sade, Sharde
Cady, Kady	Jessenia	Savannah
Cayley, Cailley	Kaylee	Sierra
Chanel, Chanelle	Keisha	Tanesha, Taniesha
Chevonne,	Kiara	Taryn, Tarin
Shavonn	Lakeisha	Taylor
Cheyenne,	Latasha	Tiana
Cheyanne	LaToya	Tiara
Chianna	Mackenzie	Whitley
Ciara, Ciera	Madison	Whitney
Daryl, Daryll	Mystique	

Names Celebrities Choose

Parents acknowledge that they get inspiration from names of real people—singers, actors, actresses, sports figures and other celebrities—and from fictional characters in books, TV and movies.

The question arises, where do celebrities get inspiration for naming *their* children?

You can draw your own conclusions from this list of baby names chosen by a number of celebrities in recent times:

Celebrities' Baby Name Choices

Prince Akishino/Princess Kiko: PRINCESS MAKO

Charles, Viscount Althorp (Di's brother)/Victoria Lockwood: ELIZA and KATYA (twins); older sister is KITTY ELEANOR

Kevin Bacon/Kym Sedgwick: SOSIE RUTH

Mikhail Baryshnikov/Lisa Rinehart: ANNA KATERINA

Michael Biehn/Gina: GAELAN MICHAEL

Robby Benson/Karla DeVito: ZEPHYR (son)

Corbin Bernsen/Amanda Pays: HENRY and ANGUS (twin sons)

Sonny Bono/Mary: CHESARE (son), CHIANNA (daughter)

Garth Brooks/Sandy: TAYLOR MAYNE PEARL

James Caan/Ingrid: ALEXANDER JAMES

Nicolas Cage/Christina Fulton: WESTON

Kate Capshaw/Steven Spielberg: SAWYER

Katie Couric/Jay Monahan: ELINOR TULLY

John Denver/Cassandra Delaney: JESSE BELLE

Brian DePalma/Gale Anne Hurd: LOLITA

Chris Evert/Andy Mill: ALEXANDER JAMES

Carrie Fisher/Bryan Lourd: BILLIE CATHERINE

Leeza Gibbons/Stephen Meadows: JENNY ROSE
Frank Gifford/Kathie Lee: CODY
Deidre Hall/Steve Sommer: DAVID ATTICUS
Jerry Hall/Mick Jagger: GEORGIA MAY AYEESHA
Mark Harmon/Pam Dawber: TY CHRISTIAN
David Hasselhoff/Pamela Bach: HAYLEY
Hugh Hefner/Kimberley Conrad: COOPER BRADFORD
Bruce Hornsby/Kathy: RUSSELL IVES and KEITH RAN-
    DALL (twins)
Earvin "Magic" Johnson/Erletha Kelley: EARVIN
Perry King/Jamison Elvidge: HANNAH PERRIN
Kevin Kline/Phoebe Cates: OWEN JOSEPH
Ivan Lendl/Samantha: MARIKA
Lee Majors/Karen Velez: DANE LUKE and TREY
    KULLEY (twin sons)
Howie Mandel/Terry: RILEY PAIGE (daughter)
Gates McFadden/John Talbot: JAMES CLEVELAND
Demi Moore/Bruce Willis: RUMER GLENN, SCOUT
    LARUE (daughters)
Robert Morse/Elizabeth Roberts: ALLYN ELIZABETH
Eddie Murphy/Nicole Mitchell: MILES MITCHELL
Dave Mustaine/Pam: JUSTIS DAVID
Vince Neal (Motley Crue)/Sharise: SKYLAR LYNNAE
Tracy Nelson/Billy Moses: REMINGTON ELIZABETH
Jack Nicholson/Rebecca Broussard: RAYMOND NICH-
    OLSON
Sean Penn/Robin Wright: DYLAN FRANCES (daughter)
Annie Potts/Jim Hayman: JAMES POWELL
Christopher Reeves/Danna Morosini: OWEN, NINNA
    PRISCILLA
Geraldo Rivera/C.C. Dyer: ISABELLA HOLMES
Meg Ryan/Dennis Quaid: JACK HENRY
Susan Sarandon/Tim Robbins: MILES GUTHRIE
Greta Scacchi/Vincent D'Onofrio: LEILA
Ed Schlossburg/Caroline Kennedy: JOHN, TATIANA

Bruce Springsteen/Patti Scialfa: EVAN JAMES
Rod Stewart/Rachel Hunter: RENEE
Maria Shriver/Arnold Schwarzenegger: CHRISTINA AU-
  RELIA
Cheryl Tiegs/Tony Peck: ZACHARY ANTHONY
Tiffany/Balmaro Garcia: ELIJAH
John Travolta/Kelly Preston: JETT (son)
Tracey Ullman/Allan McKeown: JOHN ALBERT VIC-
  TOR
Denzel Washington/Pauletta: MALCOLM and OLIVIA
  (twins)
Robin Williams/Marsha: CODY
Hank Williams Jr./Mary Jane: KATHERINE DIANA

Amazing Names, Rarities and Joke Names

A name is amazing when it shocks, jolts or surprises all
who hear it. We've come a long way from the gems of the
Puritan era, like Zeal-for-the-Lord and Flee-Fornication,
but really unusual and amazing names continue to appear
on birth registration lists.

Names like these for boys: Aladdin, Amen, Bronc,
Bum, Clever, Danish, Diploma, Doctor, Giant, Handsome,
Heartbeat, Hombre, Hoss, Ironside, Lavish, Magnum, Mis-
ter, Money, Mouser, Neon, Panache, Perfecto, Rayon, Reborn, Rocket, Sechzwan, Starlight, Suave, Tercel, Transam
and Wings.

And names like these for girls: Acquire, Amen, Aro-
ma, Beauty, Blessing, Butterfly, Cachet, California, Cam-
bridge, Caramel, Chablis, Chardonnay, Chutney, Cologne,
Coma, Corvette, Criscoe, Daiquiri, Dimple, Esprit, Essence, Ferrari, Finesse, Genuine, Holiday, Jaunty, Joyous,
Luscious, Manhattan, Martini, Meadow, Memory, Messiah,
Mystery, Naive, Novelette, Novella, Passion, Pretty, Prom-
ise, Reality, Rolaid, Secret, Sincerely, Snip, Sparkle, Spe-

cial, Spice, Starfire, Summit, Technique, Truly, Twinkle, Ultra, Vanity, Verily, Vision, Vogue and Whisper.

RARITIES. If you wished to select some rare but not totally uncommon names from the lists, you could call your child: Darling, Delight, Honey, Marvel, Miracle, Precious, Treasure or Heaven.

You could confer title and position with: Baron, Chancellor, Contessa, Duchess, Duke, General, Judge, King, Lady, Lord, Marquis, Prince, Rani or Rajah.

You could evoke the senses with luxury: Cashmere, Champagne, Diamond, Lace, Mink, Porsche, Sable, Satin, Silver or Velvet.

You could inspire the senses with color: Amethyst, Azure, Beige, Cinnamon, Ebony, Indigo, Ivory, Lavender, Magenta, Saffron, Scarlet, Silver or Viridian.

You could invoke the weather: Breezy, Dusty, Misty, Rain, Rainbow, Stormy, Sunshine, Tempest, Zephyr.

You could inspire fear or repulsion: Batman, Cobra, Demon, Desperado, Hulk, Pitbull.

A word of caution: Above all other categories of names, parents should exercise the greatest restraint when deciding to select an amazing name. Such a name can lend distinction, and some for girls are quite beautiful. Some give a sense of fun and informality. But taken to extremes, they can create a burden too heavy for a child to bear. Names intended to inspire fear or repulsion can even be dangerous, making the child a target for challenge and attack.

It's a questionable practice to give a name designed to "toughen up" a child. You run the risk of doing more harm than the song *A Boy Named Sue* might suggest. Most psychologists would agree that there are more productive ways to teach a child.

JOKE NAMES. Parents are as susceptible as any others to the temptation to make jokes of serious matters. That includes naming their children, unfortunately. The one emphatic piece of advice this book offers is, don't! A joke told once is funny. Twice told, it's tolerable. But repeated every day for a lifetime, a joke name can be sheer torture for the one bearing the name.

Try these names on for size—or rather, don't!

Carrie Carey	Honey Lamb	Vera Smart
Dick Dickers	Lily White	Hayley Fields
Peter Piper	Finn E. Fisher	Chris Cross
Raisin Cain	Akin Bach	Ferris Wheeler
Lucky Chance	Lessa Moore	Robin Banks
Gardine Angel	Minnie Moore	Raine Storm
Crystal Ball	Shanda Lear	Jim Crowe

PART II

SELECTING BY NAME TYPE

It's possible to classify names according to type, at least generally, to find a starting place in your search for the perfect name. Do you want a traditional type of name? Something a little out of the ordinary? A strong name? A very feminine name? An ethnic or Biblical name? A name from nature expressing environmental concern?

Traditional and Popular Classic Names

Most *TRADITIONAL NAMES* have been used for thousands of years. They tend to fit a pattern most people perceive as denoting stability and dignity. Traditional names are seldom mispronounced. Usually these names are so familiar that peer teasing about the name is mild or doesn't happen. Males are more often given this type of name.

Traditional Boys' Names

Aaron	Anthony	Carl	Daniel
Adam	Arthur	Charles	David
Alan, Allen	Benjamin	Christopher	Dennis
Albert	Bradley	Colin	Derek
Alexander	Brian, Bryan	Craig	Donald
Andrew	Bruce	Curtis	Douglas

Drew	Jason	Matthew	Ross
Edgar	Jeffrey	Michael	Russell
Edward	Jeremy	Mitchell	Ryan
Edwin	Joel	Nathan	Samuel
Eric, Erik	John	Nathaniel	Simon
Ethan	Jonathan	Nicholas	Spencer
Eugene	Jordan	Oscar	Steven,
Evan	Joseph	Patrick	Stephen
Frank	Joshua	Paul	Stuart
Gabriel	Julian	Peter	Theodore
Garrett	Justin	Phillip, Philip	Thomas
George	Keith	Preston	Timothy
Gerald	Kenneth	Randall	Trent
Grant	Kevin	Raymond	Victor
Gregory	Lawrence	Richard	Vincent
Henry	Louis	Robert	Walter
Ivan	Luke	Rodney	Wayne
Jacob	Mark	Roger	William
James	Martin	Ronald	Zachary
Jared			

Traditional Girls' Names

Abigail	Brooke	Deborah
Adrienne	Candice,	Denise
Alexandra	Candace	Diana, Diane
Alexis	Carol, Carole	Elizabeth
Alice	Carolyn, Caroline	Emily
Alison, Allison	Catherine	Erica, Erika
Amanda	Christine,	Evelyn
Andrea	Christina	Gabrielle
Ann, Anne, Anna	Claire	Hannah
Barbara	Claudia	Helen
Brenda	Cynthia	Irene
	Danielle	

Jane	Lindsey, Lindsay	Rebecca
Janet	Margaret	Renee
Jessica	Marie, Maria	Roberta
Joanne, Joanna	Martha	Ruth
Josephine	Mary	Sarah, Sara
Judith	Mercedes	Sharon
Julia	Melinda	Stephanie
Justine	Miranda	Susan
Karen	Natalie	Sylvia
Katherine,	Nicole, Nichole	Teresa
Kathryn	Olivia	Therese, Theresa
Kristen, Kristin	Pamela	Veronica
Laura	Patricia	Victoria
Lauren	Priscilla	Virginia
Linda	Rachel, Rachael	

POPULAR CLASSIC NAMES may be relatively modern or have long histories. Popular classic names are more informal in sound and look than traditional names. Like the traditional names, they are familiar. Some names more recently in popular use, like Brandon, Taylor and Tyler, will undoubtedly move over to the traditional list before very long.

Many popular classic names are short forms or variants of older names. As a group, they tend to have a certain liveliness that many find fresh, appealing and modern.

Popular Classic Boys' Names

Alex	Brandon	Bryant
Andre	Brendan	Bryce
Austin	Brent	Caleb
Blake	Brett	Cameron

Casey	Johnny	Ricky
Chad	Jose	Riley
Chase	Kristopher	Scott
Christian	Kyle	Sean, Shawn
Clayton	Lance	Seth
Cody	Larry	Shane
Colton	Logan	Tanner
Corey, Cory	Lucas	Taylor
Darren, Darin	Manuel	Terry
Dustin	Marcus	Todd
Dylan	Darryl	Tony
Ian	Derrick	Travis
Jack	Dominic	Trevor
Jake	Mario	Troy
Jerry	Max	Tyler
Jesse	Omar	Tyson
Jimmy	Randy	Wesley

Popular Classic Girls' Names

Adriana	Brenda	Deanna
Alicia	Brianna, Briana	Desiree
Alisha	Bridget	Emma
Amber	Brittany, Brittney	Erin
Amy	Caitlin, Caitlyn	Felicia
Ana	Carrie	Gina
Angela	Casey	Haley, Hayley
Angelica	Cassandra	Heather
April	Chelsea, Chelsey	Heidi
Ashley, Ashlee	Cindy	Holly
Bethany	Colleen	Jaclyn
Bianca	Courtney	Jamie
Brandi, Brandy	Crystal	Jasmine

Jenna	Melissa	Stacey, Stacy
Jenny	Michelle	Tabitha
Julie	Molly	Tanya
Karla	Monica	Tara
Katelyn	Monique	Tiffany
Kathleen	Nancy	Tina
Katie	Natasha	Tracy
Kayla	Raquel	Valerie
Kelly	Robin	Vanessa
Kimberly	Rosa	Veronica
Kristina	Sabrina	Wendy
Leslie	Samantha	Whitney
Lisa	Shannon	Yvette
Melanie	Sonia	

Slightly Unusual and Unusual Names

SLIGHTLY UNUSUAL NAMES. Do you want a name that is just a little bit different? But not too different? Then you'll be interested in the names in this category. Slightly unusual names often reflect or imitate the sound and look of classic and traditional names; often the difference is as simple as a change of spelling. Yet because these slightly different names are less frequently used, they are distinctive.

UNUSUAL NAMES are frankly different. A child with this kind of name is less likely to encounter another child with the same name. This category often includes contemporary variants and inventions.

Points to keep in mind: Very distinctive names can be advantageous in adult life because people tend to remember more unusual names. They can sometimes be a handicap in childhood if unusually distinctive names lead to teasing.

On the other hand, schoolchildren of all ages have been increasingly exposed to unusual names via the media and through modern-day immigration from other countries. Inventing names and changing the spelling of names also seems to be on the increase and is not limited to any particular racial group.

The following chart of names compares three stages of the same name: the basic name, a slightly unusual version and an unusual version. If you'll examine the samples, you should be able to create your own comparison chart of other names. Make use of the index. Quite a few main entry names have less frequently used variants listed under them. Cross-references will lead you to other variants of the basic name.

There are some 10,000 names listed in the index. You'll find many single names listed that will impress you as being unusual. Some have long histories, some are more recently coined. All are used today in America, though usage may be rare. Rare usage as much as distinctive spelling makes a name unusual.

Girls' Slightly Unusual/Unusual Names

BASIC NAME	SLIGHTLY UNUSUAL	UNUSUAL
Adriana	Adrianna	Adrielle
Alexandra	Alexandrea	Alyssandra
Alicia	Alissa	Aleesha
Allison, Alison	Allyson	Alisanne
Amy	Amie	Aimee
Ashley	Ashleigh	Ashlyn, Ashleen
Barbara	Barbra	Barbarella
Brianna	Bryanna	Briannon
Candice, Candace	Candyce	Kandace
Carol	Carole	Carroll

Cheryl	Cheryll	Cherrill
Crystal	Crystell	Chrystelle, Chrystalyn
Danielle	Daniela	Dhanielle
Diana	Dianna	Dionna
Elaine	Elaina	Ellaine
Emily	Emilee	Emmalee
Erin	Eryn	Erinne
Felicia	Felisha	Phylicia
Hannah	Hanna	Hannalee
Jaclyn	Jacklyn	Jackleen
Jamie	Jaimie	Jamison
Julie, Julia	Juli, Julee	Juleen
Karla	Karly	Karleigh
Katie	Katy	Katya
Kayla	Kaylee	Kaleigh, Kaylyn
Kelly	Kelley	Kellen
Laura	Lara	Laurinda
Maria, Marie	Maree	Mariah
Melanie	Melanee	Melaina
Michaela	Micaela	McKayla
Morgan	Morgana	Morgayne
Patricia	Patrice	Patrisse
Roxanne	Roxana	Roxandra
Sandra	Sondra	Xandra, Zandra
Stacy, Stacey	Stacee	Stasha
Tanya	Tonya	Tahnee, Tawnya
Tara	Terra	Taryn
Veronica	Veronika	Veronique

Boys' Slightly Unusual/Unusual Names

BASIC NAME	SLIGHTLY UNUSUAL	UNUSUAL
Alex	Alec	Alexei
Allen	Allyn	Alain
Andrew	Andre	Deandre
Brett	Bret	Bretton
Brian	Bryon	Bryant
Carl	Carlton	Charleton
Casey	Kasey	Kacey, K.C.
Colin	Collin	Colton
Curtis	Kurtis	Kurtiss
Dane	Dayne	Dayner
Darin	Daryn	Darrian
Dylan	Dillon	Daylon
Eric	Erick	Eriq
Garrett	Garth	Garrison
Jack	Jackson	Jaxon
Jared	Jarrod	Jerrod
Jason	Jayson	Jace
John	Jon	Jonte
Jordan	Jourdan	Jordi
Justin	Justyn	Jestin
Kenneth	Kent	Kendrick
Kevin	Kevan	Kevion
Lawrence	Laurence	Laurian, Lorenzo
Luke	Lucas	Lukas, Lucan
Mark	Marco	Marquez, Markell
Matthew	Mathew	Mathias
Mike	Mick	Mischa
Neil	Neal	Neilan
Riley	Ryley	Ryleigh
Sean, Shawn	Shaun	Shann
Steven, Stephen	Stephan	Steffan

Terrence	Terence	Torrance
Terrell	Tyrell	Tyree
Zachary	Zackary	Zakary, Zachariah

Dynamic Names and Cross-gender Names

DYNAMIC NAMES. Among the many possible characteristics to choose from in describing a name—lively, casual, calm, dignified—the quality defined as dynamic or strong may be most useful in our competitive modern society.

We gain impressions of strength in names from history. For example, England's King Richard the Lionhearted; Samson, the man endowed by God with superhuman strength; Russia's empress, Catherine the Great; Kate, the feisty bride in Shakespeare's *Taming of the Shrew*. All these names are associated in our minds with impressions of dynamic strength.

Perhaps none of these names seem quite right to you. You want to choose a name that has unmistakable impact, a name most people would classify as dynamic, strong. Is this possible?

STRENGTH PATTERNS. Names that are generally perceived as dynamic or strong tend to fall into certain patterns. One-syllable and two-syllable names like Brett and Jackson often sound more forceful than names with three syllables.

Many boys' and girls' names are shortened in familiar use, and the shortest form frequently seems to have the strongest impact. Matt rather than Matthew, for example, and Bree rather than Brianna. You don't have to limit yourself to choosing a short name over a long one in order to achieve the dynamic factor. Just give some thought to likely short forms and nicknames that will accompany names you do choose.

When you examine names that you yourself perceive to be strong, notice how often they include "hard" consonants. When sounds like ch, d, g, r, t and especially k are dominant or stressed, they require more force to pronounce, thereby contributing to an impression of strength. Kate has two of these stressed consonants, which may explain why it is invariably perceived as a strong name for a girl. Adding a second syllable to alter the name to Katie softens the effect. Many names for girls make use of the strong-soft combination effect.

Surnames used as first names often convey a perception of strength. Some examples are Brooke, Hayley, Morgan and Payton for girls, and Cord, Kane, Kincaid, and Tanner for boys.

CROSS-GENDER NAMES are grouped in this category because they tend to be strong names for girls. They're unique in that they may be used for either a boy or a girl.

Sometimes usage by both men and women who are prominent in the media keeps a name on the active cross-gender list. Actor Blair Underwood and actress Blair Brown, for example, help keep the name Blair open as a choice for either a boy or a girl. Robin Williams helps maintain Robin as a name for boys, though it's used more often for girls. Names like Taylor and Jordan continue to be used frequently for both genders, perhaps because they're strong-sounding surname forms. Surname forms like Whitney and Courtney move more quickly over to the girls' list, no doubt because of the two-syllable form with the "ee" ending. Many existing feminine names follow the same pattern.

Dynamic Names for Girls

Adair	Greer	Liz, Liza
Alexis	Hayley	Mackenzie
Ashton	Helen	Madison
Blaine	Honor	Margo
Blair	Jade	Morgan
Britt, Brett	Jordan	Paige
Brooke	Kady	Payton, Peyton
Brynne	Kacey, Kacie	Quinn
Callan	Kasey	Raquel
Carson	Kate	Regan
Casey	Kay	Rue
Cass	Kelcey, Kelsey	Shann
Cassidy	Kellen	Sheridan
Dale	Kelly	Sloan, Sloane
Dana	Kendall	Tate
Delta	Kendra	Taylor
Drew	Kirsten	Zandra

Dynamic Names for Boys

Barrett	Colton	Kade
Bart	Cormac	Kirk
Blake	Dane	Logan
Boone	Derek	Luke
Brad	Drake	Quinn
Brett	Garrett	Ryder
Brock	Jackson	Ryker
Caine	Jake	Tanner
Caleb	Jared	Taylor
Chase	Jordan	Zachariah

Cross-gender Names for Boys and Girls

Ali	Devon	Loren
Angel	Dominique	Morgan
Blair	Dorian	Noel
Cameron	Jamie, Jaime	Paris
Carey	Jean	Quinn
Casey	Jessie	Robin
Cassidy	Jody	Shea
Christian	Jordan	Sheridan
Cody	Kacey, Kasey	Sidney
Corey, Cory	Kellen	Skyler
Dakota	Kelly	Taylor
Dallas	Kendall	Terry
Dana	Kerry	Tory, Torrey
Daryl	Lee	Van

Feminine Names

As strong names can be characterized by their hard consonants, distinctively feminine names can be characterized by the use of the softer consonants. F, l, m, s, sh, th and v fall softly on the ear. Vowels also have a gentling effect, as do names ending with -a, -ie, and -ee. Compare Adriana with Adra. See how the softer vowels in Adriana predominate, softening the strong "d" consonant. Notice also how the multiple syllables in Adriana have an additional softening effect. Shalisa and Melissa are examples of multiple-syllable names that have only soft vowels and consonants. Say them aloud. Do you agree that they have an entirely feminine effect?

Names that are a mixture of strong and soft consonants, like Katherine, have variants that can shift the balance in either direction. For example, the variant Kaitlyn emphasizes the strong k and t consonants, while Kathleen and Kathlyn emphasize the softer "th" and "l".

It pays to examine the variants of popular names to select a version that best suits your perception of the type of name you want for your daughter. Keep in mind, too, that nicknames will give future options. Kaitlyn is almost sure to yield Kate, and Kathleen will yield Kathy or Kat.

The list below is only a sample. Very feminine names predominate in the girls' index listings, primarily due to the many diminutives used in forming variants.

Feminine Names

Alisha	Charleen	Isabel	Lucy, Lucia
Alyssa, Alissa	Cheryl	Janessa	Mallory
Amy, Aimee	Chrissie	Jocelyn	Mariana
Angela, An-gelica	Clarissa	Joyce	Marisa
Ariana	Colleen	Karla	Mary, Mari
Belinda	Daphne	Kayla	Melanie
Beth	Dawn	Keisha	Melinda
Candice, Candace	Deborah	Kimberly	Melissa
Carissa	Delores, Do-lores	Lacey	Michelle
Carla	Desiree	Lakeisha	Natasha
Cassandra	Elise, Elisa	Larissa	Noelle
Cassie	Elizabeth	Latasha	Olivia
Catherine	Farrah	Latisha	Paula
Cathleen	Felicia	Laura, Lara	Penny
Cathy	Francesca	Leila	Phylicia
Cecilia	Francine	Leslie	Rebecca
Celia	Flora	Liliana	Rose, Rosalie
Chanel	Hannah	Lillian	Roseanna
Chantel	Heather	Lisa, Lissa	Samantha
	Hillary, Hilary	Lora, Lori	Sarah
		Loretta	Sasha

Shalaine	Shelley	Tamara	Trisha
Shalisa	Sherry	Tammy	Valerie
Sharice	Stephanie	Tasha	Vanessa
Sharon	Summer	Tessa	Yvonne
Shavonne	Tabitha	Tiffany	

Environment Names—Earth, Flora and Fauna

Nature has long yielded subjects for mankind's pool of names. Earth, sky and sea, the weather, flowers, gemstones, birds and other living creatures have all contributed to this name bounty.

Classic names like Rose, Jade and Dawn belong with this name type. In modern times, environmental concerns have influenced the continued popularity of earth, flora and fauna names. Really unusual names such as River and Lark Song tend to stay unique to their original name bearers. The lists below demonstrate that names from nature are used far more often for girls than for boys.

Earth, Flora and Fauna Names for Boys

Ash	Forest	Rock, Rocky
Birch	Garnet	Sage
Clay	Hawk, Hawke	Sky
Dusty	Heath	Stone
Falcon	Rio	Thorn
Flint		

Earth, Flora and Fauna Names for Girls

Acacia	Aurora	Azalea
Amber	Autumn	Berry

Beryl
Brook
Camelia
Cherry
Coral
Crystal
Dahlia
Daisy
Ebony
Ember
Emerald
Ermine
Fawn
Fern
Gaea, Gaia
Gardenia
Garnet
Ginger
Hazel
Heather
Holly

Honey
Hyacinth
Iris
Ivory
Ivy
Jade
Jasmine
Jewel
Laurel
Lily
Linden
Linnet
Lotus
Magnolia
Marigold
Myrtle
Olive
Opal
Pearl
Peony
Poppy

Rose
Rosemary
Rowan
Ruby
Sable
Sahara
Sapphire
Savannah
Scarlet
Sierra
Sky, Skye
Spring
Star
Stormy
Summer
Sunny, Sunnie
Terra
Viola
Violet
Willow
Zinnia

Names From the Bible

Names that appear in the Bible make up a substantial proportion of traditional names. Variants in many languages greatly increase the list. For example, Elizabeth has more than 40 variants in current use in America. Maria and John yield even more.

The fact that a name comes from the Bible doesn't necessarily mean that the original name bearer was noted for virtue. Nor are all possible names listed here. Notorious names with strongly negative associations like Satan and Lucifer have been omitted, along with hundreds of other names that are too strange or cumbersome for our modern ears.

Because of the increasing secularization of American culture, the Biblical origins of some names are less well-known today. Look in the index for background notes on most of these distinctive names. Variants are shown beneath the main entry name or in cross-references.

For further information about personalities that interest you, check Bible indexes to learn where individual stories are located in the Scriptures. Bible dictionaries are also useful.

Girls' Names From the Bible

Abigail	Eunice	Myra
Adah	Eve	Naomi
Anna	Hannah	Ophrah
Bernice	Jemima,	Phoebe
Bethany	Jemimah	Priscilla
Bethel	Joanna	Rachel
Beulah	Judith	Rebecca
Candace	Julia	Rhoda
Chloe	Keziah	Ruth
Claudia	Leah	Salome
Damaris	Lois	Sarah, Sarai
Deborah	Luz	Shalisha
Delilah	Lydia	Sharon
Dinah	Mahalah	Sheba
Drusilla, Drucilla	Martha	Susanna
Eden	Mary	Tabitha
Elisabeth, Eliza-	Michal	Tamar
beth	Miriam	Zorah
Esther	Moriah	

Virtue Names For Girls

Amity	Felicity	Mercy
Charity	Grace	Modesty
Chastity	Harmony	Patience
Clemency	Honor	Prudence
Constance	Hope	Serenity
Faith	Joy	Verity

Boys' Names From the Bible

Aaron	Barnabus	Emanuel, Em-
Abel	Bartholomew	manuel
Abner	Baruch	Enoch
Abraham	Benjamin	Enos
Abram	Cain	Ephraim
Adam	Caleb	Esau
Adriel	Christian	Ethan
Alexander	Claudius	Ezekiel
Allon	Clement	Ezra
Alvah	Cornelius	Felix
Alvan	Cyrus	Gabriel
Amal	Dan	Gideon
Amos	Daniel	Haran
Andrew	Darius	Hiram
Aquila	David	Hosea
Aram	Demetrius	Ira
Aran	Eden	Isaac
Ardon	Elam	Isaiah
Arnan	Eleazar	Jabal
Asa	Eli	Jagur
Asher	Eliezer, Eliezar	Jairus
Augustus	Elijah, Elias	James
Barak	Elisha	Jareb

Jared, Jered
Jason
Jehu
Jerah, Jarah
Jeremiah
Jericho
Jeruel
Jeshua
Jesse
Jethro
Joab
Job
Joel
John
Jonah, Jonas
Jonathan
Jorah
Joram
Jordan
Joseph
Joshua
Josiah
Jotham
Jubal
Jude
Julius

Justus
Kenan
Kenath
Levi
Linus
Lucas
Lucius
Luke
Malachi
Marcus
Matthew
Matthias
Micah
Michael
Moses
Nathan
Nathanial
Noah
Omar
Oren
Paul
Peter
Philip
Rei
Reuben
Reuel
Rufus

Samson
Samuel
Sargon
Saul
Seth
Shem
Silas
Silvanus
Simeon
Solomon
Stephen
Thaddeus
Thomas
Timon
Timothy
Titus
Tobiah, Tobias
Zacchaeus
Zachariah
Zechariah
Zared

VIRTUE
NAMES
Loyal
Justice

Names From Mythology and Legend

MYTHOLOGY. Almost all cultures cherish ancient myths and legends. Worldwide, all mythology appears to have certain factors in common: the influence of higher powers on agriculture, fertility, rewards and punishments.
Western civilization in particular has been influenced by

the tales of the Greek olympiad of gods and goddesses, their servants, their human loves, offspring and victims. The Romans adopted and renamed many of these for their own pantheon. Thus Hera became Juno, Zeus became Jupiter, Artemis became Diana.

.The Celts and Scandinavians contributed their share of supernatural beings to the world's mythology. Yet, only a few Gaelic/Celtic names from mythology and legend are included in the lists of currently used American names. The original name forms and spellings have been less successfully transmitted into twentieth-century use. The same is generally true of Roman names for boys and names from Scandinavian and American Indian mythology.

LEGEND. The line that divides myth from legend is often hazy. It's known that there was a king who fit the description of King Arthur of Britain, but true names and details are shrouded in the mists of legend. The Knights of the Round Table and their ladies are known to us today through the imaginative tales transmitted by bards and poets.

Other sources of legend have preserved names for us. Finn Mac Cumhail of Ireland and England's Robin Hood are alike in legendary status, due to the tale-spinners of several centuries who told of those men's daring exploits. Homer mixed truth, legend and mythology in *The Odyssey* and *The Iliad*.

The names listed below indicate their origins. Look up individual names in the index to read fascinating tidbits about mythic and legendary name bearers.

Names From Myth and Legend

GREEK	Andromeda	Artemis
GIRLS	Appolonia	Athena, Athene
Alethea	Ariadne, Ariana	Aura

Brisa
Calista
Calliope
Calypso
Cassandra
Celina, Selena
Circe
Cleonie
Clio
Cloris
Clytie
Cybil, Sybil
Cynthia
Cyrene
Danae
Daphne
Delphi
Demetria, Demeter, Demi
Destiny
Dione, Dionna
Doris
Echo
Gaea, Gaia
Galatea
Harmony, Harmonia
Helen
Hera
Ianthe
Irene
Iris
Leda
Melissa
Nereida

Nike (see Nikki)
Oceana
Olympia
Pandora
Penelope
Peri
Phoebe
Rhea
Selena
Sirena
Sybil
Thalia

BOYS
Achilles
Adonis
Apollo
Arion
Demetrius, Dimitri
Dennis, Denis, Dion
Hector
Hercules
Hermes
Jason
Orion
Paris
Sylvanus, Silas
Troy

ROMAN

GIRLS
Aurora
Ceres

Diana
Fauna
Fortuna
Jana
Levana
Lucine
Maia
Minerva
Terra
Thea
Venus

BOYS
Jovan, Jovanus
Marcus, Mark, Marc

SCANDINAVIAN

GIRLS
Freya
Hilda
Inga, Ingrid
Rana
Tyra

BOYS
Thor
Tyrell, Terrell
Wade
Wayland, Waylon

ENGLISH LEGEND

GIRLS
Ariel

Elaine
Guinevere
Igrayne
Morgana, Morgan

BOYS
Arthur
Gareth
Lance, Lancelot
Merlin
Robin
Roland
Tristan

HINDU (Sanskrit)

GIRLS
Asha
Deva
Indira
Jaya
Kali

Kalinda
Lalita
Meena
Tara
Usha

BOYS
Dev
Hari
Jay, Jai
Kannan
Manu
Ram
Ravi
Usama

CELTIC

GIRLS
Bridget
Deirdre, Deidre
Maeve

Rhiannon
Sabrina

BOYS
Brian
Donn
Finn
Tyrell

VARIOUS

GIRLS
Cybele (Greek/Roman/Asian)
Isis (Egyptian)
Lea (Hawaiian)
Lorelei (German)

BOYS
Amon (Egyptian)
Borak (Arabic)
Rigel (Arabic)

African Names

AFRICAN NAMES are of special interest in America, especially since the 1960s, when African-American descendants have shown increasing interest in seeking out names that reflect their African heritage.

Islamic traditions have had strong influence in Africa for centuries. Names used by many tribes, Swahili among others, are often Arabic in origin.

It's possible that a number of names listed in the index as prefix names—Ka-, Sha- and Ta- names especially—are based on African or Hindi (Sanskrit) names. Parents interested in combining the sound and look patterns of some African names with patterns that are also familiar to Americans might want to give prefix names special attention.

Most of the African names on the sample lists below are currently in use in America.

African Names for Girls

Ada (Nigerian) "First daughter."
Adanna (Nigerian) "Her father's daughter."
Aisha, Aysha, Ayeisha (Swahili/Arabic) "Life."
Alika (Nigerian) "Most beautiful."
Ama, Ami (Ghanese) "Saturday's child."
Amadi (Nigerian) "Rejoicing."
Amina (Swahili/Arabic) "Trustworthy."
Ashia (Somali) "Life."
Aziza (Swahili/Arabic) "Precious."
Chika (Nigerian) "God is supreme."
Chinara (Nigerian) "God receives."
Dalila (Swahili) "Gentle."
Deka (Somali) "Pleasing."
Folasade (Yoruban) "Honor confers a crown."
Jamila (Swahili) "Chaste, holy."
Jina (Swahili) "Name."
Kalifa, Kalifah (Somali) "Chaste, holy."
Katifa (Arabic) "Flowering."
Layla (Swahili) "Dark; born at night."
Lulu (Tanzanian) "Pearl."
Marjani (Swahili) "Coral."
Nadja (Uganda) "Second born."
Neema (Swahili) "Born in prosperity."
Ola (Nigerian) "Precious."
Rasheedah (Swahili/Arabic) "Righteous."
Sade, Sharde (Yoruban) Short form of Folasade.

Safiya (Swahili) "Pure."
Shani (Swahili) "A marvel; wondrous."
Zahra (Swahili) "Flowering."
Zalika (Swahili/Arabic) "Well-born."

African Names For Boys

Abdalla (Swahili) "God's servant."
Ajani (Yoruban) "Struggles to win."
Aren (Nigerian) "Eagle."
Chike (Nigerian) "God's power."
Ekon (Nigerian) "Strong."
Faraji (Swahili) "Consolation."
Haji (Swahili) "Pilgrim to Mecca."
Hasani (Swahili) "Handsome."
Jabari (Swahili) "Valiant."
Kato (Uganda) "Twin."
Mongo (Yoruban) "Famous."
Nuru (Swahili) "Born in daytime."
Omari (Swahili) "God the highest."
Rashidi (Swahili) "Counselor."
Salim (Swahili) "Peace."
Tau (African) "Lion."

International Names

Although many names have been adopted into two or more language groups, only a relatively short list have variant forms in seven or more. The reason these names are so favored seems to be because of their religious and/or royal histories. Names of kings like Charles, George, Henry and William became solid favorites long ago, as did names of prominent saints like Francis and Gregory. Names of the early apostles and gospel writers form the majority of these special international names.

Names on the lists below can truly be termed international.

International Names for Girls

ENGLISH	GAELIC Irish/Scot/ Welsh	FRENCH	SPAN/ITAL	SCAN/GER	SLAVIC
Alexandra	Alastar, Alexina	Alixandra	Alejandra/ Allessandra	Alexandra	Aleksandra
Alice	Ailis, Alison	Alice	Alicia	Elka	Alisia
Angel, Angelica	Aingeal	Angele, Angelique	Angelita/ Angela	Angelika	Andelka
Ann	Aine	Anne	Ana/Anna	Anni, Annika	Anya
Barbara	Bairbre	Barbe	Barbara	Barbro	Barbora, Varvara
Bridget	Brigid	Brigitte	Brigida	Birgit/ Brigitta	Brygida
Carol	Carrol	Carole	Carola/ Carolina	Karel/Karol	Karol, Karola
Christine, Christina	Kirstie, Cristiona	Christine	Cristina	Kristin/ Kirsten	Krystyna, Kristina
Eleanor, Elinor	Elionora	Eleonore, Alinor	Leanor/ Eleonora	Leanora/ Eleonora	Eleni
Elizabeth	Elspeth	Elise	Isabel/ Elisabetta	Elisabet/ Elsbeth	Elzbieta
Frances	Proinseas	Francoise	Francisca/ Francesca	Frans/ Franziska	Franciszka
Helen	Aileen	Helene	Elenor/Lena	Elna/Helena	Alena, Olena

Jane	Sinead, Janet	Jeanne	Juana/ Giovanna, Gianna	Johanna	Jana, Ivana
Katherine	Caitrin, Catriona	Catherine, Cateline	Catalina/ Caterina	Karin/ Katrine	Katerina, Ekaterina
Madeline	Madailein	Madeleine	Magdalena/ Maddelena	Magdalene	Magdalina
Margaret	Mairead	Marguerite	Margarita/ Margherita	Margareta/ Margit	Marketa
Mary	Maire, Moira, Mairi	Marie, Maree	Maria	Marieke/ Marie	Marinka, Marya
Susan	Siusan	Suzanne	Susana/ Susanna	Susanne, Sanna	Zuzanna

International Names for Boys

ENGLISH	GAELIC Irish/Scot Welsh	FRENCH	SPAN/ITAL	SCAN/GER	SLAVIC
Alexander	Alasdair, Alistair	Alexandre	Alejandro/ Alessandro	Alexander	Alexsandr, Aleksander
Andrew	Aindreas, Andra	Andre	Andres/ Andrea	Anders/ Andrea	Andrei
Anthony	Antaine	Antoine	Antonio	Anton	Antoni, Anton
Benedict	Benedict	Benoit	Benito/ Benedetto	Benedikt	Benedek
Charles	Searlas, Cormac	Charles	Carlos/ Carlo	Karl	Karol, Karel
Christopher	Criostoir, Kester	Christophe	Cristobal/ Cristo- foro	Christoph, Kristoffer	Krystof
Edmund	Eamon	Edmond	Edmundo/ Edmondo	Edmund	Edmon

Edward	Eamon	Edouard	Eduardo/ Edoardo	Edvard/ Eduard	Edvard
Frank, Francis	Proinsias	Francois	Francisco/ Francesco	Frans/ Frantz	Franc, Franek
Frederick	Fardoragh	Frederic	Federico	Frederik/ Friedrich	Fryderyk, Fredek
Geoffrey, Jeffrey	Sieffre, Siofrai	Geoffroi	Godofredo/ Geoffredo	Gottfried	Gotfrid
George	Geordi	Georges	Jorge/ Giorgio	Jorgen/ Jeorg	Georgi, Yuri
Gregory	Grigor	Gregoire	Gregorio	Joris/Greger	Grigor, Grigori
Henry	Einri	Henri	Enrique/ Enrico	Hendrik/ Heinrich	Henrik
James, Jacob	Seamus	Jacques	Jaime/ Giacomo	Jakob	Yakov
John	Sean, Shaun, Shane, Ian	Jean	Juan/ Giovanni, Gianni	Jon, Johan	Jan, Ivan
Joseph	Ioseph	Josephe	Jose/ Giuseppe	Josef	Josef, Jozef
Laurence	Lorcan	Laurent	Lorencio/ Lorenzo	Lars, Lorenz	Lavrenti
Lewis, Louis	Llewelyn	Louis	Luis/Luigi	Ludvig/ Ludwig	Ludwik, Ludvik
Luke	Lucas	Luc, Lucien	Lucas/ Lucca	Lukas/ Lucius	Lukas, Luka
Mark	Marcas	Marc	Marcos/ Marco	Markus	Mark, Marko, Marek
Martin	Martainn, Mairtin	Martin	Martin/ Martino	Marten/ Martel	Martinas, Martyn

Matthew	Maitias	Mathieu	Mateo/ Matteo	Mattias/ Mathias	Matyas, Matei
Michael	Micheal	Michel	Miguel/ Michele	Mikael, Mikkel	Michal, Mikhail
Nicholas	Nicol, Nicolas	Nicholas	Nicolas/ Niccolo	Niklas, Nikolaus	Nikolai
Paul	Pol	Paul	Pablo/Paolo	Poul, Pavel	Pavlo, Pavlik
Peter	Peadar	Pierre	Pedro/Pietro	Per, Piet	Pyotr
Philip	Filip	Philippe	Felipe/ Filippo	Filip, Philipp	Filip
Richard	Rickard	Richard	Ricardo/ Riccardo	Rikard/ Richert	Rikard, Rostik
Robert	Riobard	Robert	Roberto	Robert/ Ruprecht	Rupert
Stephen, Steven	Steaphan	Etienne	Esteban/ Stefano	Stefan, Stephan	Stefan
William	Liam	Guillaume	Guillermo/ Guglielmo	Vilhelm/ Wilhelm	Vilem, Vilmos

New Variants and Created Names

Suppose you want a completely original name, or at least one that's different from any you've heard before. Perhaps you want to combine family names in a new way. You might want to create a son's name based on the mother's name, or a daughter's name based on the father's name. Perhaps you want to combine both parents' names into one new name.

Seven types of name inventions and creations are explained below. The descriptions should give you ideas for the kind of name you may have in mind. You'll want names that have originality, yet follow sound and look patterns that are not too difficult for your child to live with.

Spelling is an important consideration in this category. If you'll take special care to match up the sound you want with the most logical spelling, both you and your child will be happier with the results. See "Spell It Right, Pronounce It Right" in Part III for additional help in determining appropriate spellings.

PLACE NAMES AND SURNAMES. These are existing names that in the past have been rarely used as given names. You'll have most success with this type if your choice has some similarity to existing given names, or is especially appealing in look and sound. Barrett, Tanner, Sierra, Cheyenne and Dakota are examples of this kind of inventive transferral.

Do you have a family surname that might be a little unusual, but has a pleasing sound and look? It might make a successful name for your child. It's long been a practice in southern states to give family surnames to daughters as given names.

VOCABULARY NAMES. These are names taken from our regular vocabulary. Christian, Dusty, Porsche (the car), Satin and Charisma are all vocabulary names. Exercise caution when choosing your own vocabulary word to use as a name. Look up the word in a dictionary to be sure that the meaning is satisfactory to you. The sound of a word-name might be attractive, but not the meaning. Enema and Penicillin, for example, make embarrassing names.

PHONETIC NAMES. These are names created to ensure a specific pronunciation. For example, Britnee, Jakwalyn and Antwan. Be very careful with this type of creation. It's better to use an existing name than to produce a name most people would perceive as being misspelled. Check the index under the name you're interested in to see what phonetic variants already exist.

NAMES THAT RHYME. This is one of the most popular ways to create new names. Rhyming names are based on existing names. For example, Terrilyn and Derilyn rhyme with Marilyn, Jerrick and Terrik rhyme with Eric. You can experiment with this type of invention by substituting different letters of the alphabet for the first letter of whatever name has the basic sound you'd like to rhyme.

GENDER-CHANGE NAMES. Most names for boys can be changed into names for girls. Generally all that's necessary is to add a feminine name ending. (Danieleen or Ronalda, for example.) You can also shorten the boy's name, then add a feminine ending. This will yield names like Danine and Ronette. Many examples of this kind of name are already in use. You'll want to check existing possibilities before you invent a new version. Look in the girls' index for names that begin like the first part of the male name. Variants will be listed with the main name.

If you decide to create a new name by adding a feminine ending to a male name, consult the list of name endings at the end of this section.

To reverse the gender of a mother's name for a son, find her name in the girls' index. The entry may refer you to the male version of the name. Carlina, for example, is a feminine variant of Charles. When you look up Charles, you'll see a number of different versions of the male name.

Other names can be gender-changed by creating a new name based on a part of the female name, perhaps by changing a feminine ending to a masculine ending. Endings that work well for boys' names are fewer than for girls. See the list at the end of this section.

PREFIX NAMES. These are names formed from prefixes like La- and Sha- combined with one of the many diminutives or other name endings, or shorter names like Ana and Jon. (Latanya and DeSean are examples of this type of name.) Prefix names make up the largest group of today's new names. Before deciding to create your own new prefix name, why not check some of the prefix names already in use? They're grouped in the index alphabetically as De- names, La- names, Sha- names, etc.

Consult the list of name endings at the end of this section if you want to try creating your own prefix name.

NEW NAMES FROM OLD. This technique lets you combine parts of existing names in new ways. You can reverse syllables, changing Maribel to Bellemarie, for example. You can combine part of the father's name with part of the mother's name, changing Carl and Della into Cardell, for example. You can combine parts of the names in more than one way; Eleanor and Larry could produce either Ellary or Larellan. Still another method is to scramble the letters in a name, for example, Liana yields Niala.

You can vary almost any given name by attaching a variety of name endings to some part of the basic name. This type of name creation has a long history. Noreen, for example, was created as a variant of Nora, which was created as a short form of names like Eleanora and Leonora.

Sometimes it's necessary to insert a compatible consonant to blend the name ending with the name beginning that you've chosen. Some favorite consonant-plus-ending pairings are shown in the second list below, along with favored short forms (like sean, dean and jon) frequently used as name endings.

Basic Name Endings

a, i, ee, ie, y, ye, ia, ea, ae, an, en, in, ian, ien
ann, anne, ana, ahna, anna, ani, anni, anee, ianne, ianna
een, ene, ena, enna, ienne, ine, ina, inda, ita
ele, ell, elle, ella, iel, iell, ielle, iela, iella
ess, esse, essa, eesa, eece, iesa, iessa, isha, icia
ette, etta, iette, iara, iera, ille, ila, illa

iss, isse, issa, ise, isa, ice, ica, icka, ika
oni, onie, ona, onna, iona, ionna, ionne

Name Endings Plus Consonants

bel, bell, belle, bella
chel, chelle, chele, chella
ceen, cine, cene, cina, cinda, coya, cacia
da, die, dee, del, dell, delle, della
dine, deen, dina, dene, dena, dean, deane, dona, donna
gine, gina, geen, geena, ginny, gini
keisha, kisha, kesha, keesha
kie, kee, kia, keta, kita, keeta, kiya, kira
lana, lani, lanna, londa, linda
lane, laine, laina, layne, layna
lee, lie, lia, lea, leah, lita, leila
lin, linn, linne, linna, lyn, lynn, lynne, lynna
line, lina, leen, leena, lene, lena
lisa, lise, leese, leesa, leeza, liza, licia, lisha
liss, lisse, lissa, lyssa, lesse, lessa
mika, mica, meka, meisha, mesha, misha
nae, naya, nea, nia, nel, nell, nelle, nella
neece, neese, nice, nicia, nesha, neisha, nisha, niesha
ness, nesse, nessa, neesa, nissa, nisa
net, nette, netta, nita, nica, nika, niqua, nique
nille, neille, neil, nora
quise, quita, quetta
rae, raia, ray, raya, raye, raine, raina, rayna
ree, reese, rice, rise, risa, rysa, ressa
rell, relle, risse, rissa, reesha, rona, ronna, ronda
rene, reen, rina, rena, rienna, rill, rille
sha, shah, shay, shae, shai, saundra, sondra
shan, shana, shanna, shonna, shawna, shaunda
te, tee, tae, tai, taye, tia, tiya, tel, telle
teen, teena, tine, tina, tana, tasha, tisha, tosha

tesse, tessa, tonia, tonya, tori, tory, toria
treece, trice, trise, trisa, tricia
vette, vetta, viette, vietta
von, vonne, vonna, vonda, vona

Name Endings Favored For Boys

an, en, in, on, ano, ino, ion, ian, ien, o, yo
andre, andro, aundre, ante, ondre, onte
del, dell, tel, trel, quel
jon, juan, lon, lonn, leon
mar, mario, marco, marcus, mond, mont, monte
rik, rek, rak, rick, rel, ron, ray
sean, shawn, shaun, shane
van, von, vonn, vaughn, vonte, vel, vell

PART III

TOOL KIT FOR NAME SELECTION

Q & A to Clarify Your Choices

Think about the questions below, discuss them with your mate, then write out your answers. (Each parent can make up a separate list of answers, or you can work together to complete one list.) Your responses will help you later on when you fill in the Selection Worksheet.

1. Is there a family name you want or need to consider as a name choice? (Your own, your mate's, parents, grandparents, etc.)
2. Would you consider a variant form of the family name instead of the identical name? Perhaps a different name using just the same first initial?
3. If the first name is already determined, do you need to find a compatible middle name?
4. Do you or your mate have any family surnames (mother's, grandmother's, etc.) that might yield an interesting or appealing given name? Would you care for it as a first or a middle name? Would it work well for either a boy or a girl?
5. Do you have a particular ethnic background? Perhaps a combination of different national origins? Would you be interested in a name that reflects your origins?
6. After reading the descriptions of types of names in Part II, how would you describe the kind of names

51

you personally like? (Traditional, a little dignified, more casual, modern, slightly unusual, etc.)

7. What kind of future do you envision for your child? What type of name might best fit his or her prospects?

8. Do you want to combine name types with the first and middle name? What combination appeals to you most? (Strong/feminine, traditional/classic, classic/slightly unusual, traditional/ethnic, Biblical/Biblical, African/classic, etc.)

9. Do you want to choose a name with the fewest possibilities for shortening, nicknames, etc., or do you want a name with several potential variations?

10. Does your family have a history of twins? Be sure to select second choices for both genders, to be on the safe side. (It's not a bad idea in any case to have second choices ready. Last-minute changes of mind after a birth happen more often than you'd imagine.)

11. Will you make every effort to enjoy yourself and not get into too many arguments over name choices? (Potential name choices aren't written in stone. You'll most likely have a few months to try out various possibilities before the baby is actually born. Most conflicts over names smooth themselves out.)

Spell It Right, Pronounce It Right

American parents tend to be a bit strong-minded when it comes to achieving the pronunciation they want for a name. It's like the joke that asks, "Where does an elephant sit?" Answer: "Anywhere it wants to!"

If you decide you prefer a different pronunciation for a name than most people expect to hear, you must prepare your child to go through life correcting others who use the conventional pronunciation. The conventional pronunciation of Tristan, for example, is *TRISS-ten*. One mother decided she preferred her child to be addressed as *triss-TAHN*. She said she had to be constantly vigilant, insisting that teachers and others use the pronunciation she wanted. For parents in a similar situation, another option would be to use a phonetic spelling (Tristahn) instead of the conventional Tristan.

Sometimes parents aren't sure of the conventionally correct spelling of names like Antoine, Danielle, Desiree and Michaela. It's best not to take a chance on guessing wrong. Look up the name in the index. Pronunciation keys are given for most names that are pronounced differently from the way they're spelled. It's better to spell the name right in the first place than for your child to spend a lifetime explaining why his or her name is spelled in an unusual way. The danger is that other people are likely to assume that an awkwardly spelled phonetic variant is misspelled.

Some names have more than one conventional pronunciation. For example, look up Jacqueline in the girls' index. Six variations are indicated in the pronunciation key, and it's likely that the sound you favor is one of the six. Each sound-variant is accompanied by spellings that generally will be accepted as legitimate forms of the basic name. Some are traditional, others are creative. Note the cross-reference to Jaclyn, a contemporary phonetic form.

Because misspelling a birth name is an avoidable problem, it's important to take the time to check the spelling of any name you favor, no matter how familiar the name seems to you. Some names are particularly vulnerable to misspelling. If the names below are ones you favor, take special care in deciding on the best spelling. See Pronunciation Tips for further guidelines.

Names Frequently Misspelled

GIRLS
Alicia, Alisha
Bridget
Brittany, Brittney
Caitlin, Caitlyn
Chastity
Chelsea, Chelsey
Cheyenne
Crystal
Danielle
Desiree
Felicia
Hayley
Heidi
Jacqueline, Jacquelyn
Jennifer
Kaitlyn, Katelyn
Keisha
Kiara
Megan, Meagan,
Meghan
Michaela, Micaela
Michelle, Michele
Priscilla
Tabitha

BOYS
Aaron
Antoine, Antone
Christopher
Dante
Darren, Darin
Darryl
Demetrius, Dimitri
Derek, Derrick
Dominic, Dominick
Duane, Dwayne
Geoffrey
Jared
Jeffrey
Kaelan
Nicholas
Ramsey, Ramses
Schuyler, Skyler
Zachariah
Zachary

Pronunciation Tips

As previously mentioned, the pronunciation key given after most names in the index will help you achieve conventional (or creative) spelling and pronunciation. You might not agree with all the keys, or you might know of another way to pronounce a particular name. But the keys try to show the most common pronunciations that people in general will recognize.

An attempt to include here an extensive list of guidelines for pronunciation would only be tedious and possibly confusing. Instead, here are just two tips you can use to deal with the most common problems of pronouncing a name or name variant. First, which syllable of a name should be stressed (emphasized)? Should Tristan be pronounced *TRISS-ten* or *triss-TAHN*? Second, how can you tell whether a name like Ana should be pronounced *ANN-ah* or *AHN-ah*? Should Wynonna be pronounced *win-OHN-ah* or *win-AHN-ah*?

TIP #1—STRESS THE RIGHT SYLLABLE

This tip deals with names having only two or three syllables. It's very useful to know, particularly if you're deciding on a name with several possible name endings. (Should you choose Doris or Dorise, for example.)

Most two-syllable given names used in America (like Doris, Brian, Tristan and Roger) stress the first syllable, unless the name follows the French pattern of stressing the last syllable. The French themselves generally don't stress one part of a name more than the rest of the name. Americans rarely leave a name unstressed. Most names with French endings (see list below) end up being stressed at least slightly. The Irish "een" ending is also stressed.

French Name Endings:

aine, ayne, anne, enne, ienne, ele, elle, ielle, ette,
ille, ine, ise, isse, trice, nique, quel, quise

EXAMPLES (stress last syllable):

Charmaine (*shar-MAYNE*)   Maxine (*max-EEN*)
Jermayne (*jer-MAYNE*)   Dorise (*dor-EESE*)
Roseanne (*rose-ANN*)   Clarisse (*kla-REESE*)
Cheyenne (*shy-ENN*)   Patrice (*pa-TREESE*)
Brienne (*bree-ENN*)   Monique (*moh-NEEK*)
Michele (*mee-SHELL*)   Marquel (*mar-KELL*)
Michelle (*mee-SHELL*)   Marquise (*mar-KEESE*)
Danielle (*dan-YELL*)   Cathleen (*kath-LEEN*)
Mariette (*mar-ee-ETT*)   Maureen (*mah-REEN*)
Camille (*kah-MEEL*)   Doreen (*dor-EEN*)

TIP #2: CONSONANTS HELP DETERMINE THE VOWEL SOUND IN A NAME

Names with double consonants often indicate a short
vowel sound just before the consonants. Names with single consonants often indicate a long vowel sound. This is
particularly true with feminine name endings like:

-ena, -enna, -esa, -essa, -ila, -illa,
-ina, -inna, -isa, -issa, -ona, -onna

The name endings -ana, -anna, -ani, -anni are different
only in that the single consonant indicates the *AH* pronunciation, and the double consonant indicates the *ANN* pronunciation.

EXAMPLES:

Long vowel sounds	Short vowel sounds
Teresa (*te-REE-sah*, *te-RAY-sah*)	Teressa (*te-RESS-ah*)
Lila (*LY-lah*)	Lilla (*LILL-ah*)
Clarisa (*kla-REE-sah*)	Clarissa (*kla-RISS-ah*)
Carina (*ka-RFEN-ah*)	Carinna (*ka-RINN-ah*)
Diona (*dy-OH-nah*)	Dionna (*dy-AHN-ah*)
Ana (*AH-nah*)	Anna (*ANN-ah*)
Lani (*LAH-nee*)	Lannie (*LANN-ee*)
Mariana (*mare-ee-AH-nah*)	Marianna (*mare-ee-ANN-ah*)

Diana is an exception to the above guideline regarding single consonants. In popular usage, it's pronounced at least four ways (*dy-ANN-ah, dy-AHN-ah, dee-ANN-ah* and *dee-AHN-ah*). The index lists some of the phonetic variants that have been created to ensure each one of these four different pronunciations of Diana.

Singing star Wynonna Judd's name is different in that her chosen pronunciation is *wy-NO-nah*. One result of this choice is that when reviewers spell Wynonna in print, they sometimes use the conventional spelling Winona or Wynona. Actress Winona Ryder doesn't have the same problem since her name follows the basic guideline.

You might want to look at the list of the frequently used name endings (pages 46–48) and see for yourself how quickly you can determine the most likely conventional pronunciations. When in doubt, consult the index to find names with similar endings and see what pronunciations are suggested.

Have You Created a New Name or Name Variation?

CHECK THE RESULTS. Speak your created name out loud to test how it sounds. Consult the list above to see if you've got the right spelling for the vowel pronunciation and stressing of the syllables. Consult the index to find and compare similar names.

Show the written new name to friends. Can they pronounce the name the way you want them to without prompting? Do they have any problem with the spelling?

If no one can agree on how your created name should be spelled or pronounced, perhaps you should try again with another version of the name. Any name you create should be reasonably easy for your child to spell and logical in the way it's pronounced.

HOW TO USE THE NAME SELECTION WORK SHEETS

1. Make copies of the blank work sheets. You'll need enough to analyze all the names you're interested in.
2. On the Preliminary Selection Work Sheet, fill in the first name you want to consider. If you have a possible choice for a middle name at this time, fill that in also.
3. Write in the name type for the first and middle names.
4. Write your child's last name on each line below the surname heading; you'll see more easily how all forms of the names will look written out in full.
5. Decide what nicknames or short forms are most likely to result from the basic name. List them in the spaces below the first and middle names.
6. In the space on the top right, fill in the set of initials that results from combining first and middle names with the surname.
7. In the space provided, make notations of any points that affect how you feel about the name. What are the pos-

itive things? The negatives? Change your remarks or add to them as you continue comparing various names. Add your mate's comments. (Use the back side of the copied work sheet for additional space.)

8. Choose your favorites from the Preliminary Selection Work Sheets and enter the top three to six names on the Final Choices Work Sheet. Pencil in a number in front of each name to show the order of your preference. (Try for a Final Choices Work Sheet that combines both your list and your mate's.)

Preliminary Selection Work Sheet

NAME TYPE(S) _____/_____

FIRST NAME	MIDDLE NAME	SURNAME
_____	_____	_____
SHORT FORMS_____	_____	_____
_____	_____	_____
NICK-NAMES_____	_____	_____
_____	_____	_____

Things you like about this name:_____

_____

Things you don't like:_____

_____

Final Choices Work Sheet

ORDER OF PREFERENCE NUMBER	FIRST NAME	MIDDLE NAME	SURNAME
( )	_____	_____	_____
( )	_____	_____	_____
( )	_____	_____	_____
( )	_____	_____	_____
( )	_____	_____	_____
( )	_____	_____	_____

Final Selection Checklist

1. Have you checked the spelling of the names you like best?
2. Does the spelling fit the pronunciation you want to achieve?
3. Will the spelling be reasonably simple for your child and others to spell correctly?
4. Have you checked the set of initials—first, middle and surname—to be sure the three letters don't spell something embarrassing?
5. Have you chosen names for both a boy and a girl? (Unless modern technology has informed you in advance, you'll want to prepare for either gender.)
6. If you don't care for nicknames, have you chosen a

name that is short enough (single syllable) not to be subject to more shortening? If you've chosen a longer name, are you prepared to go to the extra effort in coming years to gently insist to all concerned that the full name should be used?

7. Have your choices pleased everyone concerned with or interested in the names you've chosen for your child? (If your answer is yes, you've accomplished wonders. Congratulations! If the answer is no, don't worry too much about it. Eventually everyone else will come around to liking the name as your child makes the name his or her very own.)

How to Use the Index

INDEX FEATURES

MAIN ENTRY NAME. This is usually the most frequently used form of the name. Related names may be listed beneath the main entry name or cross-referenced in separate main entries. Example: Helen and Elena are related but are shown as separate main entry names. Sometimes similar names (Darin/Darren, Darryl/Darrell) each have separate entries because each form follows a distinctive spelling pattern, and each has its own group of variants.

PRONUNCIATION KEY. The key shows how the name divides into spoken syllables. Commonly accepted pronunciation is shown in simple phonetics. Syllables shown in all capitals should be stressed. Alternate pronunciations are sometimes shown.

NAME ORIGIN. If more than one language origin is given, the last one listed is the older source. Example: (English/French)

NAME MEANING. Definitions are given in quotes, if known. The entry may include notes on possible or partial meanings.

MYTHOLOGICAL, HISTORICAL, BIBLICAL NOTES. These notes offer brief descriptions of significant people, nonhumans, places and events that have inspired names or made them memorable.

REMARKS. Occasionally an entry will include comments about modern usage and other facts of interest about a name.

CROSS-REFERENCES. References show the linkage of related names that have separate main entries. For example, Jeffrey cross-references to Geoffrey.

VARIANTS, RELATED NAMES. These names, grouped below the main entry name, are usually spelling variants and forms of the main name in other languages. Names with different meanings but similar spellings sometimes may be grouped together, with an explanatory note.

Sometimes one or more variant names listed below the main entry will be printed in all capitals. This indicates that those variants are used significantly more often than other variants and therefore deserve special attention.

Sample Entry

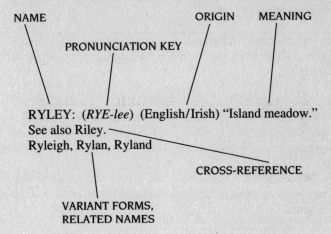

NAME

PRONUNCIATION KEY

ORIGIN MEANING

RYLEY: (*RYE-lee*) (English/Irish) "Island meadow."
See also Riley.
Ryleigh, Rylan, Ryland

CROSS-REFERENCE

VARIANT FORMS,
RELATED NAMES

PART IV

NAME INDEX

GIRLS' INDEX

A

ABIGAIL: (Hebrew) "My father rejoices." Biblical; the name of King David's third wife, described as "good in discretion and beautiful in form." See also Gail.
ABBY, Abbey, Abbie, Avagail

ABRIANA: (*ah-bree-AHN-ah*) (Italian) Feminine form of Abraham.
Abrianna, Abrienne, Abra, Abri, Abree, Abrielle

ACACIA: (*a-KAY-shah*) (Spanish/Greek) "Honorable." Biblical; acacia wood was used to build the wilderness Tabernacle. See also Casey.

ADA: (Hebrew) "Ornament." (Nigerian) "First daughter."
Adah; Ayda (Arabic) "Benefit."

ADAIR: (Scottish) "From the oak tree ford." Rare.

ADANNA: (Nigerian) "Her father's daughter." Adana is a Spanish feminine form of Adam.
Adana; Adanya

ADARA: (Arab) "Virgin."

ADELA: (Latin/German) "Of the nobility, noble." See also Adeline.
Adelle, Adele (French); Adella, Adelita, Adalia (Spanish); Adelia, Adelaide, Adalie (French)

ADELINE: (French) Variant form of Adela. See also Alina and Allena.

Adilene, Adalene, Adelynn, Adalyn, Adelina, Addie

ADELISA: (*ah-da-LEES-ah*) (French/German) Forerunner of Alice.

Adelise (French); Adaliz, Adalicia

ADINAH: (Hebrew) "Slender."

Adina

ADIRA: (*ah-DEER-ah*) (Arabic) "Strong."

ADONIA: (*ah-DON-ya*) (Spanish/Greek) "Beautiful lady." Feminine form of Adonis.

ADRIANA: (*ay-dree-AHN-ah*) (Latin) "From Adria," the Adriatic sea region. Also means "dark."

ADRIENNE (French); ADRIANNA, Adreanna, Adrianne; Adriane, Adriene (French); Adrienna, Adra, Adrea, Adria, Adrina, Adrielle

AGATHA: (Latin/Greek) "Good."

AGNES: (Latin/Greek) "Chaste." See also Anissa, Inez and Ynes.

AIDA: (*ah-EE-dah*) (Italian) The name of the Ethiopian princess in Verdi's opera *Aida*. Also a Japanese surname (*ah-ee-DAH*) "runs across the field."

AILANI: (*ah-ee-LAH-nee*) (Hawaiian paraphrase) "High chief."

AILEEN: (*eye-LEEN*) (Scottish/Irish) Variant form of Evelyn.

Aileene

AIMEE: (*ay-MEE*) (French) "Loved." Variant form of Amy.

AISHA: (*ah-EE-shah, AY-shah*) (Arabic) "Woman, life." Aisha was the name of the favorite wife of the prophet Mohammed. See also Asha, Asia, and Isha.

Aishah, Aysha, Ayesha, Ayeisha

AKIKO: (*ah-KEE-koh*) (Japanese) "Iris"; "light, bright."

AKILAH: (*ah-KEE-lah*) (Arabic) "Bright, smart."

Akili (Tanzanian)

ALAIR: (French) "Cheerful, glad." Variant form of Hilary.
Allaire

ALANA: (*ah-LAH-nah*) (Irish) "Dear child." Also used as
a feminine form of Alan. (Hawaiian) "awakening."
Alanna, Alannah, Allana, Alani, Alona, Alonna; Alaine
(French); Alaina, Alayna, Alayne

ALANDRA: (Spanish) Variant form of Alexandra.
Alondra

ALANZA: (*ah-LAHN-zah*) (Spanish) "Ready for battle."
Feminine form of Alonzo.

ALARICE: (*AL-a-riss*) (English/German) "Rules all." Feminine form of Alaric.
Allaryce

ALBERTA: (English/German) "Noble, bright." Feminine
form of Albert.
Albertina, Albertine

ALCINE: (Italian) Literary; in the Orlando poems, Alcina
is a mistress of alluring enchantments and sensual plea-
sures.
Alcina, Alcinia, Alcee

ALDA: (Spanish/Italian) "Wise, elder." Variant form of
Aldo.
Aldene; Aldona (Spanish)

ALETHA: (*ah-LEE-thah*) (Greek) "Truthful." Mythology;
goddess of truth.
Alethea, Alethia, Alathea, Alithea, Aleta

ALEXANDRA: (English/Greek) "Defender of mankind."
Feminine form of Alexander. See also Alandra, Alexis,
Drina, Lexandra, Lisandra, Olexa, Sandra, Sasha,
Xandra, and Zandra.
ALEXANDRIA, Alexandrea, Alexandrina; Alejandra
(Spanish); Alessandra (Italian); Alyssandra, Alixandra
(French)

ALEXIS: (*a-LEX-iss*) (English/Greek) "Helper, defender."

Short form of Alexandra. Used more for girls than for boys.

ALEXA, Alexia, Alyx; Alix (French); Alexi, Alexina, Alexine

ALFREDA: (*al-FREE-dah, al-FRAY-dah*) (German) Feminine form of Alfred.

ALI: (*AL-ee*) (Arabic) "Greatest." A variant form of Allah, title of the Supreme Being in the Muslim faith. Allie is a short form of names beginning with "Al-." More common for boys.

Allie, Alli

ALIA: (Israeli) "Immigrant to a new home."

Aleah, Alea, Aliyah, Aleana, Alya (Arabic) "Great one."

ALICE: (English) "Of the nobility." Variant form of the old French name Adeliz, from Adelaide. See also Adelisa, Alicia, Allison, Alyssa and Elke.

ALISA (Spanish); Alyce, Alise, Aleece, Allyce, Alyss, Alliss, Alys

ALICIA: (*ah-LEE-shah*) (Latin) Variant form of Alice. See also Alyssa and Licia.

ALISHA, Alysha, Alycia, Alecia, Aleecia, Aleesha, Alishia, Alisia

ALIDA: (*ah-LEE-da*) (Latin) "With wings."

ALIKA: (*ah-LYE-kah, ah-LEE-kah*) (Nigerian) "Most beautiful."

ALIMA: (*ah-LEE-mah*) (Arabic) "Sea maiden."

ALINA: (Latin) "Of the nobility." Variant form of Adelina.

Aline, Allina, Alyna

ALITA: (*ah-LEE-tah*) (Spanish) Short form of Adelita.

ALIZAH: (*a-LYE-zah*) (Hebrew) "Joy, joyful."

Aliza, Aleeza

ALLEGRA: (*ah-LAY-grah*) (Italian) "Lively, happy."

ALLENA: (Celtic) "Fair, good-looking." Feminine form of Allen or variant form of Helen. Alena is a Russian diminutive and a variant of Adelina.

Alena, Allene, Alene, Aleena, Aleen, Aline

ALLISON: (English/French) Diminutive form of Alice.
ALISON (Scottish); ALLYSON, Alyson, Alisanne

ALMA: (Latin) "The soul."

ALMIRA: (*al-MEER-ah*) (Arabic) "Truthful."

ALOISE: (*al-oh-eez*) (Spanish) "Famous in battle." Feminine form of Aloysius.

ALOMA: (*a-LOH-mah*) (Latin) "Dove." Short form of Paloma.

ALPHA: (*AL-fah*) (Greek) The first letter of the Greek alphabet.

ALSATIA: (*al-SAY-shah*) From Alsace, a region in France.

ALTA: (Spanish) "High." Short form of Altagracia, a reference to the "high grace" of Mary, the mother of Jesus.
Altagracia

ALTAIRA: (*al-TARE-ah*) (Arabic) "High-flying." In astronomy, Altair is a star of the first magnitude.

ALTHEA: (Greek) "Wholesome."

ALVA: (Hebrew) "Sublime." Alvarita and Alvera are Spanish feminine forms of Alvaro, meaning "speaker of truth." Alvina is the feminine form of Alvin, meaning "wise friend."
Alvarita, Alvera, Alverna, Alvina

ALYSSA: (*ah-LISS-ah*) (English) Variant form of Alice.
ALISSA, Alisse, Alysse (*ah-LISS*), Alyse (*ah-LEESE*), Allyse, Alyssia

AMA: (*AH-mah*) (Ghanese) "Saturday's child."
Ami (Ghanese)

AMABEL: (Latin) "Lovable." See also Anabel.

AMADA: (*ah-MAH-dah*) (Spanish) "Beloved."
Amadia, Amadea, Amadita, Amadi (Nigerian) "Rejoicing."

AMALA: (Arabic) "Beloved."

AMANDA: (English/Latin) "Worthy of being loved." Literary; poets and playwrights brought this name into popular usage in the seventeenth century.

AMANTHA: (*ah-MAN-thah*) (Greek) Variant form of Amarantha, a flower name, or a short form of Samantha.

AMAPOLA: (*ah-mah-POH-lah*) (Arabic) "Poppy."

AMARA: (*ah-MAHR-ah*) (Spanish) "Imperishable." Amaris, meaning "child of the moon," is the astrological name for Cancer.
Amaris, Amarissa

AMARYLLIS: (*am-ah-RILL-iss*) (Greek) Flower name; poetically, a simple shepherdess or country girl.

AMBER: (English/Arabic) A jewel-quality fossilized resin; as a color, the name refers to a warm honey shade. Contemporary variants may be rhyming variants based on Kimberly.
Amberly, Amberlee, Amberli, Amberlyn, Amberlynn

AMELIA: (*a-MEEL-yah*) (English/Latin) "Industrious, striving." See also Emily.
Amalia; Amalie, Amelie (French)

AMETHYST: (Greek) "Against intoxication." A purple or violet-colored gemstone. According to ancient Greek superstition, an amethyst protected its owner against the effects of strong drink.

AMINA: (*ah-MEEN-ah*) (Swahili/Arabic) "Trustworthy."
Amineh, Aminah, Ameena, Ameenah

AMIRA: (*ah-MEE-rah*) (Hebrew) "Princess; one who speaks."
Amirah (Arabic)

AMITA: (*ah-MEE-tah*) (Israeli) "Truth."

AMITY: (*AM-i-tee*) (English/French) "Friendship."

AMY: (English/French) "Beloved." See also Aimee.
Amie, Amia

ANA: (*AHN-ah*) (Spanish) "Grace, favor." Variant form of Anna. Ana is often used in blended names like Analee and Anarosa. See also Anna and Anne.

Analena, Anarosa, Analee, Analeigh, Anamarie

ANABEL: (Latin) "Beautiful, graceful."

Annabel, Annabelle, Anabelle, Annabella

ANAIS: (*ah-NAY-us, ah-NYE-ess*) (Latin) Variant form of Ana.

ANASTASIA: (*ahn-a-STAH-shah, ahn-a-STAY-shah*) (Greek) "Resurrection."

Annastasia (*ann-a-STAY-zhah*), Anastacia, Anastasha, Anastashia, Anastassia, Anastazia

ANDA: (*awn-dah*) (Japanese surname) "Meet at the field." Also a short form of Andrea.

ANDEE: (Contemporary) Feminine short form of Andrea.

Andi, Andie, Andena

ANDREA: (*AHN-dree-ah*) (Latin/Greek) Feminine form of Andrew. See also Ondrea.

Andria (Spanish); Aundrea, Andreya, Andreana, Andriana, Andreanna, Andrianna, Andrianne, Andrienne, Andrena, Andrina, Andra; Andree (French); Andranetta

ANDROMEDA: (*an-DRAH-ma-dah*) (Greek) Mythology; an Ethiopian princess, the wife of Perseus. Also a northern constellation.

ANEKO: (*ah-NAY-koh*) (Japanese) "Older sister."

ANGELA: (Latin/Greek) "Messenger."

ANGEL, ANGELINA, Angie, Angeline, Angelene, Angelena, Angelita, Angelia, Angelyn, Angelynn, Angelisa, Angelee, Angeli, Anjali, Angele, Angell, Angelle

ANGELICA: (Latin) "Like an angel."

Angelika (Greek/German); Anjelica (Spanish); Angelique (French); Anjelique, Angelicia

ANISSA: (English) Variant form of Anne or Agnes.

Annissa, Anyssa, Annice, Annis, Anisha, Aneisha, Anessa

ANITA: (Spanish) Diminutive form of Anne.

Anitra (Scandinavian)

ANJANETTE: (Contemporary) "Gift of God's favor." Blend of Ann and Janet.

Anjeanette, Annjeanette, Anjanique (*ahn-ja-NEEK*)

ANNA: (English/Latin) Variant of Anne. Biblical; a devout woman who saw the infant Jesus presented at the temple in Jerusalem. Anna is often used in combination with other names. See also Anne and Ana.

Annabeth, Annalee, Annamarie, Anne-Marie (French)

ANNALISA: (Latin) "Graced with God's bounty."

Annalise, Annelise, Anneliese, Annelisa, Annalissa, Analisa, Analise, Analiese, Analissa, Analicia, Analisia

ANNE: (English/French) Variant form of Hannah (Hebrew), meaning "Favor, grace." See also Ana, Anabel, Anissa, Anita, Anjanette, Anna, Annalisa, Annette, Nana, Nancy, Nanette and Ninon.

ANNIE, ANN, Anya (Russian)

ANNETTE: (French) Diminutive form of Anne.

Annetta; Annika, Anneka, Anneke (Scandinavian); Anneli (Finnish); Anni (German)

ANNORA: (*an-NOR-ah*) (Latin) English variant form of Honora.

ANTHEA: (*ANN-thee-ah*) (Greek) "Lady of flowers."
Anthia

ANTOINETTE: (*ann-twa-NET*) (French) Feminine form of Anthony.

ANTONIA: (*ann-TONE-yah*) (Latin) Feminine form of Anthony, with contemporary variants. See also Antoinette and Toni.

Antonina, Antonette, Antonetta, Antonique, Antonella

APHRA: (*AFF-rah*) (Hebrew) "Dust." Biblical place name.

APOLLONIA: (*ah-poh-LONE-yah*) (Latin) "Belonging to Apollo." Mythology; Apollo was the Greek god of sunlight, music and poetry.

APRIL: (English/Latin) The month as a given name; often used to symbolize spring. See also Averil.
Apryl, Apryll, Aprille; Abril (Spanish)

AQUANETTA: (Contemporary) Created name based on Aqua, the blue-green color of the sea.

AQUILINA: (*ah-kee-LEE-nah*) (Spanish) "An eagle; sharp-eyed."

ARABELLE: (Latin) "Calling to prayer."
Arabella

ARACELI: (*ar-ah-SAY-lee*) (Spanish) "Altar of heaven."
Aracely, Aracelia, Aricela, Arcelia, Arcilla

ARCADIA: (*ar-KAY-dee-ah*) (Greek) "Pastoral simplicity and happiness."

ARDEL: (English/Latin) "Eager, industrious." Rare.
Ardelle, Ardella

ARDEN: (English/Celtic) "Lofty, eager."
Ardena, Ardene

ARDIS: (*ARR-diss*) (Scottish/Irish) Variant of Allardyce.
Ardys, Ardyce, Ardiss

ARETHA: (*a-REE-thah*) (Greek/Arabic) "Virtuous, excellent."
Areta

ARGENE: (*ar-JEEN*) (French) "Silvery."
Arjean

ARIADNE: (*ar-ee-AD-nee*) (Greek) "Chaste, holy." Mythology; Ariadne aided Theseus to escape from the Cretan labyrinth.
Aria, Arietta

ARIANA: (Latin) Variant form of Ariadne.
ARIANNA; Ariane (French); Arianne, Arriana

ARIEL: (Hebrew) "Lion of God." Biblical; a name for Jerusalem. Shakespeare gave the name to a prankish spirit in *The Tempest*.
ARIELLE, Ariele (French); Ariela (Spanish); Ariella

ARLEIGH: (English/German) "Meadow of the hare."

ARLENE: (English) Origin uncertain. Most likely based on Carlene and Charlene.

Arleen, Arlena, Arleene, Arleena, Arline, Arlina, Arlyne, Arlana, Arleana, Arla, Arlyn, Arlenna

ARLETTE: (French) A medieval given name of uncertain origin.

Arletta, Arleta

ARLINDA: (Contemporary) Blend of Arlene and Linda.

ARLISS: (Irish) "High fort." A place name.

ARMANDA: (Spanish) Feminine form of Armando.

ARNELLE: (Contemporary) Feminine form of Arnold.

Arnette, Arnetta

ARSENIA: (ar-SEE-nee-ah) (Latin) Feminine form of Arsenio.

ARTEMIS: (AR-te-miss) (Greek) "Virgin goddess of the moon; huntress." Mythology; the equivalent of the Romans' Diana.

ARTHURINE: (Contemporary) Feminine form of Arthur.

ASENATH: (a-SEE-nath) (Egyptian) "Daughter." Biblical; Joseph's Egyptian wife.

Acenath

ASHA: (Sanskrit) "Hope." Mythology: the wife of a Hindu demigod. See also Aisha.

Ashia (Somali)

ASHLEY: (English) "Meadow of ash trees." An English surname.

ASHLEE, ASHLEIGH, ASHLIE, Ashly, Ashlyn, Ashlynn, Ashlynne, Ashlin, Ashlinn, Ashlen, Ashleen, Ashleena, Ashleah, Ashla

ASHTON: (English) "Town of ash trees."

Ashten, Ashtyn

ASIA: "The rising sun." The name of the continent used as a given name. According to the Koran, Asia was the name of the Pharaoh's wife who raised the infant Moses. Asia is also a variant form of Aisha ("life"), the name of Mohammad's favorite wife, one of the four "perfect women." See also Aisha, Fatima, Khadija and Mary.

Azia, Asianne

ASTRA: (Latin) "Star."

ASTRID: (Scandinavian) "Godly strength."

ATHENA: (*a-THEE-nah*) (Latin) Variant form of Athene, the mythological goddess of wisdom and war.

Athene

AUBERTA: (*oh-BEHR-tah*) (French) Feminine variant of Albert.

AUBREY: (English/French) "Rules with elf-wisdom."

Aubree, Aubrie, Aubry, Aubriana, Aubrianne

AUDREY: (English) "Nobility, strength."

Audra; Audree (French); Audrie, Audri, Audrea, Audria, Audriana, Audrianna, Audreana, Audreanna, Audrielle, Audrina, Audris, Audene, Audelia

AUGUSTA: (Latin) "Majestic, grand." Feminine form of August.

Augustina, Agustina

AURELIA: (*aw-REEL-yah*) (Latin) "Golden."

Aurene, Auriel, Aurielle; Arela, Arella (Spanish)

AURORA: (*ah-ROHR-ah*) (Latin) "Dawn." Roman mythology; Aurora was the goddess of dawn. Aura was goddess of breezes.

Aurore (French)

AUSTINE: (*aws-TEEN*) (French/English) Variant form of Augustine.

Austina

AUTUMN: (English) The fall season.

AVA: (*AY-vah*) (English) Meaning uncertain; possibly a variant of Avis or Aveline, medieval given names. In contemporary usage, some forms may be intended as phonetic variants of Eva and Evelyn. See also Avis.

Avah, Avalee, Avelyn, Avlynn, Avelina, Aveline

AVERIL: (English) "Opening buds of spring; born in April." See also April.

Avril, Avrill, Avriel, Averill

AVIANA: (*ay-vee-AHN-ah*) (Contemporary) Blend of Ava and Ana. Aviance is the name of a popular perfume.

Avianna, Avia, Aviance (*AH-vee-AHNSE*)

AVIS: (*AY-viss*) (English) A medieval name of uncertain meaning.

Avice

AVIVA: (*a-VEE-vah*) (Hebrew) "Springtime."

Avivah, Avivi

AYLA: (*AY-lah*) (Hebrew) "Oak tree." Literary; Ayla is the Cro-Magnon heroine of Jean Auel's *Clan of the Cave Bear.*

Ayala (Hebrew) "Doe."

AZALEA: (*a-ZAYL-yah*) (Latin/Greek) "Dry." A flower name.

Azalia

AZIZA: (*ah-ZEE-zah*) (Arabic) "Beloved"; (Swahili) "precious."

AZURE: (*A-zhure*) (English/French) "Sky-blue." The color used as a given name.

Azura, Azurine

AZUSENA: (*ah-zoo-SAY-nah*) (Arabic) "Lily."

Azucena, Asucena, Azusa

<hr>

B

BAILEY: (English/French) Courtyard within castle walls; a steward or public official. Surname. Became popularized by a character on the Eighties TV show, *WKRP in Cincinnati.*

Baylee, Bayley, Baylie, Bailee

BAMBI: (Italian) "Little child, bambino." Pet name.

BARBARA: (English/Greek) "Traveler from a foreign land." Used since medieval times. In Catholic custom,

St. Barbara is invoked as a protectress against fire and lightning. See also Bobbi.

Barbra, Barbie, Barbi; Babette (*ba-BET*) (French); Barbarita, Barbarella

BEATA: (*bee-AH-ta*) (Latin) "Happy, blessed."

BEATRICE: (*BEE-a-triss*) (Latin) "Brings joy."

BEATRIZ (Spanish); Beatrix (Italian); Beatriss, Bea, Bee

BECKY: (English) Short form of Rebecca.

Becki, Becca

BELEN: (*bay-LEN*) Spanish word for "Bethlehem."

BELINDA: (English/Latin) "Very beautiful."

BELLA: (Latin) "Fair, lovely one." Also a short form of Isabel.

Belle, Bel (French); Bellissa (Italian); Belva

BENECIA: (*ba-NEE-sha*) (Latin) "Blessed one."

Benicia

BENITA: (Latin) "Blessed." Feminine variant of Benedict.

BERNADETTE: (French) Feminine form of Bernard. Most famous name bearer was St. Bernadette, canonized in 1933. See also Lourdes.

Bernadina, Bernadine, Bernarda, Bernadea, Bernette, Bernetta, Bernita, Berdine, Bernelle, Berneen

BERNICE: (*ber-NEECE*) (French/Greek) "One who brings victory." Variant form of Berenice.

Bernyce, Berniss (*BER-niss*); Bernicia (Spanish); Bernisha, Berenice (*BARE-a-neece*), Berenise, Berenisa, Berrie, Berry

BERONICA: (Spanish) "True image." Variant form of Veronica.

BERTHA: (German) "Bright."

Berta (Spanish, Czech); Bertine, Berthe (French); Bertina

BERYL: (English/Greek) A gemstone of varying colors,

most often yellow-green. Biblical; the eighth foundation stone of the wall of New Jerusalem was made of beryl.

BETH: (Hebrew) Short form of Elizabeth.

BETHANY: (*BETH-a-nee*) (Hebrew) The name of a village near Jerusalem where Jesus visited Mary, Martha and Lazarus.

Bethanie, Bethani, Bethanee, Bethann

BETHEA: (*BETH-ee-ah, be-THE-ah*) (Hebrew) "Maid-servant of Jehovah."

Bethia

BETHEL: (Hebrew) "House of God."

BETTY: (English) Short form of Elizabeth.

Betsy, Betsey; Bettine, Bette (French); Bettina, Bessie, Bessy, Bess

BEULAH: (*BEW-lah*) (Hebrew) "Claimed as a wife." Biblical; a name symbolic of the heavenly Zion.

BEVERLY: (English) "Beaver stream."

Beverley, Beverlee

BIANCA: (*bee-ONK-ah*) (Italian) "White, shining." Variant form of Blanche.

BLANCA (Spanish); Blanche (French); Bianka, Byanca

BIBI: (Arabic/Persian) "Lady." Bibiana is a Spanish form of Vivian.

Bibiana

BILLIE: (English) "Determination, strength." Originally a nickname for William. Now a feminine name, often combined with other names.

Billie-jean, Billie Jo

BIRDENA: (Contemporary) "Little bird." May also be a variant form of Bernadene. See Bernadette.

Birdine, Byrdene, Birdie

BIRGITTA: (*ber-GIT-ah*) (Scandinavian) Variant form of Bridget. See also Bridget and Britt.

Birgit, Birgitte, Brita

BLAINE: (Scottish/English) Surname, meaning uncertain.

BLAIR: (Scottish) "Field of battle."
  Blaire
BLISS: (English) "Joy, cheer." Bliss and its variants date
  from medieval times.
  Blyss, Blysse, Blisse; Blix (Swedish)
BLONDELL: (English/French) "Fair-haired, blonde."
  Blandina is a Spanish name meaning "coaxing, flatter-
  ing."
  Blondelle, Blondene, Blandina
BLYTHE: (English) "Blithe, lighthearted."
BO: (English/Scandinavian) Nickname and short form.
  Brought into popularity by actress Bo Derek. Also a
  Chinese name meaning "precious."
BOBBI: (Contemporary) Nickname of Roberta and Bar-
  bara. Bobbie is often combined with other names, with
  or without a hyphen. Bobbie, Bobbiejo, Bobbijo,
  Bobbie-Jean
BONITA: (*boh-NEE-tah*) (Spanish) "Pretty little one."
BONNIE: (Scottish) Diminutive of the French word *bon*;
  "good." In Scottish usage, "bonnie" means "pretty,
  charming."
  Bonny, Bonni, Bonnibelle, Bonnie-Jo, Bonny-Jean,
  Bonny-Lee
BRANDY: (Contemporary) The name of the beverage used
  as a given name, with contemporary variants. Brandi is
  also an Italian surname form of Brand, "fiery beacon."
  BRANDI, Brandee, Brandie, Brandice, Brandyce,
  Branda, Brandelyn, Brandilyn, Brandyn
BREANNA: (Contemporary) See also Bree, Brianna and
  Briona
  BREANNE, Breana, Breann, Breeann, Breeanne,
  Breeanna, Breeana, Breonna, Breona, Breonda
BRECK: (Irish) "Freckled."
BREE: (Irish) "Hill." May also be used as a short form of
  names like Brina and Breanna. See also Brianna.

Bria, Brea, Brielle

BREENA: (Irish/Gaelic) "Fairy palace." May also be used as a short form of Brianna and Sabrina. See also Brina.
Breen

BRENDA: "Beacon on the hill." Feminine form of Brendan.
Brendalynn, Brendolyn, Brynda

BRENNA: (Irish) Variant form of Brenda.

BRETT: (English/French) "Brit." A native of Britain (England) or Brittany (France). Lady Brett Ashley was Hemingway's heroine in *The Sun Also Rises*.
Bret, Brette, Bretta, Brettany

BRIANNA: (Contemporary/Celtic) "She ascends." Feminine form of Brian. See also Breanna, Bree, Breena and Briona.
BRIANA, BRIANNE, Briannah, Brianna, Briann, Briannon, Brienna, Brienne, Bryanna, Bryanna, Bryana, Bryann, Bryanne

BRIDGET: (Irish) "Strength." Mythology; the Celtic goddess of fire and poetry. See also Birgitta.
Bridgette, Bridgett, Brigette, Brigitte (French); Brigid, Brigida (Scandinavian)

BRINA: (*BREE-nah*) Short form of Sabrina. See also Breena.

BRIONA: (*bree-OH-nah*) Variant form of Brianna.
Brione, Brionna (*bree-AHN-ah*), Brionne (*bree-AHN*)

BRIONY: (*BRY-o-nee*) (English/Greek) The name of a flowering vine used in folk medicine.
Bryony, Brioni, Bryani

BRISA: (*BREE-sah*) Short form of the Spanish name Briseida, from Briseis, the Greek name of the woman loved by Achilles in Homer's *Iliad*.
Brissa, Bryssa, Briza, Breezy, Brisha, Brisia

BRITT: (Scandinavian) "Strength." Short form of Birgit, from the Irish name Bridget.

Britta, Brit, Brita (*BREE-ta*)

BRITTANIA: (*bri-TAHN-yah*) (Latin) A poetic name for Great Britain.

Britania, Brittanya

BRITTANY: (*BRIT-'n-ee*) (English) From the name of an ancient duchy (Bretagne) in France. Celtic Bretons emigrated from France and became the Bretons of England; later the name "Britain" came to signify the entire country. See also Brittney.

BRITTANI, Brittaney, Britani, Brittanie

BRITTNEY: (*BRITT-nee*) Very popular modern variant of Brittany; the phonetic spelling ensures a two-syllable pronunciation.

BRITNEY, Brittnee, Brittni

BRONWYN: (*BRON-win*) (Welsh) "White-breasted."

Branwyn, Bronwen

BROOKE: (English) "Water, stream." Actress Brooke Shields has made the English surname familiar as a girl's given name today.

Brook, Brooklyn, Brooklynn, Brooklynne

BRYNN: (Irish/Celtic) "The heights."

Bryn, Brynne, Bren, Brenne, Brynna, Brynnan, Bryna, Brynelle

C

CADY: (*KAY-dee*) (Irish/English) "Hillock." A surname, also used as a given name, perhaps due to the phonetic similarity to Katy and Cody. Cadence literally means "a rhythmic flow of sounds." See also Kady.

Cadi, Cadee, Cadie, Cadence

CAILIN: (*KAY-lin*) (Gaelic) "Girl, lass." Possibly a contemporary variant of Cailean (Scottish). See also Kaylyn.

Caylin, Cailyn, Cailyn, Caelan, Caileen

CAITLIN: (*KATE-lin*) (Irish) Variant form of Katherine. See also Catherine, Katherine, Kaitlin and Katelyn.
CAITLYN, Caitlynn, Caitlan, Catelyn, Caitlinn; Cateline (French); Cait, Caitrin, Catriona (Scottish/Irish); Caitland, Catlin, Catline, Catlyn

CALANDRA: (*ka-LAHN-drah*) (Italian/Greek) "Lark." Calinda and Calynda are contemporary variants or blends with Linda.
Calendre, Calinda, Calynda

CALISTA: (*ka-LEES-tah, ka-LISS-tah*) (Greek) "Most beautiful." A saint's name. Mythology; an Arcadian nymph who metamorphosed into a she-bear, then into the Great Bear constellation. See also Kallista.
Calisto, Callista, Calysta, Calissa, Cali

CALLAN: (Gaelic) "Powerful in battle." See also Kallan.
Callen, Calynn

CALLIE: (Irish/Gaelic) Variant form of Cayley, also short forms of names beginning with "Cal-." See also Kallie.
Calli, Callee

CALLIOPE: (*ka-LIE-ah-pee*) (Greek) "Beautiful voice." Mythology; the muse of epic poetry.

CALVINNA: (Latin) Feminine form of Calvin.

CALYPSO: (*ka-LIP-so*) (Greek) Mythology; a nymph who beguiled Odysseus for seven years. Music; a West Indies style of extemporaneous singing.

CAMELIA: (*ka-MEEL-yah*) (Latin) A flower name often associated with the name Camille. See also Camille and Kamelia.
Camella, Camellia

CAMEO: (*KAM-ee-o*) (English) A gem portrait carved in relief.

CAMERON: (Scottish) "Bent nose." Clan surname based on the nickname given a valorous ancestor. See also Kameron.

CAMILLE: (*ka-MEEL*) (French/Latin) "Free-born, noble."

Literary; in Virgil's *Aeneid*, Camilla was a swift-running warrior maiden. See also Kamille.

Camilla, Camile, Camila, Cammi

CANDICE: (*KAN-diss*) (English) Variant of Candace, an ancient hereditary title used by the Ethiopian queens, as Caesar was used by Roman emperors. See also Kandace.

CANDACE, Candyce, Candiss

CANDIDA: (*kan-DEE-dah*) (Latin) "Bright, glowing white."

Candide (French)

CANDY: (English) Short form of Candace, also used as an independent name meaning "sweet." Candi is a Spanish diminutive of Candida.

Candi, Candie

CAPRICE: (*ka-preese*) (French) "Whimsical, unpredictable." Capri, as in the Isle of Capri, is rarely used as a given name.

Capricia (*ka-PREE-sha*), Capri, Capriana

CARA: (Latin) "Beloved." Cari is a Spanish short form of Caridad, "dear, darling," and is also the name of a star in the Orion constellation. See also Kara and Caroline.

Cari, Carita, Carella, Caralea, Caralee, Carillie, Caralisa

CARESSE: (*ka-RESS*) (French) "Tender touch." See also Charis.

Caress, Caressa, Carressa

CARINA: (*ka-REEN-ah*) (Latin) "Little darling." See also Karina.

Carrina, Carena, Carine, Carin, Carinna, Cariana

CARISSA: (*ka-RISS-ah*) (Latin/Greek) "Very dear." See also Karissa.

Carrissa, Carrisa; Carisa (Spanish)

CARLA: (Latin) Feminine form of Charles. See also Carol, Charla and Karla.

CARLY, Carley, Carlie, Carli, Carlee, Carleigh, Carlene;

Carleen (Irish); Carlyn, Carlynn, Carlisa; Carletta, Carlena, Carlina, Carlita (Spanish)

CARLOTTA: (Italian) Variant form of Charlotte.

Carlota (Spanish)

CARMELA: (*car-MAY-lah*) (Latin) "Fruitful orchard," a reference to Mount Carmel in Palestine. See also Karmel.

Carmel, Carmelle, Carmelita, Carmella

CARMEN: (Spanish) Variant form of Carmel. See also Karmen.

Carmina (Italian); Carmencita

CAROL: (English) Feminine form of Carl. See also Caroline and Karol.

Carole (French); Carola, Carrola (Spanish); Carroll (Irish); Caryl

CAROLINE: (English) Feminine variant form of Charles. Carolan is an Irish surname. See also Cara, Carla, Carlotta, Carol, Carrie, Charla, Charlene, Charlotte, Karla, Karol and Sharlene.

CAROLYN, CAROLINA, Carolyne, Carolynn, Carolann, Carolanne, Carolan, Caro, Caralyn, Carilyn, Carilynne, Caroliana

CARRIE: (English) Short form of Carol and Caroline often used as a given name. The Irish surname Carey is used more for boys than for girls.

Carey, Caree, Carree

CARSON: (Scottish) Surname. Rare.

CARYN: (Contemporary) Variant form of Karen.

Carynn

CASEY: (Irish) "Vigilant." Caycee and Cacia are short forms of Acacia. See also Kasey.

Cacey, Casee, Caycee, Cacia

CASSANDRA: (*ka-SAN-dra, ka-SAHN-dra*) (Greek) "Unheeded prophetess." Literary; in Homer's *The Iliad*,

Cassandra foretold the fall of Troy but was unheeded.
See also Cassie and Kassandra.
Casandra (Spanish); Cassondra, Cassaundra, Cassandrea
CASSIA: (*KASH-ah*) (Greek) "Spicy cinnamon." See also
Kassia.
CASSIDY: (Irish) "Curly-headed."
CASSIE: (English) Short form of Cassandra frequently
used as an independent name. See also Kassie.
Cassi, Cassy
CATHERINE: (Latin/Greek) "Pure." One of the great tradi-
tional names for women, with variations in many lan-
guages. Historical; the name of several saints and
queens including Catherine the Great, Empress of Rus-
sia. See also Cathy, Caitlin and Katherine.
Catarina (Italian); Cathryn, Catharine, Cathleen (Irish);
Cathrine (*kath-REEN*), Caitrin, Catriona (Gaelic); Cata-
lina, Catrina, Caterina (Portuguese)
CATHY: (English) Short form of Catherine. See also Kathy.
Cathie, Cathi, Cathia
CATRICE: (*ka-TREECE*) (Contemporary) Blend of Catrina
and Patrice.
CAYLEY: (Gaelic) "Slender." Variant form of Caley or
Cailley (French) "from the forest." Caela is also a short
form of Micaela. See also Callie, Kayla and Kaylee.
Cailley, Caleigh, Caylee, Caylie, Caileigh, Caela, Caila,
Cayla
CECILIA: (*sess-SEEL-ya*) (Latin) "Blind." The blind St.
Cecilie, patron saint of music, was herself a talented
musician. See also Celia and Celina.
Cecelia, Cicilia (*siss-SEEL-yah*), Cecily, Cecilie, Cecilee
(*SESS-a-lee*); Cicely, Cicily (*SISS-a-lee*) (English);
Cecille, Cecile (*sess-SEEL*) (French); C'Ceal, Ceci (*see-
see*)
CEDRICA: (*sed-REE-kah*) (Contemporary) Feminine form
of Cedric.

Cedrika, Cedrina, Cedra (*SED-rah*)

CELESTE: (*seh-LEST*) (French/Latin) "Heavenly."
Celesta, Celestina (Spanish); Celestine, Celestyna, Celestia, Celestiel, Celesse, Celisse

CELIA: (*SEEL-yah*) (Latin) Short form of Cecilia.
Celie (French); Ceil, Cele

CELINA: (Latin) Variant form of Celia or Selena. Mythology; one of the seven daughters of Atlas who were transformed by Zeus into stars of the Pleiades constellation. See also Selena.
Celena, Celene; Celine (French); Celinda, Celinna, Celenia, Celicia, Celenne

CERES: (*SAIR-ees*) (Latin) "Of the spring." Mythology; the Roman goddess of agriculture and fertility.

CERISE: (*ser-REESE*) (French) "Cherry; cherry red."

CHA- names: (Contemporary) Blends of Cha- plus various name endings, with pronunciation emphasis on the second syllable. See also Charis, Cherie and Sha- names.
Chalia, Chalise, Chalon, Chalonn, Chalonne, Chalyse, Chanae, Chanee, Chenay, Chanice, Chanise, Chaquita, Charita, Charelle, Charice, Chevelle, Chavonne, Chevonne, Chevon

CHALINA: (*sha-LEEN-ah*) (Spanish) Diminutive form of Rosa.

CHANA: (Hebrew) Variant form of Hannah. Also a Spanish diminutive of names ending in -iana.
Channa

CHANDELLE: (*shan-DELL*) (French) "Candle."
Chandel

CHANDRA: (*SHAN-drah, SHAHN-drah*) (Sanskrit) "Of the moon."
Chandy, Chandara, Chandria, Chaundra, Chanda "foe of evil," Candra, Canda "shining"

CHANEL: (*sha-NELL*) (French) "Canal, channel." Recent

popularity is probably influenced by the perfume and the "Sha-" name pattern.

Chanelle, Channelle, Chanell, Chenelle

CHANTEL: (*shahn-TELL*) (French) "Singer." See also Shantel.

Chantelle, Chantell, Chauntel, Chantal, Chantalle, Chantrell, Chante (*shawn-TAY*) "to sing," Chantay, Chantae, Chaunte

CHANTILLY: (*shahn-TEE, shan-TILL-ee*) (French) A delicate lace from Chantilly, France.

CHARIS: (*KARE-iss*) (Greek) "Grace." Mythology; a reference to the three Graces, symbols of womanly beauty, charm and inspiration. Charisma is the related English word used as a given name. See also Cherise, Karisma and Sherisa.

Charissa (*sha-RISS-ah* or *ka-RISS-ah*), Chariss (*ka-RISS*), Charisse, Charise (*sha-REESE*), Charice, Charisa, Charisma, Carisma (*ka-RIZ-mah*)

CHARITY: (English/Latin) "Benevolent goodwill and love."

CHARLA: (*SHAR-la*) (Contemporary) Feminine form of Charles. Charlie as a name for girls may be influenced by the perfume Charlie. See also Charlene and Sharlene.

Charlee, Charli, Charlie, Charly, Charlyn, Charlynn

CHARLENE: (*shar-LEEN*) Diminutive feminine form of Charles. "Char-" is also used as a blend prefix. See also Sharlene.

Charleen, Charleene; Charline (French); Charlena, Charleena, Charlaine, Charlayne, Charlita, Charlisa, Chardae

CHARLOTTE: (French) Feminine form of Charles. See also Carlotta.

Charlotta, Charlette

CHARMAINE: (*shar-MAYNE*) (French) Possibly a variant

form of Charmian, the name of one of Cleopatra's attendants in Shakespeare's *Antony and Cleopatra.*
Charmayne, Charmain, Charmine

CHARO: (*CHAR-oh*) (Spanish) Pet name for Rosa.

CHASTITY: (*CHASS-ta-tee*) (Latin) "Purity, innocence." A virtue name. Chasity (*CHASS-a-tee*) is a slurred phonetic variant.
Chasity, Chasta, Chastine (*chass-TEEN*), Chastina

CHAVELA: (*sha-VAY-lah*) (Spanish) Variant form of Isabel.
Chavelle

CHAYA: (*CHYE-ah*) (Spanish) Short form for names ending in "-ario." Also (Hebrew) "life."

CHELSEA: (*CHELL-see*) (English) Place name, especially in reference to the district in London.
CHELSEY, CHELSIE, Chelsi, Chelsee, Chelsy, Chelsa

CHERIE: (*sha-REE*) (French) "Dear one, darling." Contemporary variants of Cherie follow the "sha-" name pattern. See also "Cha-" and "Sha-" names, Cheryl and Sherry.
Cher, Chere, Cheri, Cheree, Cherree, Charee, Chereen, Cherina, Cherine, Cherita, Cherrelle, Cherelle, Cherell

CHERISE: (*sha-REESE*) (Contemporary) Blend of Cherie and Cerise. See also Charis.
Cherisse, Cherice, Cherese, Cherisa, Cheresse (*sha-RESS*)

CHERRY: (English) Fruit-bearing tree of the rose family.
Cherrie, Cherri

CHERYL: (*CHARE-el, SHAR-el*) (English) Rhyming variant of names like Meryl and Beryl, developed early this century. Cherilyn is a further variant based on Marilyn. See also Cherie and Sheryl.
Cheryll, Cherrell, Cherrill, Cherilyn, Cherilynn

CHESSA: (Slavic) "At peace."
Chessie

CHEYENNE: (*shy-ENN*) (French/American Indian) Name

of an Algonquian tribe of the Great Plains and of the
capital city of Wyoming.

Cheyanne, Cheyanna, Chiana, Chianna

CHIARA: (*chee-AR-ah, kee-AR-ah*) (Italian) "Light." Variant form of Clare. See also Ciara.

CHIKA: (*CHEE-kah*) (Nigerian) "God is supreme." The
Spanish pet names Chica and Chiquita mean "little
girl." Chiko (*CHEE-koh*) is a Japanese name with the
potential meanings "arrow", "pledge."

Chica, Chiquita, Chiko

CHINA: (Contemporary) Place name. Chynna Phillips is a
popular singer.

Chynna, Chyna

CHINARA: (Nigerian) "God receives."

CHIYO: (*chee-yoh*) (Japanese) "Thousand years; eternal."

CHLOE: (*KLO-ee*) (Greek) "Fresh-blooming."

CHRISANN: (*kriss-ANN*) (English/Greek) Variant form of
Chrysantus, a saint's name. Chrysandra is a contemporary blend using Sandra. See also Krisandra.

Chrisanne, Chrisanna, Chrysann; Crisann, Crisanna
(Spanish); Chrysantha, Chrysandra

CHRISTA: (Greek) "Anointed one; a Christian." Chrysta's
spelling may refer to the Greek word for "gold" or
"golden." See also Christine and Krysta.

Crysta, Chrysta, Chrystie, Chryssa; Crista (Spanish)

CHRISTABEL: (Latin) "Beautiful Christian."

Cristabel, Cristabell, Christabella

CHRISTEN: (Contemporary) Variant form of Christian.
Spanish and Italian forms begin with Cr-. See also
Christina and Kristen.

Christin, Christyn, Christan, Christanne, Christana,
Christaine, Cristin, Cristen, Cristyn

CHRISTIAN: (Greek) "Follower of Christ." Spanish and
Italian forms begin with Cr-. See also Christina.

Christiana, Christianna; Christiane (French);

Christianne, Chrystian, Cristian, Cristianne, Cristiana, Cristianna

CHRISTINA: (English/Latin) Variant form of Christiana. See also Christa, Christabel, Christen, Christian, Christy, Crystal, Khristina, Kirsten, Krista, Kristen, Kristina, Kristine and Krystal.

CHRISTINE (French); CRISTINA, Cristine (Spanish/Italian); Christene, Christeen, Christena, Chrystina, Christeena

CHRISTY: (Scottis/Irish) Short form of Christine. See also Krista.

Christie, Christi, Chrissy, Chrissie, Chrissa, Cristy, Cristie, Crissa, Crissie, Crissy

CIANA: (*see-AHNA* or *chee-AHNA*) (Italian) Feminine variant of John. Pronounced *kee-AHN-ah*, may also be a contemporary feminine variant of an Irish name meaning "ancient." See also "Ki-" names.

Ciandra

CIARA: (*kee-ARR-ah* or *see-ARR-ah*) (Irish) "Dark." Feminine form of Ciaran, the name of two major Irish saints. See also Chiara, Kiara and Sierra.

Ceara, Ciarra, Ciaran, Cierra, Ciera

CINDY: (English) Short form of Cynthia and Lucinda.

Cindi, Cyndi, Cyndy, Cyndee, Cinda, Cindia, Cindel

CIRA: (*SEER-ah*) (Spanish/Italian) Variant of Cyril. See also Cyrilla and Cyrah.

Ciri, Ceri, Ceria

CIRCE: (*SIR-see*) (Latin) Mythology; a sorceress who tempted Perseus and changed his men into swine and back again.

CLAIRE: (French) "Bright, shining and gentle; famous." See also Claribel and Clarissa.

Clara, Clare, Clair, Clarita, Clarinda

CLARIBEL: (English) "Bright, beautiful." Blend of Clare

and Bella. Literary; a name used by Shakespeare in *The Tempest.*

CLARISSA: (English) Variant of Claire or Clarice.
Clarisa (Spanish); Claressa, Clarrisa; Clarisse (French); Clarice

CLAUDIA: (English/German) Feminine form of Claude.
Claudine, Claudette, Claudelle

CLEMENCE: (*klem-awnse*) (French/Latin) "Clemency, mercy." Mythology; the Roman goddess of pity.
Clementina, Clementine

CLEO: (*KLEE-oh*) (Greek) Short form of Clotilde and Cleopatra. Clio (*KLY-oh*) is the mythological Muse of historic poetry.
Clea, Clio

CLEONE: (*KLEE-a-nee*) (Greek) "Glorious." Mythology; daughter of a river god.
Cleonie, Cliona (Irish)

CLEOPATRA: (*klee-oh-PAT-trah*) (Greek) "Glory of her father." Historical; the queen of Egypt who was immortalized by Shakespeare in *Antony and Cleopatra.* See also Cleo.

CLETA: (*KLEE-tah*) (Latin/Greek) "Illustrious."

CLORIS: (*KLOR-iss*) (Greek) "Blooming." Mythology; the goddess of flowers.
Chloris

CLYTIE: (*KLY-tee*) (Greek) Mythology; a nymph in love with Helios, god of the sun. Clytie was changed into a sunflower, which always turns its face toward the sun.

COCO: (Spanish) Diminutive form of Soccoro. Also a French pet name.

CODY: (Irish/English) "Helpful."
Codi, Codee

COLBY: (English) "Dark-skinned." See also Kolby.

COLETTE: (French) "Victorious." Variant of Nicolette.
Collette, Coletta, Colletta; Coleta (Spanish)

COLLEEN: (*kah-LEEN*) (Irish) "Girl." See also Cailin.
Collene, Collena, Colene (*koh-LEEN*)

CONCETTA: (Latin) Italian form of Concepcion, referring to the doctrine of the Immaculate Conception of Mary.
Concepcion, Conchita (Spanish)

CONNIE: (English) Short form of Constance.

CONSTANCE: (English/French) "Constancy, steadfastness."
Constancia, Constantia (Spanish); Constantina (Italian)

CONSUELO: (*kohn-SWAY-loh*) (Spanish) "Consolation."

CONTESSA: (Italian) Title, the feminine equivalent of Count.
Countess (English)

CORA: (English) Possibly a variant of Kore (Greek) "maiden."
Coralee, Coralie, Coralia, Coralyn, Corlene, Corella, Coretta, Corissa, Corrissa

Coral: (English/Latin) A semiprecious natural sea growth, often deep pink to red in color.
Coraline

CORAZON: (*kor-a-SOHN*) (Spanish) "Heart."
Corazana

CORDELIA: (*kor-DEEL-yah*) (English) Literary; in *King Lear,* Shakespeare portrays Cordelia as a woman of rare honesty.
Cordella

CORINA: (*ko-REE-nah*) (Latin) Variant form of Corrinne. The "-een" spellings are Irish endings.
Corrina, Corrine (French); Corine, Coreen, Correen, Coreene, Correena.

CORINNE: (*ko-RINN*) (French) Variant of Cora.
Corinna, Corynne, Corryn, Coryn, Corynn, Corrin

CORINTHIA: (*ko-RIN-thee-ah*) (Greek) "Woman of Corinth."

CORLISS: (English) "Carefree."

CORNELIA: (*kor-NEEL-yah*) (Latin) Feminine form of Cornelius.
Cornella

CORY: (English/Irish) Rare. Corrie and Corry are Scottish surnames. Cori is also used as a prefix in contemporary blended names. See also Kori.
Cori, Corey, Corie, Corri, Corrie, Corry, Coriann, Corianne, Corrianne, Corrianna, Coretta, Corisa

COURTNEY: (English/French) "Courtly, courteous." Place name and surname. Courtlyn is a contemporary variant.
Cortney, Courtlyn

COZETTE: (*koh-ZETT*) (French) "Little pet." Literary; in Victor Hugo's *Les Miserables,* Cosette is Jean Valjean's beloved adopted daughter.
Cosette

CRECIA: (*KREE-shah*) (Latin) Short form of Lucrecia.

CRYSTAL: (English/Greek) "Ice." A transparent quartz, usually colorless, that can be cut to reflect brilliant light. Cr- spellings are Spanish/Italian. Chrys- spellings could refer to a Greek word meaning "golden." Chris- spellings may refer to Christ rather than to "ice." See also Christina and Krystal.
Crystall, Crystell, Crystalann, Crystalynn, Crystalina; Christal, Christel (German); Christelle, Christella; Chrystal, Chrystalann, Chrystalyn; CRISTAL, Cristalle, Cristella, Cristalyn

CYBELE: (*si-BELL*) (Greek/Roman/Asian) Mythology; an ancient nature goddess worshiped as the Great Mother in Asia Minor. The mother of all gods, men and wild nature, lions were her faithful companions. She was identified with Rhea by the Greeks, with Maia and Ceres by the Romans.

CYBIL: (Contemporary) Variant form of Sibyl, the name given in Greek mythology to a prophetess or fortune-teller.

Cybill

CYDNEY: (Contemporary) Variant form of Sydney.
Cydnee, Cidney

CYNTHIA: (Greek) Mythology; one of the names of Artemis, the goddess of the moon, referring to her birthplace on Mount Cynthus. See also Cindy.
Cinthia, Cyntia (Spanish); Cinzia (*CHIN-tsee-ah*) (Italian)

CYRAH: (*SEER-ah, SYE-rah*) (Contemporary) "Enthroned," if Cyrah and variants are feminine forms of Cyrus. "Lady," if variants of Kyria (Greek). Greek mythology; Cyrene was a maiden-huntress loved by Apollo. See also Cira and Kyra.
Cyra, Cyrena, Cyrina, Cyrene (*si-REE-nee*)

CYRILLA: (*sir-ILL-ah*) (Contemporary) "Mistress, lady." Feminine form of Cyril.
Cirilla, Cerella, Cerelia

CZARINA: (*zar-REEN-ah*) (Latin/Russian) Feminine form of czar, the Russian equivalent of a female caesar or empress.

D

DA- names: (Contemporary) Blends of Da- plus various endings, with pronunciation emphasis on the second syllable. See also Dale and De- names.
Dalynn, Dameshia, Danessa, Danisha, Daniesha, Danille, Daneille, Dashay, Davisha, Davonne

DACIA: (*DAY-shah*) (Spanish) "From Dacia."
Daisha, Dacia, Dacey, Dacy, Deyci

DAGMAR: (Scandinavian) "Glorious."

DAHLIA: (*DAL-yah*) (Swedish) "Valley." The flower was named for botanist Anders Dahl. See also Dalia.
Dahl

DAISY: (English) "Day's eye." A flower name.
Daizy, Daysi, Daisey, Daisie, Daisi, Deysi

DAKOTA: (American Indian) "Friend, ally." Tribal name.

DALE: (English) "Small valley." Rare. Dalena and Dalenna are also short form variants of Madeline.

Dayle, Dalene, Dalena, Dalina, Dalenna; Dael (Dutch); Daly, Daelyn

DALIA: (*dal-yah*) (Tanzanian/Arabic) "Gentle." See also Dahlia.

Daliah (Israeli); Dalila (Swahili)

DALLAS: (Scottish) "From the dales, the valley meadows." Name of the Texas city used as a given name. Used more for boys than for girls.

Dallis

DAMARIS: (*DAM-a-riss*) (Latin) "Gentle." Biblical; an educated woman who heard Paul speak at Mar's Hill, the open-air supreme court of Athens.

Damara, Damariss, Damaress

DAMIANA: (*day-mee-AHN-ah*) (Greek) "One who tames, subdues." Feminine form of Damian.

DANA: (*DAY-nah*) (English) "From Denmark." A surname also used as a variant form of Daniel. Used more for girls than for boys.

Dayna, Danah, Daena, Daina, Dayne, Daney, Dania

DANAE: (*dan-ay*) (Greek) Mythology; the mother of Perseus by Zeus.

Danay, Danaye, Danee, Denae, Denay, Danea

DANICA: (*DAN-i-kah*) (Slavic) "Morning star."

Dannica, Danika, Dannika

DANIELLE: (*dan-YELL*) (French) Feminine form of Daniel.

DANIELA (Spanish); Daniella, Daniele, Danyelle, Dhanielle, Donielle

DANNA: (Contemporary) Feminine variant form of Daniel. Dannah is a Biblical place name.

Dani (Spanish/Italian); Dannee, Danni, Dany, Danelle, Dannell, Dannelle, Dannon, Danitza, Danice, Danise,

Danette, Danita, Dannia, Danya, Dania, Dannalee, Dantina, Dannah

DAPHNE: (*DAFF-nee*) (Greek) "The laurel tree." Mythology; virtuous Daphne was transformed into a laurel tree to protect her from Apollo.

Daphney; Dafne (Israeli); Daphna

DARA: (Hebrew) "Wise." Biblical; the name of a descendant of Judah noted for his wisdom. Also, Dara and Darra are Gaelic names meaning "oak tree." See also Derry.

Darah, Darra, Darrah, Dareen, Darissa, Darice

DARCY: (Irish/French) "Dark." See also Dorcey.

Darcie, Darci, Darcey, D'Arcy, Darcia, Darcel, Darcell, Darcelle, Darchelle

DARIA: (Latin) Feminine form of Darius, a Persian royal name. Variants may also be feminine forms of names like Daryl and Darin.

Darya (Russian); Darielle, Dariele, Darrelle, Darian, Darienne, Darianna; Darina (Czech)

DARLENE: (English) Contemporary form of the Old English "dearling; darling."

Darla, Darline, Darleen, Darlena, Darlina, Darleena, Darleane

DARNELL: (English) "Hidden." Place name and surname.

Darnelle, Darnae, Darnisha, Darnetta

DARYL: (English) Actress Daryl Hannah has probably influenced the occasional use of Daryl and variants as names for girls.

Daryll, Darryll, Darrill, Darylene, Darylyn, Darolyn, Darrellyn, Darrylynn

DARYN: (Greek) "Gift." Contemporary feminine form of Darin.

Darynn, Darynne

DAVENEY: (*DAV-nee, DAV-a-nee*) (French) Name of a

town and castle in Flanders. May be used as a rhyming variant of Daphne.

DAVIDA: (*dah-VEE-dah*) "Beloved." Feminine form of David.

Davita, Davina, Davinia, Davia, Davonna, Davy, Davynn, Daveen, Davine, Davianna

DAWN: (English) "The first appearance of light; daybreak."

Dawna, Dawne, Dawnika, Dawnette, Dawnetta, Dawnelle, Dawnielle

DE- names: (Contemporary) Blends of De- plus various name endings, with pronunciation emphasis on the second syllable. See also Da- names, Delicia, Deandra and Danae.

DeAngela, Dejana, Dejanee, Dejeanee, Delana, Delaree, Delena, Deleena, Delise, Deloise, Delyse, Delinda, Delyn, DeLynden, Demeisha, Denell, Denesha, Deneisha, Denita, DeShay, DeShawna

DEANDRA: (*dee-AHN-drah, dee-ANN-drah*) (Contemporary) Blend of Deanne plus variants of Andrea and Sandra.

Deandrea, Deandria, Deeandra, Diandra, Diandre, Dianda, Deanda

DEANNA: (English) Variant form of Diana. See also Dionna.

Deanne, Deann, Deeana, Deeann, Deeanna, Deana, Deena, Deane, Deonna, Deonne, Deona, Deondra

DEBORAH: (Hebrew) "Bee." Biblical; a prophetess who summoned Barak to battle against an invading army. The victory song she wrote after the battle is part of the Book of Judges. See also Devora.

DEBRA, DEBBIE, Debrah, Debby, Debralee

DEE: (English) Short form of names beginning with the letter D.

DeeDee, Dede, DiDi

DEIDRE: (*DEE-drah*) (Irish) "Melancholy." A phonetic spelling of the older name "Deirdre" (*DEER-drah*). Mythology; from a Celtic legend comparable to Tristram and Isolde. The Celtic Deirdre died of a broken heart.
Deirdra, Deidra, Deedra, Deidra, Diedre

DEITRA: (*DEE-tra*) (Greek) Variant form of Demetria.
Deetra, Detria

DEJA: (*DAY-hah*) (Spanish) Short form of Dejanira, from the Greek name Deianeira, the wife of Hercules. Sometimes a use of the French "déjà vu," (*day-zhah*) "remembrance."
Dejah, Deija, Daija

DEKA: (*DEE-kah*) (African/Somali) "Pleasing."

DELANEY: (*de-LAY-nee*) (Irish) Surname.
Delaina, Delaine (*de-LAIN*) (French); Delayne, Delayna

DELFINA: (*del-FEEN-ah*) (Spanish/Latin) "Dolphin." Variant form of Delphine, the name of a thirteenth-century French saint. Delphi refers to the Oracle of Delphi on Mount Parnassus.
Delphi (*DELL-fye*), Delphia; Delphine (French)

DELIA: (Greek) "From Delos." Mythology; the island of Delos was Artemis's birthplace. Delia is also used as a short form of Cordelia and Adelia.

DELICIA: (*de-LEE-shah*) (Latin) "Gives pleasure." Variant forms follow the "De-" name pattern.
Delisa, Delisha, Delissa, Delyssa, Deliza, Delice, Delight

DELILAH: (*dee-LYE-lah*) (Hebrew) "Languishing." Biblical; the woman who beguiled Samson into revealing the secret of his superhuman strength. Dalila (Tanzanian) "gentle."
Delila, Dalila

DELLA: (English/German) "Noble."
Dell

DELMA: (*DEL-mah*) (German) "Noble protector." Short

form of Adelma. May also be an Irish short form of Fidelma.

Delmy, Delmi, Delmira

DELORES: (English/Latin) Variant form of Dolores.

Deloris, Delora

DELTA: (*DEL-tah*) (Greek) Fourth letter of the Greek alphabet.

DEMELZA: (*de-MELL-zah*) (English) "Fortified." A place name in Cornwall.

DEMETRIA: (*da-MEE-tree-ah*) (Greek) "Of Demeter." Feminine form of Demetrius. Mythology; Demeter was the goddess of corn and harvest. See also Deitra and Demi.

Demetra, Demitra, Dimetria, Demitras, Demeter

DEMI: (*DEH-mee*) (English) Short form of Demetria.

DENA: (*DEE-nah*) (English) Variant form of Deana and Dina. See also Deanna and Dinah.

Dene, Denia, Deneen, Denni, Denica

DENISE: (*de-NEES*) (French) Feminine form of Denis, from the Greek name "Dionysus."

Denice, Deniece, Denisse, Denisha; Denisa (Spanish); Dennise, Denyse, Denissa

DERICA: (Contemporary) "Gifted ruler." Feminine form of Derek.

Dereka, Derrica, Dericka

DERRY: (Irish) "Oak grove." Rare. See also Dara.

DESIREE: (*dez-a-ray*) (French) "The one desired." Often spelled phonetically to ensure the French pronunciation.

Desirae, Dezirae, Desarae, Desaree, Deziree, Dezirae; Desire (English), Desyre

DESSA: (Latin) From the Greek name Odysseus, meaning "wandering."

DESTINY: (English/French) "One's certain fortune; fate." Mythology; the Greek deity of fate.

Destina (Spanish); Destinee, Destinie, Destini, Destanee, Destine (*dess-TEEN*)

DEVANY: (*DEV-a-nee*) (Irish) "Dark-haired." Variants may be contemporary rhyming blends of Devon and Bethany.

Devenny, Devaney, Devanie, Devinee, Devony

DEVI: (*DEV-ee*) (Sanskrit) "Divine." Hindu Mythology; title, especially relating to Shiva's wife, who is known by various names according to her exercise of power for good or ill. Devika means "little goddess."

DEVON: (English) The name of a county in England noted for beautiful farmland.

DEVIN (English/French) "Divine," Devan, Devyn, Devynn, Devana, Devanna, Devonna, Devonne, Devona, Devondra

DEVORA: (*DEV-or-ah*) (Hebrew) "Bee." Variant form of Deborah.

Devorah, Devra, Devri, Devery, Devi

DEXTRA: (Latin) "Adroit, skillful."

DHANA: (*DAHN-ah*) (Sanskrit) "Wealthy."

Dhanna

DIAMOND: (English) "Of high value; brilliant." The gemstone.

Diamonique, Diamante, Diamanda, Diamontina

DIANA: (*dy-ANN-ah, dee-AHN-ah*) (Latin) "Divine." Mythology; Diana was an ancient Roman divinity who came to be associated with the Greek Artemis. Noted for her beauty and fleetness, Diana is often depicted as a huntress. Popularized by the Princess of Wales. See also Deanna, Diantha and Dionna.

DIANE (French) (*dy-ANN, dee-AHN*); Dianna, Dianne, Diahna, Diahann, Diannah, Diahann, Di, Dian, Diandra, DiAnne, Dyanna, Dyann, Dyana

DIANTHA: (*di-ANN-thah*) (Contemporary) Blend of Diana and Anthea.

DILYS: (*de-LEES*) (Welsh) "Perfect, true."

DINAH: (*DYE-nah*) (Hebrew) "Judged and vindicated." Biblical; Jacob's only daughter. Dina and Dinora are Spanish forms of Dinah. See also Dena.
  Dina, Dynah, Dinora, Dinorah

DIONNA: (English) "From the sacred spring." Mythology; Dione was the wife of Zeus and the mother of Aphrodite. See also Diana and Deanna.
  Dionne, Diona, Dione, Diondra

DIOR: (*dee-ORR*) (French) Surname. Rare. D'Or is a French variant meaning "golden."
  D'Or

DITA: (*DEE-tah*) (Spanish) Short form of Edith.

DIVINA: (*dih-VEEN-ah*) (Latin) "Divine one."
  Devina

DIXIE: (English) Surname and short form of Richard. The American name refers to the French word for "ten" or to the region of the southern states below the Mason-Dixon line.

DOLORES: (Spanish) "Sorrows." Refers to the Virgin Mary as "Mary of the sorrows." See also Delores and Lola.

DOMINIQUE: (*dom-min-NEEK*) (French/Latin) "Of the Lord." Variant form of Dominic.
  Dominica, Domenica, Dominga (Spanish); Domenique, Dominee

DONNA: (Italian) "Lady." A title of respect, equivalent to "Don" for men. See also Madonna.
  Dona (Spanish); Donni, Donnie, Donielle, Donelle, Donella, Donisha, Donetta, Donya, Dahnya, Dahna, Donnalee, Donnalyn, Donna-Marie

DORA: (Latin/Greek) "Gift." Short form of Dorothy. Also used as a prefix in blended names.
  Dorah, Doria, Dorae, Doreina; Dorlisa (German);

Doreen (Irish); Dorene, Dorena, Dorina, Dorine, Doralee, Doralyn, Dorinda, Dorelia, Dodie, Dodi

DORCAS: (*DOR-kuss*) (Greek) "Gazelle." Biblical; a woman who "abounded in good deeds and gifts of mercy."

DORCEY: (English) Variant form of Darcy.
Dorsey

DORIAN: (Greek) "Descendant of Dorus." Variant form of Doris.
Dorianna, Dorianne, Dorrian, Dorienne, Doriana

DORIS: (Greek) "Gift." Mythology; a daughter of the sea god Oceanus. See also Dorian.
Dorrie, Dorri, Dorry, Dori, Dorie, Doree, Dorris, Dorice, Dorisa

DOROTHY: (Greek) "Gift of God." See also Dora.
Dorothea; Dorotea (Spanish); Dorothee, Dorotha, Dortha, Doro, Dottie, Dolly, Dollie, Dorit

DREW: (Scottish) Short form of Andrew. Popularized by actress Drew Barrymore.

DRINA: (*DREE-nah*) (Spanish) Short form of Alexandrina.
Dreena

DRUSILLA: (*drew-SILL-ah*) (Latin) Feminine form of Drusus, a Roman family name.
Drucilla, Dru

DUANA: (*D'WAY-nah*) (Irish) Feminine form of Duane.
Duayna

DULCE: (*DOOL-cee*) (Latin) "Sweet, sweetness." Dulcinea was a name created by Cervantes's *Don Quixote* for his idealized lady.
Dulcie, Dulcy, Dulcea, Dulcia, Dulcine, Dulcina, Dulcinea (*dul-see-NAY-ah*)

DUSTY: (English) Nickname.
Dusti, Dustee

E

EARLINE: (*er-LEEN*) Feminine form of Earl. Erlina (Spanish) is from the German name Herlinde, meaning "shield."
Earlene, Earlina, Earlena, Erlene, Erlina

EARTHA: (*ER-thah*) (German) "The earth." See also Terra and Tierra.
Ertha

EBONY: (*EBB-o-nee*) (Greek/Egyptian) "Black."
Eboni, Ebonee, Ebonique (*ebb-o-NEEK*)

ECHO: (*EK-koh*) (Greek) "Sound." Mythology; a nymph who faded away until only her voice was left behind.
Ekko

EDANA: (Irish) "Fiery." Feminine form of Aidan.

EDDA: (German) "Strives." Variant form of Hedda or Hedwig.

EDEN: (*EED-'n*) (Hebrew) "Pleasure." Biblical; the name of the gardenlike first home of Adam and Eve.
Edenia (Spanish)

EDITH: (English) "Spoils of war." See also Dita.
Edythe, Edytha, Edie, Edee, Eda, Edelina; Edita (Spanish)

EDNA: (Hebrew) "Pleasure."

EDWINA: (*ed-WEEN-ah*) (English) "Rich in friendship." Feminine form of Edwin.
EDWINNA (*ed-WIN-ah*)

EFFIE: (English/Greek) Short form of Euphemia, a Greek name meaning "well spoken."

EILEEN: (*eye-LEEN*) (Irish) Variant form of Evelyn. See also Ilene and Aileen.
Eilene, Eilena, Eileene, Eila

ELAINE: (*ee-LAYNE*) (French) "Shining light." Variant form of Helen.
Elaina, Elayna, Ellaine, Ellayne (*ell-ayne*)

ELANA: (*ee-LANN-ah*) (Israeli) "Oak tree." See also Ilana.
Elanna, Elanah, Elanie (*ELL-a-nee*)

ELDORA: (Spanish/Greek) "Gift of the sun." Variant form of Heliodorus, the name of many saints.
Eleadora

ELEANOR: (*ELL-a-nor*) (English/French) "Shining light." Variant form of Helen. See also Elnora, Leonora and Nelly.
Eleonora (Italian); Eleanora (Spanish); Eleonore (French); Eleni (Russian); Elinor (English)

ELEKTRA: (Greek) "The fiery sun." Mythology; the daughter of Agamemnon. Literary; a central character in three Greek tragedies. Also the inspiration for Lavinia in Eugene O'Neill's trilogy of plays, *Mourning Becomes Electra.*
Electra

ELENA: (*eh-LAYN-ah*) (Spanish) Variant form of Helen.
Eleni (Russian); Elina, Eleena

ELFRIDA: (*el-FREE-dah*) (German) "Peaceful ruler." Variant form of Frieda. See also Frederica.

ELIANA: (*ell-ee-AH-nah*) (Latin/Greek) "Daughter of the sun." See also Liana.
Elianna, Elianne; Eliane (French); Eleana

ELISE: (*ell-EESE*) (French) Short form of Elisabeth. See also Elissa and Ellyce.
ELISA, Elisha, Elicia, Elishia, Elisamarie

ELISSA: (Greek) "From the blessed isles." Mythology; another name for Dido, Queen of Carthage. Variants may also be intended as forms of Elise and Elisabeth.
Elissa, Elisse, Elyssa, Elysse, Elyse, Elysa, Elysia, Elysha, Elisia

ELITA: (*el-LEE-tah*) (Latin) "Chosen one." Also a short form of names like Carmelita.

ELIZABETH: (English/Hebrew) "My God is bountiful; God of plenty." Biblical; the mother of John the Baptist.

Since the reign of Queen Elizabeth I, Elizabeth has been one of the most frequently used names, with variants and short forms still being created today. See also Beth, Betty, Elise, Elissa, Elsa, Elspeth, Ilse, Isabel, Libby, Liesl, Lilibeth, Lisa, Liza, Lizbeth and Lizette.

ELISABETH; Elisabet, Elizabet (Scandinavian); Elisabetta (Italian); Elizabel; Elzbieta (Polish); Eliza, Elyza

ELKE: (German) "Noble." Variant form of Alice.

ELLA: (English) Short form of Eleanor and Ellen. Also a French medieval given name meaning "all."
Ellie, Elly, Elle, Ellee, Ellia, Ellesse

ELLEN: (English) Variant form of Helen.
Ellyn, Elynn, Ellena, Ellene; Elleen (Irish); Elin (Welsh)

ELLYCE: (*ell-EESE*) (English) Variant forms of Elias, the Greek form of Elijah. See also Elise.
Elyce, Ellice, Ellecia, Ellisha, Ellison

ELMA: (German) "God's protection."

ELNORA: (*el-NOR-ah*) (English) Variant form of Eleanor.

ELOISA: (*ell-o-WEE-sah*) (Spanish/Italian) Variant form of Louise. See also Heloise.
Eloise (French); Eloiza

ELORA: (*eh-LOR-ah*) (Contemporary) Blend of "El-" and Lora, "God gives the Laurel, the crown of victory." Ellora is a name given to the cave temples of India.
Ellora

ELSA: (German) Short form of Elisabeth. See also Ilse.
Else (Scandinavian); Elsie, Elsy, Elza

ELSPETH: (*ELLS-peth*) (Scottish) Variant form of Elisabeth.
Elsbeth

ELVA: (English/Irish) "Elfin."
Elvia, Elvie, Elvina, Elvinia

ELVIRA: (*ell-VYE-rah, Ell-VEER-ah*) (Spanish) "Truth."
Elvera, Elvita

EMBER: (English) "Anniversary." Usage today may be as a rhyming variant of Amber, or refer to "Ember day," a day in Lent devoted to fasting and prayer.

EMILY: (Latin) "Industrious, striving." See also Amelia and Emmaline.

Emilia, Emilie, Emilee, Emelia, Emalee, Emmalee, Emmalei

EMMA: (English/German) "Whole, complete."

EMMALINE: (French/German) "Hardworking." Variant form of Emily.

Emmeline, Emeline (French); Emmalyn, Emmy

ENID: (*EE-nid*) (Welsh) "Life."

ENRICA: (*ahn-REE-kah*) (Spanish) "Rules her household." Feminine form of Henry.

ERICA: (Scandinavian) "Ever kingly." Feminine form of Eric.

ERIKA, Ericka, Erikka, Eryka

ERIKO: (*air-EE-koh*) (Japanese) "Child with a collar." The suffix -ko, meaning child, is frequently used as an ending for Japanese girls' names.

ERIN: (Gaelic) Poetic name for Ireland.

Erinn, Eryn, Erynn, Erinne, Erienne, Erina, Erinna

ERMA: (German) "Complete." See also Irma.

ERNESTINA: (Latin/German) "Serious, determined." Feminine form of Ernest.

Ernestine, Erna; Ernesta (Spanish); Ernesha

ESME: (*es-may*) (French) "Esteemed."

ESMERALDA: (*ez-mer-AHL-dah*) (Spanish) Variant form of emerald, the prized green gemstone.

Ezmeralda, Emerald

ESPERANZA: (*ess-per-AHN-zah*) (Spanish) "Hope."

ESTEFANY: (*ess-STEFF-a-nee*) (Spanish) Feminine form of Stephan.

Estefania, Estephanie, Estefani

ESTELLA: (*ess-STEL-ah*) (Latin) "Star."

Estelle, Estee (French); Estela, Estelita, Estrella, Estrellita (Spanish)

ESTHER: (*ESS-ter*) (Persian) "Myrtle leaf." Biblical; a young Hebrew woman who became the wife of the Persian ruler Xerxes and risked her life to save her people. See also Hester.

Ester (Spanish)

ETHEL: (English/German) "Noble."

ETTA: (English/Latin) Short form of names ending in -ette and -etta, especially Henrietta and Harriette.

Ettie, Etty

EUGENIA: (*you-GEEN-yah*) (Greek) "Wellborn." Feminine form of Eugene.

Eugenie (*you-ZHAY-nee*) (French); Eugena, Eugina

EULALIE: (*you-LAY-lee*) (Greek) "Sweet-spoken."

Eulalia, Eula, Eulah (*YOU-lah*), Eulia

EUNICE: (*YOU-niss*) (Greek) "She conquers." Biblical; a woman who was noted for being "without hypocrisy."

EUSTACIA: (*you-STAY-shah*) (Latin/Greek) "Productive." Feminine form of Eustace.

EVA: (*AY-vah, EE-vah*) (Latin/Hebrew) "Living one." Variant form of Eve, used much more frequently than the original name. Biblical; Adam's wife, the first woman. See also Ava.

Eve, Evette, Evetta, Evie, Evita, Evia, Eviana

EVANGELINA: (Greek) "Brings good news."

Evangeline, Evangelyn, Evangela, Evangelia

EVANIA: (*ee-VAHN-yah*) Possibly a variant form of the Greek name Evadne meaning "goodness" or a feminine form of Evan.

Evin, Evanna, Evanee

EVELYN: (*EV-lin, EEV-lin*) (English/French) Meaning uncertain; a male surname used in this century as a given name for girls. See also Aileen, Ava and Eileen.

Evelin, Evalyn, Evelina, Eveline, Evaline, Evalina, Evaleen, Evelyne, Evelynn, Evelynne

EVONNE: (French/German) Variant form of Yvonne, from Yves. See Yvonne and Ivonne.

Evon, Evonna, Evony (*EV-oh-nee*)

F

FABIOLA: (*fah-bee-OH-lah*) (Latin) Feminine variant of Fabian, from the Roman family clan name Fabius.

Fabianna; Fabienne (French); Fabianne, Favianna, Faviola, Fabia, Fabra

FAITH: (Latin/Greek) "Confidence, trust; belief." See also Faye.

Faythe

FALLON: (Irish) "In charge."

Falon, Fallyn, Faline

FANNY: (English) Pet name; variant form of Frances.

Fannie, Fanni, Fannia, Fanceen, Fantine

FARRAH: (English) "Fair-haired"; (Arabic) "happy."

Farah, Fara (English) "traveler."

FARREN: (English) "Adventurous."

Faryn, Farrin, Farryn; Farran (Irish); Farron, Faren, Farin, Ferran, Ferryn

FATIMA: (*FAH-tee-mah*) (Arabic) The name of a daughter of the Prophet Muhammad; one of the four "perfect women" mentioned in the Koran. See also Aisha, Khadijah and Mary.

Fatimah

FAUSTINE: (*foss-TEEN*) (Latin) "Fortunate one." Feminine form of Faustus, the name of many saints.

FAWN: (English) Literally, "young deer." Greek mythology; Fauna, a deity of fertility and nature, was famous for her chastity.

Fawna, Fawne, Fauna

FAYE: (English/French) Variant form of Faith.

Fay, Fae, Fayanna

FELICIA: (*feh-LEE-shah*) (Latin) "Happy." Feminine form of Felix. Felicity (English) is one of the "virtue" names.
Felisha, Felicity; Felicitas, Felicita (Spanish); Felice, Felisa, Falisha, Feliciona

FERN: (English) A green shade-loving plant. A name from nature.
Ferne

FERNANDA: (*fer-NAHN-dah*) (Latin/German) "Adventurous." Feminine form of Fernando.

FIALA: (*fee-AH-lah*) (Czech) "Violet."

FIAMMETTA: (*FEE-a-MET-tah*) (Italian) "A flickering fire."
Fia (*FEE-ah*)

FIDELIA: (*fee-DAYL-yah*) (Latin) "Faithful."
Fidelina, Fidessa; Fidelma (Irish)

FILOMENA: (*fee-lo-MAY-nah*) (Italian/Greek) "Beloved." Variant form of Philomena.

FIONA: (*fee-OWN-nah*) (Scottish) "Fair."
Fionna (*fee-AHN-nah*) (Irish)

FLAIR: (English) "Style, verve."

FLAVIA: (*FLAH-vee-ah*) (Latin) "Yellow-haired." Feminine form of Flavius, a Roman clan name.

FLORA: (Latin) "Flower." Mythology; the Roman goddess of flowers.
Flor, Florita (Spanish); Florinda, Floressa, Floriana, Florida, Floretta, Flori, Florrie, Floria; Fleur (French)

FLORENCE: (English/Latin) "Flowering." From a medieval given name once used mostly for boys.
Florencia (Spanish); Florentina, Florenza (Italian)

FONTANNE: (*fawn-TAN*) (French) "Fountain, spring."

FORTUNA: (*for-TOON-nah*) (Latin) "Fortune, fortunate." Mythology; the Roman goddess of fortune, chance. Also a saint's name.

FRANCES: (Latin) "From France." Feminine spelling of Francis. See also Francesca and Francine.

Frankie, Franki, Francie, Franci, France, Francia; Francoise (French); Fran

FRANCESCA: (*fran-CHESS-kah*) (Italian) Variant form of Frances. Francisca (Spanish); Franchesca, Franchesa, Franceska

FRANCINE: (French) Variant form of Frances.

Francene, Francina, Francena, Francille (*fran-SEEL*)

FREDERICA: (German) "Peaceful ruler." Feminine form of Frederick.

Frederika, Fredrika, Fredda, Freddi, Frieda, Freda

FREYA: (*FREE-yah, FRAY-ah*) (Scandinavian) Mythology; Freya, wife of Odin, was the goddess of love and fertility. Friday is named for Freya.

FRITZI: (*FRIT-zee*) (German) Nickname for Frederica.

G

GABRIELA: (*gab-ree-ELL-ah*) (Latin/Hebrew) "God's able-bodied one." Feminine form of Gabriel.

GABRIELLE (French); Gavriella (Italian); Gabriele (German); Gabriell, Gavrielle, Gabi, Gaby

GAEA: (*GYE-ah*) (Greek) "The earth." Mythology; the womanly personification of the earth; mother of the Titans.

Gaia

GAIL: (English) "Joyful." Short form of Abigail. Gael is a term for descendants of the ancient Celts, especially in Scotland, Ireland and the Isle of Man. See also Gayle.

Gale, Gaila, Gala, Gael, Gaylene

GALATEA: (*gal-ah-TEE-ah*) (Greek) Mythology; Galatea was a statue loved by the sculptor Pygmalion. She was brought to life for him by Aphrodite.

GALIANA: (Arabic) The name of a Moorish princess for whom a splendid palace was built in Spain.

GALINA: (*ga-LEEN-ah*) (Russian) Variant form of Helen.

GARDENIA: (English) The flower; a name from nature.

GARNET: (English/French) A dark-red gemstone named for the pomegranate that the garnet crystals resemble. Also a surname.

GAVINA: (*gah-VEE-nah*) (Latin) "From Gabio." Variant form of Gabinus, a saint's name.

GAYLE: (English) Variant form of Gail. Gala literally means "festive party." Gay has declined in usage as a given name due to its general appropriation as a term denoting homosexuality.

Gayla, Gala, Galea, Gaylen, Galen, Galena, Gay

GEMMA: (Latin) "Gem; a jewel." See also Jemma.

Gemmalyn, Gemmalynn, Gem

GENESIS: (*JEN-eh-siss*) (Hebrew) "Origin, birth." Biblical; name of the first book in the Bible. In Catholic tradition, Genisia, Virgin Mary of Turin, is invoked as a protectress against drought.

Genessa, Genisa, Genisia, Genisis

GENEVIEVE: (French/German) "Of the race of women."

Geneva; Genevra, Ginevra (Italian); Geneve, Genevie, Genivee

GENNA: (Contemporary) Variants based on Jenny. See also Jenna and Jenny.

Genny, Genae (*je-NAY*), Genaya

GEORGIA: (*JOR-jah*) (English/German) "Farmer." Feminine form of George.

GEORGINA: (Latin) Diminutive form of Georgia.

Georgiana, Georgianna, Georgeanne, Georgegina; Georgine, Georgette (French); Georjette

GERALDINE: (English/German) "Rules by the spear." Feminine form of Gerald.

Geraldina, Geralyn, Geralynn

GERI: (Contemporary) Feminine form of Gerry. Variant

forms listed here are blends of Geri plus Erica and Marilyn.

Gerri, Gerica, Gerika, Gericka, Geralyn, Geralynn, Gerrilyn

GERMAINE: (*jer-MAYNE*) (French/Latin) Feminine form of Germain, from a Roman name meaning "brotherly."

GERTRUDE: (German) "Spear's strength."

GIANNA: (*jee-AHN-ah*) (Italian) Feminine form of Jane, from John.

Gia, Giana, Gianina, Giannina, Gianella, Gianara, Gionna, Geonna

GIGI: (*JEE-jee, zhee-ZHEE*) (French) Nickname for Gabrielle and other French names like Georgine.

GILANA: (*je-LAHN-ah, gil-ann-ah*) (Hebrew) "Joy."
Gilah

GILDA: (*JILL-dah, GEEL-dah*) (English) "Golden." Also a short form of Teutonic names containing "gilde."

GILLIAN: (*GILL-ee-an, JILL-ee-an*) (English/Latin) Variant form of Juliana. See also Jillian.

GINA: (*GEE-nah*) Short form of names ending in "-gina." Also used as a name prefix to form new variants.

Gena, Geena, Ginamaria, Genelle, Ginelle (je-NELL), Geneene, Gineen, Genina, Genie, Genalyn, Geana, Geanndra, Genette

GINGER: (English) Nickname for Virginia. Literally, "pep, liveliness," referring to the pungent root used as a spice.

GINNY: (English) Short form, usually of Virginia.
Ginnie, Genny, Ginnette, Ginnelle, Ginna, Ginnilee

GIORDANA: (Italian) Feminine form of Jordan. Refers to the Jordan River. See also Jordana.

GIOVANNA: (*jo-VAHN-ah*) (Italian) Feminine form of John.

Giovana, Giavanna, Geovana, Geovanna

GISELLE: (*je-ZELL*) (French/German) "Pledge."

Gisela (German); Gisele (French); Gizelle, Gisella, Giselda

GIULIANA: (*JOO-lee-AHN-nah*) (Italian) Variant form of Juliana.
Giulia

GLADYS: (*GLAD-iss*) (Welsh) Variant form of Claudia.
Gladis

GLENDA: (Welsh) "Fair, good." See also Glynnis.
Glinda, Glynda, Glyn, Glynn

GLENNA: (Gaelic) "Valley." The name Glenn popularized by actress Glenn Close.
Glenn, Glenne, Gleniesha

GLORIA: (Latin) "Glory."
Glorianne, Gloriana, Glorianna, Glory, Gloribel, Gloribell

GLYNNIS: (Welsh) Variant form of Glenda.
Glynis, Glenys, Glynice, Glynae (*glen-NAY*), Glennis

GOLDIE: (English) The precious metal. Golda is a variant made prominent by Golda Meir, the late prime minister of Israel.
Golda

GRACE: (Latin) "Favor, blessing." Mythology; the three graces were goddesses of nature: Aglaia (brilliance), Thalia (flowering), and Euphrosyne (joy).
Graciela, Gracielle, Gracella, Gracelynn, Gracelynne, Gracia, Gracie

GREER: (Scottish) Surname. Variant form of Gregory.

GRETA: (German/Scandinavian) "Pearl." Short form of Margaret.
Gretta, Gretel (German/Dutch)

GRETCHEN: (German) Variant form of Margaret.

GRISELDA: (*gri-ZELL-dah*) (Latin/German) "Gray, gray-haired." Italian author Giovanni Boccaccio's use of the name in a tale about an exceptionally patient wife has made the expression "patience of Griselda" proverbial.

Gricelda, Grizelda, Gryselda, Griselle, Grisella

GUADALUPE: (*gwah-da-LOO-pay*) (Spanish/Arabic) "Wolf valley." Refers to Mary as Mexico's "Our Lady of Guadalupe."

GUINEVERE: (*GWIN-a-veer*) (Welsh) "Fair one." An early form of Jennifer. Mythology; King Arthur's queen.
Guenevere, Gwenevere

GWEN: (Welsh) "Fair, blessed."
Gwyn, Gwenna, Gwenda, Gwendi, Gweneth, Gwenyth, Gwyneth, Gwynne, Gwynn, Gwinn

GWENDOLYN: (Welsh) "Fair, blessed."
Gwendolynn, Gwyndolyn, Gwyndolynne, Gwendelyn

GYPSY: (English) Nickname derived from "Egyptian," used to describe migratory tribes of dark Caucasians who came from India to Europe in the fifteenth century.
Gipsy, Gitana (Spanish)

H

HADARA: (Hebrew) "Adorned with beauty."
Hadarah

HADASSAH: (*ha-DAHS-sah*) (Hebrew) "Myrtle tree." Biblical; the Persian Queen Esther's Hebrew name.

HADLEY: (English) "Field of heather." Surname. Rare. It was the name of Hemingway's first wife.

HAIDEE: (*HAY-dee*) (Greek) "Well-behaved."
Haydee; Hadya (Arabic); Hadiya (Swahili) "gift"

HALEY: (*HAY-lee*) (English) "Field of hay." The surnames listed here as variants undoubtedly came into popular use as girls' names due to actress Hayley Mills.
HAYLEY, HAILEY, Haylee, Haylie, Hailee, Haleigh

HALIA: (*hah-LEE-ah*) (Hawaiian paraphrase) "Remembrance of a loved one."

HALIMA: (Swahili) "Gentle."

HALLIE: (*HAL-lee*) "From the Hall."
Halli, Halley

HANA: (*ha-NAH*) (Arabic) "Happiness"; (Japanese) "Flower"; (Hawaiian) "work"; (Slavic) Variant form of Johanna. See also Hannah.

HANAKO: (*hah-NAH-koh*) (Japanese) "Flower child."

HANNAH: (English/Hebrew) "Favor, grace." Biblical; mother of the prophet Samuel. See also Hana.
HANNA; Hanah (Israeli); Hannalee, Hanalise

HARLENE: (English) "Meadow of the hares." Feminine form of Harley.
Harleen, Harlee, Harlie

HARMONY: (English) "Unity, concord; musically in tune." Mythology; Harmonia was the daughter of Aphrodite.
Harmonie, Harmoni, Harmonee, Harmonia

HARRIET: (English/French) "Rules her household." Feminine form of Harry, from Henry. See also Etta.
Harriett, Hattie

HASINA: (*hah-SEE-nah*) (Swahili) "Good."

HAYLEY: (English) See Haley.

HAZEL: (*HAY-zel*) "The hazel tree." A name from nature.
Hazell

HEATHER: (English) An evergreen flowering plant that thrives on peaty barren lands, as in Scotland.

HEDDA: (German) "Warfare." Variant form of Hedwig.
Hedy (*HED-ee*)

HEIDI: (*HYE-dee*) (German/Swiss) "Little Miss." Short form of Adelheid.
Heide

HELEN: (English/Greek) "Shining light." Mythology; the abduction of Zeus's mortal daughter, Helen, resulted in the Trojan War. See also Allena, Elaine, Eleanor, Elena, Ellen, Elnora, Galina, Ilona and Leonora.
Helena (*HELL-a-nah, hel-LAY-neh, hel-LEE-nah*); Helene, Helaine (heh-LAYNE) (French); Helaina (heh-LAYNE-ah), Heleena, Helana; Halina (Polish); Helenna

HELGA: (*HEL-gah*) (Scandinavian) "Holy, devout."

HELOISE: (*HEL-oh-ees*) (French) "Renowned fighter." Variant form of Eloise, a feminine form of Louis. See also Eloisa.

HENRIETTA: (French) "Rules her household." Feminine form of Henry. See also Etta.
Hetta, Hettie

HERA: (*HARE-ah*) (Greek) Mythology; Hera (Juno to the Romans) was the Greek Queen of Heaven, wife of Zeus. Dealing with her husband's infidelities resulted in her also being called the goddess of marriages.

HERMINIA: (*air-MEEN-ee-ah*) (Latin) Feminine form of Herman. A saint's name.
Hermine: Hermione (*her-MY-oh-nee*) (Greek)

HESPER: (*HESS-per*) (Greek) "Evening star."

HESTER: (English) Variant of Esther.

HILDA: (German) "Warfare." Scandinavian mythology; Hildegard was a Valkyrie, sent by Odin to escort battle heroes to Valhalla.
Hildagarde, Hildegard, Hilde, Hulda, Hylda

HILLARY: (*HILL-a-ree*) (English/Latin) "Joyful, glad."
HILARY; Hilaire (*hih-LARE*) (French)

HOLLY: (English) "The holly tree." Often given to daughters born on or near Christmas.
Hollie, Holli, Hollee, Hollyann, Hollis

HONEY: (English) "Nectar." Nickname and name of endearment.

HONOR: (*AHN-er*) (Latin) Literally, one's good name and integrity. A virtue name. See also Annora and Nora.
Honora (*ah-NORE-ah*); Honore (*ah-NORE*) (French); Honour, Honoria

HOPE: (English) "Expectation, belief."

HORTENCIA: (*or-TEN-see-ah*) (Spanish) "Garden." The English form Hortense is rare.
Hortensia, Hortense

HOSANNA: (*ho-ZAN-ah*) (Greek/Hebrew) A prayer of acclamation and praise for salvation.

HYACINTH: (*HYE-a-cinth*) (Greek) "Alas." Name of a flower and a color that ranges from sapphire to violet. A saint's name. See also Jacinda.

I

IANTHE: (*eye-AN-thee*) (Greek) "Violet flower." Mythology; a sea nymph, daughter of Oceanus.
Iantha

IDA: (English/Scandinavian) "Diligent." Mythology; a Greek nymph who cared for the infant Zeus on Mt. Ida.

IDALIA: (*eye-DAYL-yah*) (Greek) "Behold the sun."

IDELLE: (*eye-DELL*) (Welsh/Celtic) "Bountiful."
Idella, Idelisa

IGRAYNE: (*ee-grayne*) (English) Mythology; in Arthurian legend, the mother of Arthur.
Igraine, Ygraine

ILANA: (*ee-LAHN-ah*) (Hebrew) "Tree." See also Elana.

ILENE: (*eye-LEEN*) (English) Variant form of Eileen.
Ileen, Ilena, Ila (*EYE-lah*); Ilane (Irish/Gaelic) "island."

ILIANA: (*ee-lee-AHN-ah*) (Spanish) Variant form of Elena. See also Liana.
Ileana, Ileanna

ILIMA: (*ee-LEE-mah*) (Hawaiian) "The flower of Oahu."

ILONA: (Hungarian) Variant form of Helen.

ILSE: (*ILL-sah*) (German) Short form of Elizabeth.
Ilsa

IMAN: (*ee-MAHN*) (Arabic) "Believes."

IMELDA: (*ee-MEL-dah*) (Spanish/German) "Powerful fighter." The name of a fourteenth-century Spanish saint.

IMOGENE: (*EYE-mah-jeen*) (Latin) "Blameless, innocent."

INA: (*EYE-nah, EE-nah*) Diminutive ending of many names, used as an independent name.

INDIA: (*IN-dee-ah*) (English) The name of the country.
Indiana, Indee, Inda

INDIRA: (*in-DEER-ah*) (Sanskrit) "Splendid." Hindu mythology; the wife of Vishnu.

INEZ: (*ee-NEZ*) (Spanish) "Chaste." Variant form of Agnes. See also Ynes.
Ines (Italian/Spanish); Inessa (Russian); Inetta

INGA: (Scandinavian) "Ing's abundance." Feminine form of Ing. See also Ingrid.
Inge, Inger

INGRID:, (Scandinavian) "Ing rides." Norse mythology; Ing, god of the earth's fertility, rides the land each year to prepare it for spring planting.

IOLA: (*eye-OH-lah*) (Greek) "Violet-colored dawn."

IOLANA: (*ee-oh-LAH-nah*) (Hawaiian) "To soar like the hawk."

IONE: (*eye-OHN*) (Greek) "Violet."
Iona (Scottish/English)

IRENE: (*eye-REEN, eye-REE-nee*) (Greek) "Peace." The three-syllable pronunciation is mostly British. Mythology; Greek goddess of peace.
Irena (Slavic); Irayna, Irenee; Irina (Russian); Iriana

IRIS: (Greek) "Rainbow." A flower name. Mythology; Iris was a messenger-goddess who rode rainbows between heaven and earth to deliver messages from Olympus.
Irisa (Russian); Irisha (*eye-REE-shah*)

IRMA: (German) "Complete." Short form of names like Ermintrude. See also Erma.

ISABEL: (Latin/English) Variant form of Elizabeth. See also Bella, Chavela, Sabelle and Ysabel.
Isabelle, Isabeau (French); Isobel (Scottish); Isabela, Isabelita, Isabella (Spanish); Izabel (Portuguese)

ISADORA: (*iz-a-DOR-ah*) (Greek) "Gift of Isis." Feminine

form of Isadore. Notable name bearer: Isadora Duncan, acclaimed American dancer in the 1920s.

ISHA: (*ee-shah*) (Hebrew) "Woman." See also Aisha.

ISIS: (*EYE-siss*) (Egyptian) Mythology; the most powerful of all the female goddesses; sister to Osiris.

IVANA: (*ee-VAH-nah*) (Czech) Feminine form of Ivan, from John.

Ivanna, Ivania

IVETTE: (Spanish) Variant form of Yvette.

IVONNE: (*ee-VON*) Variant form of Yvonne. See also Evonne.

IVORY: (*EYE-vree*) (English) Literally, a reference to the creamy-white color, or to the hard tusk used for carving fine art and jewelry.

IVY: (*EYE-vee*) (English) Name from nature; an evergreen climbing ornamental plant.

Ivey, Ivie, Iva, Ivalyn, Ivyanne

J

JA- names: (Contemporary) Blends of Ja- plus various endings, with pronunciation emphasis on the second syllable. The second syllable may or may not begin with a capital. See also Je- and Jo- names, Jay, Janae and Janessa.

Jacodi, Jaconda, JaCoya, Jadeana, Jadine, Jakeisha, Jakisha, Jakira, Jakiya, Jalaine, Jalaina, Jalayna, Jalena, Jaleesa, Jaleese, Jalicia, Jalisa, Jalessa, Jalissa, Jamaine, Jamari, Jamesha, Jamisha, Jameisha, Jamiesha, Jamika, Jameka, Janika, Janique, Janecia, Janeesa, Janeese, Janeil, Janeille, Janielle, Janisa, Janisha, Janora, Jarae, Jarai, Javona

JACEY: (Contemporary) Phonetic variant based on the initials J.C. or a short form of Jacinda.

Jaci, Jacee, Jacy, Jaicee, Jacelyn, Jaycee, Jaycie

JACINDA: (Greek) "Hyacinth."

Jacinta (Spanish); Jacinthe (French); Jacenia
JACKIE: (English) Short form of Jacqueline.
Jacque, Jackee, Jacqui, Jacquie, Jacki; Jacquetta (Italian)
JACLYN: (*JAK-lin*) (Contemporary) Two-syllable phonetic form of Jaqueline.
JACKLYN; Jacklynn, Jaclynn, Jackleen, Jakleen, Jaklyn
JACQUELINE: (*JAK-kwa-lin; jak-LEEN; zhak-leen; ZHAK-ah-leen; JAK-ah-lin; JAK-lin*) (French) Feminine form of Jacques, from James and Jacob. See also Jackie and Jaclyn.
JACQUELYN; Jaqueline, Jacquelyne, Jacquelynn, Jacqualine, Jacqualyn, Jacquelynne, Jacquelina, Jacqueleen, Jaquelyn, Jaquelin, Jaquelynn, Jacalyn, Jacalynn
JADA: (*JAY-dah*) (Arabic) "Goodness." Jade (English) refers to the gemstone and the color green.
Jadira, Jadee, Jady, Jaeda, Jaida, Jaide, Jayde, Jaydra
JAE: (Contemporary) Feminine variant form of Jay; some variants follow the pattern of "Ja-" names. See also Jaya.
Jaelana, Jaeleah, Jaeleen, Jaena, Jaenelle, Jaenette, Jayleen, Jaylene, Jaylee, Jaylynn
JAIRA: (Spanish/Hebrew) Feminine form of Jairus.
JAMAICA: (*ja-MAY-kah*) The name of the West Indies island.
JAMEELAH: (Arabic) "Beautiful"
Jameela; Jamila (Somali-Swahili) "chaste"; Jamilah, Jamilla, Jamilia, Jemila, Jamelia, Jamille
JAMIE: (Scottish) Pet form of James.
JAIME (Spanish/Scottish); Jaimie, Jaimee, Jaimi, Jaimelynn, Jami, Jamee, Jamey, Jaymie, Jaymee, Jamia, Jamielee, Jamilyn, Jamison
JAN: (Dutch/Slavic) Variant form of John.
JANA: (Polish/Czech) Feminine form of Jan, from John, with contemporary variant forms. Roman mythology; Jana (*JAY-nah*) was the wife of Janus.

Janna, Jannie, Janny, Janah, Jannah, Janne, Janica, Janceena, Janalee, Jannalee, Janalyn, Janalynn

JANAE: (*ja-NAY*) (Contemporary) An especially favored Ja- name with contemporary variants based on Jane or Jean. Janai is a Biblical male name with the meaning "God has answered."

Janae, Janai, Janaye, Jannae, Jeanae, Jeanay, Jenae, Jenay, Jenee, Jenai, Jennae, Jennay, Jenaya, Janaya, Janais

JANE: (English/Hebrew) "Jehovah has been gracious, has shown favor." Variant form of Joan, from John. See also Gianna, Giovanna, Ivana, Jan, Jana, Janae, Janelle, Janessa, Janet, Janice, Janine, Jean, Jeanelle, Jeanette, Jeannine, Jenny, Jiana, Joan, Johnna, Juanita, Seana, Sheena, Siana, Sinead and Siobhan.

Janie, Jayne, Janee, Janey, Jaina, Jayna, Jaynie, Jayni; Jenica (Rumanian); Jenika

JANELLE: (Contemporary) Variant form of Jane. See also Jeanelle.

Janel, Janell, Jannelle, Janella

JANESSA: (Contemporary) Blend of Jan or Jane and Vanessa. See also "Ja-" names.

Janesse, Jannessa, Janissa

JANET: (Scottish) Variant form of Jane, from the French Jeanette.

JANETTE, Jannet, Janett, Janetta, Janeth, Janneth

JANICE: (English) Variant form of Jane.

Janiece, Jannice, Janise, Janeece, Janicia, Janis, Jannis

JANINE: (English) Variant form of Jeannine. See also Jeannine.

Janina, Janeen, Janene, Jannine, Jannina

JASMINE: (*JAZ-min, jaz-MEEN*) (French/Arabic) A flower name, from the earlier form Jessamine. See also Yasmin and Jazlyn.

JASMIN, JAZMIN, JAZMINE, Jasmyn, Jasmyne,

Jasmina, Jasmeen, Jazmyn, Jazzmyn, Jazmyne, Jazzmine, Jessamine, Jessamyn

JAVIERA: (*HA-vee-ER-ah*) (Spanish) "Bright." Feminine form of Xavier.

JAXINE: (Contemporary) Variant form of Jacinta. May also be a contemporary blend of Jack and Maxine.

JAYA: (Sanskrit) "Victorious." Mythology; a Buddhist female deity and one of the names of the wife of Shiva.

JAZLYN: (Contemporary) Variant forms of Jasmine, influenced by Jocelyn and the musical term jazz. See also Jasmine.

Jazzlyn, Jazlynn, Jaslyn, Jaslynn, Jasleen, Jazzalyn, Jasmaine, Jazmaine, Jasminique, Jazmina, Jazma, Jazzy

JE- names: (Contemporary) Blend of Je- plus various endings, with pronunciation emphasis on the second syllable. The second syllable may or may not begin with a capital. See also Ja- and Jo- names.

Jelani, Jelisa, Jelissa, Jemelle, Jenessa, Jeondra, JeRae, JeRaine, Jeree, Jeressa, Jerona

JEANELLE: (Contemporary) Diminutive form of Jeanne. See also Janelle.

Jeannell, Jeannelle, Jenelle, Jenell, Jennelle, Jenneil, Jenella

JEANETTE: (*je-NET*) (French) Diminutive form of Jeanne. A favorite name in France and Scotland. See also Janet.

Jeannette, Jeanetta, Jenette, Jennet (Scottish)

JEANNE: (*jeen*) (French) Variant form of John. See also Sheena.

Jean, Jeana, Jeane, Jeanna, Jeanice, Jeena, Jeannie, Jeanie, Jeanee

JEANNINE: (French) Diminutive form of Jane or Jeanne. See also Janine.

Jeanine, Jeanina, Jenine, Jenina, Jennine, Jineen

JELENA: (*ya-LAY-nah, je-LEE-nah*) (Russian) "Shining light." Variant form of Helena.

JEMIMA: (*je-MYE-mah*) (Arabic/Hebrew) "Little dove."
  Biblical; one of the three daughters of Job (see also
  Keziah and Keren), renowned as the most beautiful
  women of their time.
  Jemimah
JEMMA: (English) Variant form of Gemma.
JENEVIEVE: (*JEN-nah-veeve*) (Contemporary) Phonetic
  variant form of Genevieve.
  Jennavieve, Jenavieve, Jenneva, Jeneva,
JENNA: (Contemporary) Variant form of Jenny and
  Jennifer. Jenna is also used for blends and compound
  names. See also Jenny and Genna.
  Jennah, Jennabel, Jennalee, Jennalyn, Jennarae,
  Jennasee
JENNIFER: (English/Welsh) "Fair one." Variant form of
  Guinevere. Mythology; in Arthurian tales, Guinevere
  was Arthur's queen. Jenifer is a spelling variant used es-
  pecially in Cornwall. See also Jenna.
  Jenifer
JENNY: (English) Diminutive of Jane and Jennifer. Also
  used for blends and compound names. See also Jenna.
  Jennie, Jenni, Jeni, Jinny, Jinni, Jen, Jennyann, Jenny-
  lee, Jennilee, Jenalee, Jennilyn, Jenilynn, Jenalyn,
  Jenalynn, Jena, Jeneen, Jenene, Jenetta, Jenita, Jennis,
  Jenice, Jeniece, Jenise, Jenarae, Jennessa, Jennika
JEORJIA: (Contemporary) Phonetic variant form of Geor-
  gia.
  Jorja
JEOVANA: (*joe-VAH-nah*) (Contemporary) Feminine form
  of Giovanni or variant of Jovana. See also Jovita.
  Jeovanna (*joe-VAN-ah*)
JERALDINE: (English) Variant spelling of Geraldine.
JERALYN: (Contemporary) Blend of Jerry and Marilyn.
  Jerelyn, Jerilyn, Jerilynn, Jerralyn, Jerrilyn
JERI: (Contemporary) Feminine form of Jerry.

Jerri, Jeralee

JERICA: (*JARE-ah-kah*) (Contemporary) "Strong, gifted ruler." Blend of Jeri and Erica.

Jerrica, Jerika, Jerrika

JERUSHA: (*je-ROO-shah*) (Hebrew) "He has taken possession." A Biblical name that James Michener used for the missionary heroine in his novel *Hawaii*.

JESSENIA: (*jes-SEE-nee-ah*) (Spanish) Probably a created name, made popular by the Gypsy title character of a Seventies Spanish soap opera. See also Yessenia and Llessenia.

Jesenia, Jasenia

JESSICA: (English/Hebrew) Feminine form of Jesse. For *The Merchant of Venice*, Shakespeare is said to have devised this name for Skylock's daughter, a young Jewish woman who elopes with Lorenzo and converts to Christianity. See also Jessie.

Jessika

JESSIE: (English) Short form of Jessica. Also a spelling variant of the male name Jesse. Jess- is a popular prefix in contemporary girls' names, especially blends that sound like Jocelyn.

Jessi, Jessye, Jessa, Jessalyn, Jessalynn, Jesselyn, Jessilyn, Jesslyn, Jesslynn, Jessamae, Jessina, Jessana, Jessandra, Jeslyn, Jesirae, Jeziree

JETTA: (English) Refers to jet, an intensely black, shiny gemstone.

JEWEL: (English/French) "Playful." Literally, a precious gem.

Jewell, Jewelle, Jewelene, Jewelissa, Jewelyn

JEZEBEL: (*JEZ-a-bel*) (Hebrew) "Where is the prince?" Rare. Name of the notorious Biblical Jezebel, a queen of Israel condemned by God.

JIANA: (*jee-AHN-ah*) (Contemporary) Phonetic form of Gianna, an Italian form of Jane.

Jianna

JILL: (English) Short form of Jillian. See also Gillian.

Jyl, Jyll, Jilly

JILLIAN: (*JIL-ee-an*) (English) "Jove's child." Variant form of Gillian, from Julian. See also Jill and Gillian.

Jillianne, Jilliann, Jilliane, Jillianna, Jilian, Jillanne, Jillayne (*jil-LANE*), Jillesa, Jillene, Jyllina

JIMI: (Contemporary) Feminine form of Jimmy.

Jimmi

JINA: (*JEEN-ah*) (Swahili) "Named child." See also Gina.

JISELLE: (*ji-ZELL*) (Contemporary) "Pledge." Phonetic spelling of Giselle.

JO and JO- names: (Contemporary) Jo is an independent name and short form of names like Joanna and Josephine, frequently used as a prefix in blends and compound names. See also Ja- and Je- names, Jolene and Jodelle.

Jobeth, Jobelle, Jodean, Joetta, Joette, Joleesa, Jolisa, Jolise, Jolissa, Jolynn, Jolyn, JoLyn, Jolinda, JoMarie, Jonelle, Jonell, Jonetia, Jonessa, Joniece, Jonique, Jonisa, Joquise, Jorene, Josanna, Josanne, Joselle, Jozelle, Jozette, Jovelle

JOAN: (English) Feminine form of John. See also Jane, Joanna and Siobhan.

JOANNA: (English/Latin) Variant form of Joan. Biblical; the name of several women who were disciples of Christ. See also Jane and Joan.

JOANNE (English/French); JOHANNA, Johannah (Hebrew/German); Joana, Joann, Joanie, Joeanna, Joeanne

JOAQUINA: (*wah-KEE-nah*) (Spanish) Feminine form of Joaquin.

JOCELYN: (*JOSS-lin, JOSS-sa-lyn*) (English/French) Medieval male name adopted as a feminine name. Josalind is a contemporary blend of Jocelyn and Rosalind.

Jocelynn, Jocelyne, Joceline, Jocelina, Joscelyn, Josalyn, Josalynn, Josilyn, Joslyn, Joslin, Jozlyn, Josalind

JODELLE: (*joh-DELL*) (French) Surname used as a given name.

Jodell, Jo Dell

JODI: (English) Feminine form of nicknames for Joseph and Jude. Biblical; Joda (Hebrew) is the name of an ancestor of Christ.

Jody, Jodie, Jodee, Joda

JOELLE: (*jo-EL*) (French) "Jehovah is God." Feminine form of Joel.

Joella, Joellen, Joellyn, Joell

JOHNNA: (Contemporary) Feminine form of John and Jon.

Johnette, Johnetta, Johnelle, Johnnie, Jonette, Jonetta, Jonalyn, Jonalynn, Jonna, Jonnie, Joni, Jonni, Jonita, Jonay, Jonell, Jonnelle

JOLENE: (English) A well-established Jo- name.

Joleen, Joline, Jolena, Jolina, Jolleen, Jollene

JOLIE: (*zho-LEE*) (English/French) "Cheerful, pretty."

Joli, Jolee, Joleigh (*joe-LEE*)

JONINA: (*yo-NEE-nah, jo-NEE-nah*) (Israeli) "Little dove."

JORDAN: (*JOR-dan*) (Hebrew) "Down flowing." The river in Palestine where Jesus was baptized, used as a given name since the time of the Crusades.

Jordana (Spanish); Jourdan, Jordane, Jordaine (French); Jordanne, Jordann (*jor-DAN*), Jordanna (*jor-DAN-ah*), Jordyn, Jori, Jorry

JORGINA: (Contemporary/Latin) Variant form of Georgina.

Jorgeanne, Jorgelina, Jorjana (*jor-JAN-ah*)

JOSEPHINE: (French) Feminine form of Joseph. See also Josie.

Josephina; Josefina (Spanish); Josefa (German)

JOSIE: (English) Diminutive form of Josephine.

Josette (French); Josina

JOVITA: (*hoe-VEE-tah, joe-VEE-tah*) (Spanish) Feminine form of Jovian, from Jove, the Roman Jupiter, "father of the sky." A saint's name. See also Jeovana.

Jovena, Jovina, Jovana, Jovanna

JOY: (English/French) "Rejoicing."

Joya; Joie (French); Joi, Joia, Joyanna, Joyann, Joyanne, Joyelle

JOYCE: (English/Latin) "Cheerful, merry."

Joycelyn, Joycelynn, Joyceanne

JUANITA: (*wah-NEE-tah*) (Spanish) Diminutive form of Juana, from John.

Juana (*WAH-nah*), Juanetta, Juanisha

JUDITH: (Hebrew) "From Judea."

JUDY, Judi, Judie, Judeana, Judeena, Juditha

JULIANA: (Latin) "Jove's child." Feminine form of Julius. See also Gillian, Giuliana, Jillian, Julie and Juliet.

JULIANNE, Julieann, Juliann, Julieanne, Juliane, Julianna, Julieanna

JULIE: (*JOO-lee, zhoo-lee*) (French) Feminine form of Julian. See also Juliana and Juliet.

JULIA, Julee, Juli, Juleen, Julena; Julina (Spanish); Julisa, Julissa, Julyssa, Julisha, Julita, Julayna, Juliza

JULIET: (*joo-lee-ET*) (English/French) Variant form of Julia. Shakespeare used the name Juliet twice, in *Romeo and Juliet* and in *Measure for Measure*.

Julieta (Spanish); Juliette (French); Julietta (Italian)

JUNE: (Latin) "Young." Roman mythology; Juno was the protectress of women and of marriage, hence June is known as the bridal month.

Junel, Junelle, Junette, Junae, Juno

JUSTINE: (*juss-TEEN*) (English/French) "Just, upright." Feminine form of Justin.

Justina (Latin); Justyne, Justene, Justeen, Justeene; Jestine, Jestina (Welsh)

K

KA- names: (Contemporary) Blends of Ka- plus various endings, with pronunciation emphasis on the second syllable. See also Ke- names.

Kalana, Kalania, Kalea, Kaleah, Kaleila, Kalia, Kalisha, Kaleesha, Kalisa, Kalissa, Kalyssa, Kamara, Kamari, Kamesha, Kaneisha, Kanisha, Karaina, Karisa, Karisha, Karysa, Kasaundra, Kashana, Kashonna, Katana, Katasha, Katisha, Katiya, Katessa, Katrice, Katrisa, Kavonna

KACIE: (Contemporary) Kacie and its variants are probably phonetic forms of the initials K.C. or variants of the Irish name Casey, meaning "alert, vigorous." See also Kasey.

Kacey, Kaci, Kaycee, Kaycie, Kayci, Kacy, Kacee, K.C., Kayce, Kacia, Kaesha

KADY: (*KAY-dee*) (Contemporary) Rhyming variant of Katy or Cady.

Kadie, Kadi, Kadee, Kaedee, Kadia, Kadian, Kadienne

KAI: (*kye*) (Hawaiian) "The sea." Rare. See also Kay.

Kaia

KAILA: (*KYE-lah, KAY-lah*) (Israeli) "The laurel crown." Also a Hawaiian name (*kye-EE-lah*) meaning "style." See also Kayla.

Kaela, Kaylah, Kailah, Kaelah, Kayle

KAITLIN: (Contemporary) Phonetic form of the Irish name Caitlin, from Catherine. See also Katelyn, Katherine and Caitlin.

KAITLYN, Kaitlynn, Kaitlan, Kaitleen

KALANI: (*kah-LAH-nee*) (Hawaiian paraphrase) "The sky; chieftain." See also Keilani.

Kaloni, Kalanie, Kailani (*kye-LAH-nee*) "Sea and sky."

KALEI: (*kah-LAY-ee*) (Hawaiian) "The flower wreath; the beloved."

KALI: (*KAH-lee*) (Hawaiian) "Hesitation." Mythology; Kali, wife of Shiva, is a Hindu goddess symbolizing the essence of destruction. See also Kallie.

KALIFA: (*kah-LEE-fah*) (Somali) "Chaste, holy."

KALILAH: (*kah-LEE-lah*) (Arabic) "Darling, sweetheart."

KALINA: (*kah-LEE-nah*) (Polish/Czech) A flower name and place name. Kalena is the Hawaiian equivalent of Karen.

Kalena, Kaleen, Kalene, Kaleena

KALINDA: (*ka-LEEN-dah*) (Sanskrit) "The sun." Hindu mythology; a reference to the mountains of Kalinda or the sacred Kalindi river.

Kalynda, Kalindi

KALLAN: (Scandinavian) "Flowing water." See also Callan.

KALLIE: (Contemporary) Variant form of Callie. Kalle is a Finnish form of Carol. See also Kali and Callie.

Kalli, Kalle, Kally, Kahli, Kallita

KALLISTA: (*kah-LISS-tah*) (Greek) "Beautiful." See also Calista.

KAMBRIA: (*KAM-bree-ah*) Spelling variant of Cambria, referring to Wales.

KAMEA: (*kah-MAY-ah*) (Hawaiian) "The one (and only)."

Kameo (See also Cameo)

KAMELIA: (*kah-MEEL-yah*) See Camelia.

Kamella

KAMERON: (Contemporary) Variant form of Cameron. Also occasionally used for girls.

Kamryn, Kamron, Kamrin, Kamren

KAMI: (Japanese) "Lord." Variants may also be short forms of names like Kamelia and Kamille.

Kammi, Kammie, Kamlyn

KAMILAH: (Arabic) "Perfection." Kamille is a variant form of Camille.

Kamille, Kamila, Kamilla, Kamillia

KANANI: (*kah-NAH-nee*) (Hawaiian) "The beautiful one."

KANDACE: (Contemporary) See Candace.

Kandice, Kandis, Kandyce, Kandiss, Kandy, Kandi, Kandee

KANI: (*KAH-nee*) (Hawaiian) "Sound." Also the Hawaiian equivalent of Sandy.

KAPRI: (Contemporary) See also Caprice.

Kaprice, Kapricia, Kaprisha

KARA: (Scandinavian) Short form of Katherine. See also Cara, Cari and Kerry.

KARI, Karah, Karrah, Karalyn, Karalynn, Karalee, Karalie, Kaira, Karie, Karrie, Karri, Karee, Kary, Karianne, Kariann, Karianna, Kariana, Karielle

KAREN: (English/Danish) Short form of Katherine. See also Karina, Keren and Caryn.

Karin (Norwegian); Karyn, Karon, Karren, Karrin, Karan

KARIDA: (Arabic) "Virgin."

KARIMA: (*kah-REE-mah*) (Arabic) "Generous, a friend." Feminine form of Karim.

KARINA: (*kah-REE-nah*) (Contemporary) Variant form of Katherine. See also Karen and Carina.

Karena (Scandinavian); Karyna, Kareena, Kareina, Karenah, Karene, Kareen, Karine, Karinna, Karinne

KARIS: (*KARE-iss*) (Greek) "Grace." Phonetic variant of Charis.

KARISMA: (*ka-RIZ-mah*) (Contemporary) "Favor, gift." See also Charis.

KARISSA: (*ka-RISS-ah*) (Greek) "Very dear." See also Carissa.

Karessa, Karyssa, Karisa, Karess

KARLA: (German/Scandinavian) "Womanly, strength." Feminine form of Karl. See also Carla.
Karly, Karli, Karlie, Karlee, Karley, Karleigh, Karlesha, Karleen, Karlene, Karline, Karlina, Karlyn, Karlen, Karlin

KARMA: (Sanskrit) "Actions are fate." In Buddhism and Hinduism, Karma is the inevitable effect of actions during life.

KARMEL: "Fruitful orchard." See also Carmela.
Karmelle

KARMEN: (Contemporary) Variant form of Carmen.
Karmina

KAROL: (Hungarian) Variant form of Carol.
Karole, Karolyn; Karoline, Karolina (German/Scandinavian)

KASEY: (Contemporary/Irish) "Alert, vigorous." Variant form of Casey. See also Casey and Kacie.
Kasie, Kasia

KASHMIR: (*kazh-meer*) (Sanskrit) The name of a state in India. See also Cashmere.
Kasmira, Kazhmir, Kasha

KASSANDRA: (Greek) "Unheeded prophetess." Contemporary variants are based on some of the preferred pronunciations of Sandra. See also Cassandra and Kassie.
Kasandra (Spanish); Kassondra, Kasondra, Kasaundra

KASSIA: (*kah-SEE-ah*) (Polish) Short form of Katharine. Also a variant form of Cassia.

KASSIDY: (Contemporary) "Curly-headed." See also Cassidy.

KASSIE: (Contemporary) Short form of Kassandra and other names that being with "Kas-." See also Cassie.
Kassi, Kassy, Kassie

KATELYN: (English) Phonetic form of Caitlin, an Irish form of Katherine. Kateline is a medieval English form. See also Kaitlin and Caitlin.

Katelynn, Katelin, Kateline, Katelinn, Katlin, Katlyn, Katlynn, Katlynne, Kitlyn

KATHERINE: (English/Greek) "Pure." A name in use at least since the third century A.D. The early Latin forms Katerina and Caterina became Katharine and Catherine. The French Cateline and English Catlyn came into wider use during the medieval period, and variant spellings and forms multiplied. Preference in modern times is for the K- spelling, which is closest to the original Greek versions. See also Caitlin, Catherine, Cathy, Kaitlin, Kara, Karen, Karina, Kassia, Katelyn, Kathleen, Kathy, Katie, Katrina, Kay, Kayla, Kaylee, Kaylyn, Kitty and Kolena.

KATHRYN, KATHARINE, Kathrine, Kathryne, Kathrynn, Kathrina, Katheryn, Katharyn, Katherina; Katarina (Hungarian, Polish); Katerina, Katrya, Katria (Russian); Katriane (French); Katriana; Katalina, Katina (Greek); Katena

KATHLEEN (Irish) Variant form of Caitlin, from Katherine.

Kathlene, Kathlena, Kathleena, Kathlyn, Kathlynn

KATHY: (English) Short form of Katherine.

Kathie, Kathia, Kathi, Kathe (German)

KATIE: (English) The most popular English short form of Katherine. See also Kady.

KATE, KATY; Kati (Hungarian); Katee, Katey; Katya, Katiya, Katinka (Russian); Katia (Spanish); Katianne, Kaydee, Kaydi; Kata (Czech); Kat, Katilyn

KATRIEL: (ka-tree-ELL) (Hebrew) "My crown is God."

KATRINA: (Scottish/German) Variant short form of Katherine.

Katrin (Iceland); Katrine (Scandinavian/German)

KAY: (English/Scandinavian) "Keeper of the keys." Though Kay is most often used as a short form of Katherine and its variants, it is also a surname and independent given name. Sir Kay was one of King Arthur's knights. See also Kayla, Kai, Kaylee and Kaylyn.

Kaye, Kayanna, Kayana

KAYA: (*KAH-yah*) (Japanese) "Adds a place of resting." Also an African name of uncertain meaning.

KAYLA: (Contemporary) Variant form of Kay. Initial popularity of the name is attributable to the character named Kayla on the daytime TV drama, *Days of Our Lives*. See also Kaila, Kaylee, Kaylyn and Cayley.

Kaylah, Kaela, Kaelah, Kayle

KAYLEE: (Contemporary) Variant form of Kay and Kayla. See also Cayley, Kayla and Kaylynn.

Kayleigh, Kaylie, Kayley, Kayli, Kaylei, Kaylea, Kayleen, Kaylene, Kailee, Kailey, Kaley, Kalie, Kaleigh, Kalee, Kaeley, Kaeli, Kaeleigh, Kaelee, Kaelie

KAYLYN: (Contemporary) Variant form of Kay and Kayla. See also Cailin and in the boys index, Kaelan.

Kaylin, Kaylen, Kaylynn, Kaylan, Kalyn, Kalynn, Kalin, Kalen, Kalan, Kaelyn, Kaelin, Kaelynn, Kailyn, Kailynne, Kailin, Kailan, Kayleen, Kaelene, Kaileen, Kailene, Kayleena

KE- names: (Contemporary) Blends of Ke- plus various endings, with pronunciation emphasis on the second syllable. See also Ka- names.

Keandra, Keaundra, Keona, Keonna, Keosha, Kevonda

KEALA: (*kay-AH-lah*) (Hawaiian) "The pathway."

KEELY: (Irish) "Lively, aggressive." Variant form of Kelly.

Keeley, Keelie, Keelyn, Keila, Keilah

KEENA: (Irish) Possibly a feminine variant form of Keane, meaning "ancient." See also Kiana.

Keana, Keeana

KEIKI: (*kay-EE-kee*) (Hawaiian) "Child."

KEIKO: (*KAY-koh*) (Japanese) "Be glad"; "rejoicing child."

KEILANI: (*kay-ee-LAH-nee*) (Hawaiian) "Glorious chief."
Keilana; "glory, calmness." See also Kalani.
Keilana

KEISHA: (*KEE-shah*) (Contemporary) Short form of
Lakeisha.
Keshia, Kisha, Kesha, Keesha, Kiesha, Kecia

KEITHA: (English) "Woodland." Feminine form of Keith.

KELBY: (Gaelic/Scandinavian) "Place by the fountain;
spring."

KELLEN: (Gaelic) "Slender, fair." Used more for boys
than for girls.
Kellyn, Kellan

KELLY: (Irish/Gaelic) "Lively, aggressive." Occasionally
used for boys.
KELLI, KELLIE, KELLEY, Kellee, Kellye, Kelleen,
Kelleigh, Kellyann, Kellyanne, Kelianne

KELSEY: (English/Irish) "Brave." Popular preference for
Kelsey and its variants may be influenced by names like
Chelsea and Casey.
KELSIE, Kelsi, Kelsy, Kelsee, Kelsa, Kellsey, Kellsie,
Kelcie, Kelcey, Kelcy

KENDALL: (English) "Royal valley." Surname referring to
Kent, England.
Kendal, Kendahl, Kendyl, Kindall, Kyndall, Kyndal

KENDRA: (Contemporary) Blend of Ken and Sandra or
Andrea.
Kenna, Kindra, Kenndrea, Kendria, Kyndra

KENISHA: (*ken-NEE-shah*) (Contemporary) Possibly a
prefix name or a feminine variant form of Ken.
Kennesha

KENZIE: (Scottish) "The fair one." Short form of
McKenzie.
Kenza, Kenzy, Kinzie

KEREN: (Hebrew) "Beauty." Short form of Keren-happuch. Biblical; one of the three daughters of Job. See also Karen.

Kerrin, Keryn

KERRY: (Irish) "Dusky, dark." See also Kara.

Keri, Kerri, Kerrie, Kera, Keriann, Kerianne, Keriana, Kerianna, Kerilyn, Kerrianne, Kerra

KETIFA: (*ke-tee-fah*) (Arabic) "Flowering."

KETURAH: (*ke-TOO-rah*) (Hebrew) "Sacrifice." Biblical; the second wife of Abraham.

KEVINA: (*ke-VEEN-ah, KEV-i-nah*) (Contemporary) "Beautiful child." Feminine form of Kevin.

Kevia, Keva

KEZIAH: (*ke-ZYE-ah*) (Hebrew) "Cassia; sweet-scented spice." Biblical; one of the three fair daughters of Job.

Kezia

KHADIJAH: (*kah-DEE-jah*) (Arabic) Muhammad's first wife, named in the Koran as one of the four perfect women. (The others were Fatima, Mary and Aisha.)

KHRISTINA: (Russian) Variant form of Kristina, a Scandinavian form of Christina. See also Christina, Kirsten and Kristina.

Khrystyna (Polish); Khristyna, Khristina, Khristine, Khrystyne, Khristeen, Khrystyn, Khristin, Khristen, Khristyana

KIANA: (*kee-AHN-ah*) (Contemporary) May be a favored prefix name or a variant form of Kian, an Irish name meaning "ancient." See also Cian and Keena.

Kiana, Kianna, Kiani, Kianni, Kiauna, Kiahna, Keiana, Keanna, Kiona, Kionah, Kionna, Kioni, Kiandra, Kiandria

KIARA: (*kee-AR-ah*) (Contemporary) Rhyming variant of Ciara. Kiera (*KEER-ah*) is a feminine form of the Irish Gaelic Kieran, meaning "dusky, dark-haired." See also Kira and Kyra.

Kiera, Kierra, Keira, Kiarra

KIKI: (*kee-kee*) (Spanish) Pet form of Enriqueta, from Henrietta.

Kiko (Japanese)

KILEY: (Irish) "Near the church (or the wood)." See also Kylie.

Kilee

KILLASHANDRA: (Irish) "Church of the fortress." A place name used as a woman's given name by science-fiction writer Anne McCaffrey in the *Killashandra* novels. See also Shandra.

KIM: (English) An independent name and short form of Kimberly. Also a Vietnamese name meaning "precious metal, gold."

KIMBERLY: (English) "King's wood." Place name and surname.

Kimberley, Kimberlee, Kimberli, Kimberlyn, Kimberleigh, Kymberly, Kymberlee, Kymberlie, Kym

KIMI: (*kee-mee*) (Japanese) "Upright, righteous."

Kimiko (*KEE-mee-koh*) "righteous child"

KINA: (*KEE-nah*) (Hawaiian) "China." Also the Hawaiian equivalent of Tina.

KIOKO: (*kee-OH-koh*) (Japanese) "Child born with happiness."

KIRA: (Russian) "Lady." See also Kiara and Kyra.

Kiri, Kirra, Kiran, Kiriana

KIRBY: (English) "Church farm." Place name and surname.

KIRSTEN: (Scandinavian/Scottish) Variant form of Christine.

Kirstin, Kiersten; Kerstin (Swedish); Kirstyn, Kyrstin, Kierstin, Kirstine; Kirstie, Kirsty, (Scottish); Kirsti, Kirstee

KISHI: (*kee-shee*) (Japanese) "Happiness to the earth."

KITRA: (Hebrew) "Crowned one."

KITTY: (English) Pet name for Katherine.

Kitlyn

KLARISSA: (German) "Bright, shining and gentle." Variant form of Klara. See also Clarissa.

Klara, Klaire

KODI: (Contemporary) "Helpful." See also Codi.

Kodie, Kodee

KOEMI: (*koh-AY-mee*) (Japanese) "A little smile."

KOLBY: "Dark, dark-haired." See also Colby.

KOLINA: (*ko-LEEN-ah*) (Swedish) Variant form of Katharine.

KORA: (Greek) "Maiden." See also Cora.

Korena, Koren, Koreen, Koral, Koralise, Korissa, Koressa

KORI: (Greek) See also Cory.

Korie, Kory, Korey, Korri, Korrie, Koree, Korry

KORIN: (Contemporary) "Maiden." Variant form of Corrine.

Korrin, Korinne, Koryn, Korynn, Korynne, Korine, Korina, Korinna, Korrine, Koreena, Korrina

KOURTNEY: (Contemporary) Variant form of Courtney.

Kortney

KRISANDRA: (Contemporary) Variant form of Chrysandra.

Krisanne

KRISTA: (Czech) Variant form of Christine. Also a variant spelling of Christa. See also Christa and Christy.

KRISTY, KRISTI, Kristie; Krysta (Polish); Krysti, Krystie, Khristie, Khristy, Khrysta, Khris, Krissa, Kryssa, Krissie

KRISTEN: (Scandinavian) Variant form of Christian. See also Christen and Kirsten.

KRISTIN, Kristyn, Krysten, Krystin, Kristan, Krystyn, Krystynn

KRISTINA: (Scandinavian/Czech) Variant form of Christina. See also Khristina and Kristine.

Krystina (Czech); Krystyna (Polish); Krysteena, Kristena, Kristyna, Kristena, Kristeena, Kristiana, Kristianna, Kristiane, Kristianne, Krystiana, Krystianna

KRISTINE: (English) Variant form of Christine. See also Christine, Krista, Kristina, Kristen, and Kirsten.

Krystine, Kristeen, Kristyne; Kristian (Danish)

KRYSANTHE: (Greek) "Golden flower." See also Crysantha.

KRYSTAL: (Contemporary) Variant spelling of Crystal. The "K" reflects the Greek spelling, *krystallos*. See also Crystal.

Kristal, Kristel, Kristell, Krystel, Khristal, Khrystal, Krystelle, Kristella, Krystalyn, Krystalynn, Kristalyn, Kristalena, Krystabelle, Kristabelle, Khrystalline

KUMIKO: (*KOO-mee-koh*) (Japanese) "Companion child; drawing together."

KYLIE: (Gaelic) Feminine form of Kyle. See also Kiley.

Kyla, Kylah, Kylee, Kyley, Kyli, Kyleigh, Kylea, Kalene, Kyleen, Kylianne, Kylin

KYOKO: (*kee-OH-koh*) (Japanese) "Mirror."

KYRA: (*KEER-rah, KYE-rah*) "Enthroned." Variant form of Cyra, feminine form of Cyrus. See also Kiara, Kira and Cyrah.

Kyrie (Greek) "lady," Kyria, Kyrene

L

LA- names: (Contemporary) Blends of La- plus various endings, with pronunciation emphasis on the second syllable, which might or might not begin with a capital. Lakeisha, Latasha, Latisha and LaToya are listed separately.

Lacacia, Lachelle, Lacinda, Lacretia, Lacoya, Laday, Ladonya, LaDonna, LaGina, Lajuana, LaJoyce, Lakendra, Lakia, Lalani, Lanae, Lanai, Lanelle, Lanesha, Lanessa, Laniece, Lanetta, Lanette, Lanika,

Lanisha, Lanita, Lanora, Laporsha, Laquana, Laquanda,
Laquesha, Laquita, Larae, LaRay, LaRee, LaRhonda,
Laronda, Larisha, Lasandra, LaShae, Lashanda,
LaShawn, Lashawnda, Latanya, Latavia, Latina,
Latonia, Latonya, Latoria, Latrice, Latreece, LaTricia,
Latrisha, Lavette, Lavonda, Lavonna, Lavonne,
LaWanda

LACEY: (French) Nobleman's surname carried to England
and Ireland after the Norman conquest.
Lacy, Lacie, Lacee, Laci, Laycie, Lace, Lacene, Lacina,
Lacyann, Laciann

LAEL: (*LAY-el*) (Hebrew) "Belonging to God." Traditionally a Biblical male name.

LAILA: (*LAY-lah*) (Persian/Arabic) "Born at night." Variant
form of Leila. See also Leila and Lyla.
Layla, Laylah (Sanskrit)

LAINA: (*LANE-ah*) (Contemporary) "Path, roadway."
Feminine variant form of surnames like Lane and Laine.
Laine, Laney, Lanie

LAKEISHA: (*lah-KEE-shah*) (Contemporary) Lakeisha and
its variant forms are rhyming variants of Leticia. See
also Keisha.
Lakesha, Lakisha, Lakeshia, Lakiesha, Laquisha

LALIA: (*LAH-lee-ah*) (Spanish) Short form of Eulalie. Lala
is the Hawaiian equivalent of Lara.
Lali, Lala; Lalla

LALITA: (Sanskrit) "Playful." Hindu mythology; the
mistress-playmate of the young Krishna.

LANA: (*LAN-ah, LAHN-ah*) (English) "Fair, good-
looking." Short form of Alana. Also (Hawaiian) "afloat;
calm as still waters." Some La- names might be variants
of Lana.
Lanna, Lanice, Lanette

LANDRA: (*LAHN-drah*) (Spanish/German) "Counselor."
Short form of Landrada, a saint's name.

LANI: (*LAH-nee*) (Hawaiian) "The sky; heavenly; royal."

LARA: (*LAR-ah*) (Latin) "Protection." From *lares*, referring to the individual gods of Roman households, the protectors of home and fields. Lara is popular in Russia and is also a Spanish surname and place-name. See also Larissa.
Laralaine, Laramae, Larinda, Larina, Larita

LARAINE: (English) Variant form of Loraine. Lareina; LaRayne, Larraine; Lareina (Spanish) "the queen," Larena

LARISSA: (*la-RISS-ah*) (Russian) Variant form of Lara.
Larisa (*la-REES-ah*), Laryssa, Lari

LATASHA: (*la-TAH-shah*) (Contemporary) A La- name based on Natasha, "birthday." See also Natasha and Tasha.

LATISHA: (*la-TEE-shah*) (Contemporary) A modern variant of the medieval name Letitia. See also Leticia and Tisha.
Laticia, Latesha, Lateisha, Letitia

LATOYA: (Spanish) "Victorious one." Derived from a short form of Victoria, LaToya has been made familiar today by singer LaToya Jackson. See also Toya.

LAURA: (English/Latin) "The laurel tree." In use for at least eight centuries, Laura has many variant forms. See also Laurel, Lauren, Liora, Lora, Loren, Lorena, Lorenza, Loretta and Lori.
Laurie, Laureen, Laurene, Laurena, Lauraine, Lauralee, Lauralyn, Lauretta; Laurette (French); Laurita (Spanish); Laurinda, Laurana

LAUREL: (English) Literally, the laurel tree, also called the sweet bay tree; symbolic of honor and victory.
Laurelle, Laural, Lauriel

LAUREN: (English/Latin) "From Laurentium, the place of the laurel trees." Feminine form of Lawrence. The earliest feminine form of the name was Laurentia, dating from the time of the early Romans; Lauren has come into use only in the twentieth century. See also Loren and Lorna.

Lauryn, Laurenne

LAVERNE: (*la-VERN*) (French) "Woodland."

Lavern

LAVINA: (*la-VEEN-ah*) (Spanish) From Levinia, a Roman given name of uncertain meaning.

Lavinia, Levina, Luvina, Luvenia

LEA: (*LAY-ah*) (Hawaiian) Mythological; the goddess of canoe makers. Also a Spanish form of Leah. Lia is a short form of names like Amalia and Rosalia. See also Leah and Lee.

Lia, Leatrice (*LEE-ah-triss*)

LEAH: (*LEE-ah*) (Hebrew) Biblical; Jacob's first wife, the mother of Dinah and six of Jacob's 12 sons. See also Lea.

LEALA: (*lee-AL-ah*) (Spanish/French) "Loyal, faithful."

Leola (*ee-OH-lah*)

LEANDRA: (*lee-AN-drah*) (Greek) "Lioness." Feminine form of Leander.

LEANNA: (Contemporary) Possibly derived from an Irish Gaelic form of Helen; may be a variant form of Liana. See also Liana.

Leanne, Leann, Leeann, Leana, Leeanne, Leianna

LECIA: (*LEE-shah*) (Contemporary) Short form of names like Alicia and Felecia, used as an independent name.

Lisha

LEDA: (*LEE-dah*) (Greek) Mythology; queen of Sparta, mother of Helen of Troy.

Leyda, Lyda, Leta

LEE: (English) "Meadow." Surname. Lee is often chosen as a middle name.

Leigh

LEILA: (*LEE-lah, LAY-lah, LYE-lah*) (Persian/Arabic)

"Born at night." Lela (French) refers to loyalty. See also Laila and Lyla.

Leilah, Lela, Leyla; Lelia (Latin); Leela (Sanskrit) "play"

LEILANI: (*lay-LAH-nee*) (Hawaiian) "Child of heaven; heavenly flowers."

Lei (Hawaiian) "wreath of flowers," Leia

LENA: (English/German/Scandinavian) Originally a name ending. Also an Irish name meaning "wet meadow." See also Lina.

Leena

LEONIE: (*LAY-o-nee, LEE-oh-nee, lay-OH-nee*) (French) "Lion, lioness." Feminine form of Leon. See also Loni.

Leona, Leonela, Leondra, Leondrea, Leonda

LEONORA: (Italian) "Shining light." Variant of Eleanor.

Leonor, Leonore (French/German); Lenore (English); Lenora (English/Russian); Leora

LEONTYNE: (*LEE-'n-teen, LAY-'n-teen*) (Contemporary) Feminine form of Leon made familiar by operatic star Leontyne Price.

Leontine (French); Leontina

LEORAH: (*lee-OR-ah*) (Israeli) "Light to me."

Leora

LESLIE: (*LESS-lee, LEZ-lee*) (Scottish) Name of a prominent Scottish clan. Used mainly for boys in England and Scotland. In America, Leslie is used almost exclusively for girls. The Lezlie spelling preserves the original Scottish pronunciation.

Lesley, Leslee, Lezlie

LETICIA: (*le-TEE-shah*) (Latin) "Great joy." Variant of Letitia. See also Latisha.

Letitia, Letisha, Letty, Laetitia

LEVANA: (*le-VAHN-ah*) (Latin) "Raise up." Mythology; Levana was the Roman goddess/protectress of the newborn.

Livana; Livaun, Levane (Irish) "the elm tree"

LEXANDRA: (*lex-ANN-drah, lex-AHN-drah*) (Contemporary) Variant of Alexandra.

Lexann, Lexi, Lexie, Lexine; Lexa (Czech)

LIANA: (*lee-AHN-ah*) (Contemporary) "Daughter of the sun." Diminutive of Eliana. See also Eliana and Leanna.

Lianna, Lianne, Liane, Liann; Lian, Li (Chinese)

LIBBY: (English) Diminutive of Elizabeth.

LIBERTY: (English) Literally, freedom.

LICIA: (*LEE-shah*) (Contemporary) Short form of Alicia.

LIDA: (*LEE-dah, LYE-dah*) (Russian) Originally a diminutive name ending. Variant form of Lydia (Czech).

LIESL: (*LEES-ul, LEE-zul*) (German) Short form of Elizabeth.

Liezel, Liezl

LILIANA: (Latin) Variant of Lillian, from Lily, the flower name.

LILLIAN, Lilian (English); Liliane (French); Lilianne, Lilianna, Lilliana, Lilliane, Lilliann, Lillianna

LILIBETH: (English) Blend of Lily and Elizabeth.

Lilibet, Lilybeth, Lilybell

LILY: (English) A flower name; the lily is a symbol of innocence and purity as well as beauty. See also Lillian.

Lilia (Latin); Lilly, Lillie; Lilli (German); Lili (French)

LIN: (Chinese) Family name. (English) Short form for names like Linden and Linnette.

LINA: (*LEE-nah*) (English/Latin) Originally an ending of names like Carolina. (Arabic) "Palm tree." See also Lena.

Lyna

LINDA: (English/German) "Lime tree; linden tree." Originally derived from linde, a Germanic name element referring to the lime tree, today Linda is associated by most parents with the Spanish word meaning "beautiful." See also Lynda.

Lindy, Lindee, Lindi, Lindalee

LINDEN: (English) "The linden tree."

LINDSEY: (Scottish/English) May refer to a lake or to a place of linden trees. Lindsay is a surname of some of the major Scottish and English noble families. See also Lyndsey.

LINDSAY, Linsey

LINNEA: (*le-NEE-ah, le-NAY*) (Scandinavian) A small blue flower.

Linnae, Lenae, Lynae, Lynnae, Linna

LINNET: (*LIN-et*) (English) "Songbird." See also Lynette.

Linnette (*li-NET*)

LIORA: (*lee-OR-ah*) (Israeli) "Light."

LISA: (*LEE-sah*) (English) Short form of Elisabeth. See also Liza.

Lise (French)

LISANDRA: (*le-SAN-drah, li-SAHN-drah*) (Greek) "Liberator." Feminine form of Lysander. Lissandra is an Italian variant form of Alexandra; Lizandra is a contemporary blend of Liz/Alexandra; Lizann, a blend of Liz/Ann.

Lissandra, Lizandra, Lizann

LISSA: (Contemporary) Short form of names like Melissa, Lissandra and Alyssa.

Lyssa

LITA: (*LEE-tah*) (Latin) Originally a diminutive ending.

Leta

LIV: (Rhymes with give.) (Scandinavian) "Life." Made familiar by actress Liv Ullman. Livia is an ancient Roman name as well as being a short form of Olivia.

Livia, Lyvia

LIZA: (*LYE-za, LEE-zah*) (English) Short form of Elizabeth and Eliza. See also Lisa.

Liz, Leeza, Lyza, Lizzie

LIZBETH: (*LIZ-beth*) (English) Short form of Elizabeth.

Lyzbeth, Lizabeth, Lisabeth, Lizbet, Lisbet, Lisabet

LIZETTE: (Contemporary) Variant of Elizabeth.
  Lissette, Lisette (French); Lyzette, Lizeth
LLESENIA: (*yeh-SEE-nee-ah*) (Spanish) Contemporary, probably created for the gypsy female lead in a seventies soap opera. See also Jessenia and Yessenia.
LOIDA: (*LOY-dah*) (Latin) Variant form of Leda.
  Loyda
LOIS: (Greek) "Pleasing." Biblical; a first-century Christian, the grandmother of Timothy.
LOLA: (Spanish) Short form of Dolores.
  Lolita
LONI: (*LAH-nee*) (Contemporary) Variant form of Alona or Leona. Modern usage is probably due to actress Loni Anderson, who pronounces the name to rhyme with Lonnie.
  Lona (*LOH-nah*), Lonnie, Lonni, Lonna
LORA: (German) Variant form of Laura. See also Lori and Loretta.
  Lorah, Lorinda, Lorita, Loree, Loranna, Loreana
LORELEI: (*LOR-a-lye, LOR-a-lay*) (German) A rocky cliff on the Rhine river, dangerous to boat passage, has been poetically personified as the Lorelei whose singing lures men to destruction.
  Loralei
LOREN: (English) Variant of Lawrence, from the Latin Laurentius, meaning "from Laurentium." See also Lauren and Lorna.
  Lorin (French); Loryn, Lorren, Lorrin, Lorryn
LORENA: (*lor-EEN-ah, lor-AY-nah*) Variant form of Laura or Lora. See also Lorraine.
  Lorene, Lorenia, Loreen, Loreene, Lorenna, Lorrina
LORENZA: (*lo-REN-zah*) (Italian) Feminine form of Lorenzo, from Lawrence.
LORETTA: (English/Latin) Diminutive form of Laura or Lora. Loreta is a saint's name.

Lorette, Loreta

LORI: (Contemporary) Variant of Lora and Laurie.
Lorianne, Loriann, Lorian, Loria, Loriana, Loriel, Lorilee, Lorilynn, Lorinda, Loris

LORNA: (Scottish) Feminine form of Lorne, from Loren, made familiar by the heroine of Blackmoore's novel *Lorna Doone*.

LORRAINE: (French) Name of the province in France and a family name of French royalty. See also Laraine and Lorene.
Lorraina, Loraine, Loraina, Lorayne

LOUISE: (*loo-EEZ*) "Renowned fighter." Feminine form of Louis. See also Luisa.
Louisa, Louella

LOURDES: (*loourd*) (Basque) Place name. Miracles of healing are attributed to the site in France where the Virgin Mary reportedly appeared to a young girl. See also Bernadette.

LUANA: (*loo-AHN-ah*) (Hawaiian) "Content, happy." Also contemporary blends based on Lou and Ann, Anna.
Luann, Luanna, Luanne, Luanda, Louann

LUCIA: (*loo-CEE-ah*) (Latin) "light, illumination." Feminine form of Lucius. See also Lucille and Lucine.
LUCY, Luci (English); Luciana, Lucianna (Italian); Lucie, Lucienne, Lucette (French); Lucita (Spanish)

LUCILLE: (*loo-CEEL*) (French) Diminutive form of Lucia.
Lucila, Lucilia (Spanish); Lucilla, Luciela (Italian); Lucienne, Lucile (French)

LUCINE: (*loo-CEEN*) (Latin) "Illumination." Mythology; the Roman goddess of childbirth, giver of first light to the newborn. Also a reference to Mary as the Lady of the Light. See also Lucia and Luz.
Lucina (German); Lucena (Spanish); Lucinda, Lucinna

LUCRETIA: (*loo-KREE-shah*) (Latin) The name of a Roman matron who committed suicide in public protest against dishonor. During the Renaissance, darker associations were added to the name through Lucrezia Borgia, sister to Cesare Borgia. See also Crecia.

Lucrecia (Spanish); Lucrezia (Italian); Lucrece (French)

LUISA: (*loo-EE-sah*) (Spanish) Feminine form of Louis. See also Louisa.

Luiza, Luisana, Luella

LULU: (Swahili) "Precious" (Tanzanian) "pearl" (Hawaiian) "calm, peaceful; protected." Also a pet form of names like Louise and Louella.

LUMINA: (*loo-MEEN-ah*) (Latin) "Brilliant, illuminated."

LUNA: (*LOO-nah*) (Latin) "The moon." Mythology; one of the names of Artemis, goddess of the moon.

LUPITA: (*loo-PEE-tah*) (Spanish) Short forms of Guadalupe.

Lupe

LUZ: (*looz*) "Almond tree." Biblical; an early name of the town of Bethel. Also a reference to Mary as "Our Lady of Light."

Luziana, Luzelena, Luzette

LYDIA: (Greek) "From Lydia." Biblical; a Christian woman called "a seller of purple." One of the rare descriptions of a woman of business, probably affluent, in Biblical times.

Lidia (Polish)

LYLA: (English) Possibly a feminine form of Lyle, or a variant short form of Delilah. See also Leila.

Lila, Lilah

LYNDA: (Contemporary) Variant form of Linda.

Lyndi, Lyndee, Lyndall

LYNDSEY: (Contemporary) Variant form of Lindsey.

Lyndsay, Lyndsie, Lynsey, Lynzee, Lynzie

LYNETTE: (*le-NET*) (English/Welsh) Variant of an ancient Welsh given name. In the Arthurian tales, Lynette ac-

companied Sir Gareth on a knightly quest. See also
Lynn and Linnet.

Lynnette, Lynnet, Lynelle, Lynessa

LYNN: (English) Possibly a short form of Lynnette, or a
variant form of *lann*, an Irish Gaelic word meaning
"house, church." Used especially as a middle name and
as a feminine beginning or ending in many name
blends, like Kaylyn and Lynlee.

Lynne, Lyn, Lynna, Lynlee, Lynley

LYRIC: (*LEER-ick*) (Latin/French) "Of the lyre." Literally,
the words of a song.

Lyrica (*LEER-ick-ah*), Lyra

M

MABEL: (*MAY-bel*) (English) "Lovable." Short form of
Amabel.

Mable, Maybell, Mabelle (French)

MACHIKO: (*MAH-chee-koh*) (Japanese) "Child who learns
truth; beautiful child." Machiko is the name of the current Empress of Japan.

MACKENZIE: (*ma-KEN-zee*) (Scottish) "Son of Kenzie;
fair, favored one." See also McKenzie, Mc- names and
Kenzie.

MACY: (*MAY-see*) (English/French) From a medieval male
name, possibly a form of Matthew.

Maci, Macey, Macie, Macee

MADELINE: (*MAD-a-linn*) (English/French) "Woman
from Magdala." Variant form of Madeleine. See Magdalena.

Madeleine (*mad-LAYNE*), Madelaine, Madelon
(French); Madalyn, Madalynn, Madelyn, Madelynn,
Madilyn; Madalena (Spanish); Maddelena (Italian);
Madelena, Madelina, Madelene, Madalene, Maddie,
Maddy; Madia, Madina, Madena (Spanish); Malena
(Scandinavian)

MADISON: (English) Surname derived from Matthew, "gift of Jah," or Matilda, "strong fighter." The mermaid heroine Madison in the hit film *Splash* probably influenced the adoption of the surname as a girl's name.

MADONNA: (Italian) "My lady." A form of respectful address, like the French "madame." Also used to signify the Virgin Mary, or a work of art depicting her as a mother. See also Donna and Mona.

MAEKO: (*mye-EE-koh*) (Japanese) "Truth child."

MAEMI: (*mah-AY-mee*) (Japanese) "Smile of truth."

MAEVE: (*ma-EEVE*) (Irish) "Joy." Maeve, the legendary warrior queen of ancient Connacht, is described in the *Tain*, the Celtic equivalent of the *Iliad*, as "tall, fair . . . carrying an iron sword."

MAGDA: (Slavic/German) Short form of Magdalena.

MAGDALENA: (Spanish/Czech) "Woman from Magdala." Biblical; Mary Magdalene came from the Magdala area near the sea of Galilee.
Magdalen, Magdalene

MAGGIE: (English) Short form of Margaret: usage as an independent name has risen due to a revival of interest in "old-fashioned" names.
Maggy, Maggi

MAGNOLIA: (*mag-NOL-yah*) A name from nature; the magnolia flower.

MAHALA: (*ma-HAH-lah*) (American Indian) "Woman."
Mahalia (Hebrew)

MAHINA: (*mah-HEE-nah*) (Hawaiian) "Moon, moonlight." The Hawaiian equivalent of Diana, goddess of the moon.

MAI: (French) "May." Roman mythology; Maia (source of the name May for the calender month) was the goddess of spring growth. Maiya (*MY-ah*) is a Japanese surname meaning "rice valley." See also May and Maya.
Maia, Maiya, Mae, Maelee, Maelynn

MAIDA: (*MAY-dah*) (English) "Maiden, virgin."

MAIRA: (*MAY-rah*) (Irish) Variant form of Mary. See also Mayra.

MAISIE: (*MAY-zee*) (English) Nickname for Margaret or Marjorie.

Maysa (*may-sah*) (Arabic) "graceful"

MAJESTA: (Latin) "Royal bearing, dignity." Mythology; Majestas was the Roman goddess of honor.

Majesty, Majida (*MA-jee-dah*) (Arabic) "glorious"

MALANA: (*ma-LAH-nah*) (Hawaiian) "Buoyant, light."

Malina "calming, soothing."

MALIA: (*ma-LEE-ah*) (Hawaiian) Variant of Mary. Also a Spanish variant of Maria

Malea, Maleah, Maleia

MALLORY: (English/French) Surname that came into great favor as a girl's name during the Eighties, primarily due to the character Mallory on the TV series *Family Ties*.

Malorie, Mallorie, Malori, Mallori

MAMIE: (*MAY-mee*) Short form of Mary and Miriam. See also Mimi. Mayme

MANDISA: (*man-DEE-sah*) (Africa) "Sweetness."

MANDY: (English) Short form of Amanda.

Mandi, Mandie, Manda, Mandalyn

MANON: (*man-awn*) (French) Diminutive form of Marie.

MANUELA: (*mahn-WAY-lah*) (Spanish) "With us is God." Variant form of Manuel.

MARA: (*MAHR-ah*) (English/Hebrew) "Bitter." Biblical; Naomi, mother-in-law of Ruth, claimed the name Mara as an expression of grief after the deaths of her husband and sons. May also be used as a variant form of Mary and as a short form of Tamara. See also Mary and Tamara.

Maralinda, Maraquina

MARCELLA: (Latin) "Of Mars." Feminine form of Marcellus. Mythology; Mars, the Roman god of fertility, for whom the spring calender month March was named, came to be identified with the Greek god Ares, god of war. See also Marcia and Maricela.

Marcelle, Marchelle (French); Marcelina, Marceline, Marcelyn, Marcelline, Marcellina, Marcelinda

MARCIA: (*MAR-shah*) (Latin) "Of Mars." Feminine form of Marcus. See also Marsha and Marcella.

Marcy, Marci, Marcie, Marcena, Marciana, Marcianne, Marcila, Marcine

MARGARET: (Greek) "Pearl." A saint's name. Historical; the name of nine queens of England, Scotland, France and Austria. See also Greta, Gretchen, Maggie, Maisie, Margo, Marjorie, Megan, Peggy and Rita.

MARGARITA (Spanish); Marguerite (French); Margit, Margret, Margrit (German); Margrete, Margareta, Margarete (Scandinavian); Margita, Marketa (Czech/Polish); Margarette, Madge, Margie, Margeen, Margette, Meg, Meggie

MARGO: (French/German/Hungarian) Variant of Margaret. Margot, Margaux, Margeaux (French)

MARI: (Welsh) Variant of Mary; also a favored prefix for blending with other names. See also Maribel and Maria.

Marisol (Latin) "Mary soledad; Mary alone," Maricruz "Mary of the Cross," Marycruz, Marilu, Marilou, Marilena, Marilene, Marilee, Maribeth, Marilisa, Maridel, Marita

MARIA: (*ma-REE-ah*) (Latin) Variant of Mary, popular with both Spanish and non-Spanish cultures. Marie, the French variant, was the preferred form of Mary in England until about the time of the Reformation. Mariah (*ma-RYE-ah*) is quietly but steadily used today. Maria and Marie are very often blended with other names and suffixes. See also Mari, Manon, Maribel, Marisa, Mary, Mia and Ria.

MARIE, Maree (French); Marya (Slavic); Mariah,

Marielena, Marialena, Marialinda, Marialisa, Marieanne, Mariette; Marietta (Italian); Marika (Slavic)

MARIANA: (*mar-ee-AHN-ah*) (Latin) Variant of Mary. Shakespeare gave the name Mariana to a woman noted for her loyalty in *Measure for Measure*. See also Mary and Miriam.

Marianne, Marian, Marianna, Mariann; Mariane (French); Maryan, Maryon (English surname forms); Marien (Dutch); Mariam; Maryam (Greek/Arabic); Marianda

MARIBEL: (Latin) "Beautiful Marie." Blend of Mari and Belle. See also Mary.

Maribell, Maribelle, Maribella

MARICELA: (*mar-a-SEE-lah*) (Spanish) Variant of Marcella.

MARISELA, Maricella, Maricelia, Maricel

MARIELA: (*mar-ee-ELL-ah*) (Latin) Diminutive form of Maria. See also Meriel.

Mariel (English); Marielle, Mariele (French); Mariella (Italian)

MARIGOLD: (English) "Mary's gold," a reference to the flower and to the mother of Jesus.

MARIKO: (*mah-REE-koh*) (Japanese) "Ball, circle."

MARILLA: (*ma-RILL-ah*) "Shining sea." Variant of Muriel. Marilis is a short form of Amaryllis.

Marilis, Marella

MARILYN: (English) Blend of Marie or Mary and Lyn.

Marilynn, Marylynn, Marylin, Marylyn, Maralyn, Marlyn

MARINA: (*mah-REE-nah*) (Latin) "Of the sea." See also Marnie.

Marin, Maryn, Marena, Mareen, Mareena, Marinna, Marinella, Marinelle, Marinda

MARISA: (*ma-REES-ah*) (English/Latin) Variant of Maria.

Marise (*ma-REESE*), Mareesa; Marysa, Maryse (Dutch)

MARISE: (*mah-ree-say*) (Japanese) "Infinite, endless."

MARISSA: (*ma-RISS-ah*) (Latin) "Of the sea." Variant of Marie and Mary.

MARITZA (German); Marisha (Russian); Mariza, Maryssa, Maressa, Maris, Marisabel, Maricia, Merissa, Meris

MARJAN: (Polish) Variant form of Mary.

Marjanne, Marjon

MARJORIE: (English) Variant of the French Margerie, from Margaret.

Marji, Marja, Marjo, Margie, Margerie, Margery (English)

MARK- names: (Contemporary) Feminine names that probably are based on Mark, though Marketa is a Czech form of Margaret. See also Marquise.

Markie, Markee, Markia, Marketa, Markita, Markeda, Markeeta, Markeia, Markeisha, Markesha, Markisha, Markiesha, Marqui, Marquee; Marquel, Marquita (Spanish); Marquette, Marquetta, Marqueta

MARLA: (Contemporary) Variant form of Marlene or Marlo. Also used as a prefix to form other variants. See also Marlee.

Marlo, Marlowe, Marlette; Marlisa, Marlise, Marliss, Marlissa, Marlyssa, Marlyse, Marlys

MARLEE: (English) "Marshy meadow." May also be used as a variant of Marlene. See also Marla.

Marley, Marlie, Marleigh

MARLEN: (Contemporary) Feminine form of Marlon or variant of Marlene.

Marlyn, Marlin, Marlynn, Marlenne

MARLENE: (*mar-LEEN, mar-LAYNE*) (English/German) Variant of Madeline. Some contemporary names are spelled phonetically to ensure the desired pronunciation. See also Marla, Marlee and Marlen.

Marlena, Marleen, Marleene, Marleena, Marlina, Marline, Marleina, Marlaina, Marlayna, Marlayne, Marlinda, Marlana

MARNI: (Israeli) "Rejoicing." Marnie is a variant of Marina.

Marnie, Marnee, Marnell, Marnisha

MARQUISE: (*mar-KEES*) (French) The feminine equivalent of the French title Marquis. See also Mark- names.

Marquisha, Marquisa; Marquesa (*mar-KAY-sah*) (Italian)

MARSHA: (English) Variant form of Marcia.

MARTHA: (Aramaic) "Lady." Biblical; the sister of Mary and Lazarus.

Marta (Spanish/Scandinavian/Slavic)

MARTINA: (*mar-TEEN-ah*) (Spanish) Feminine form of Martin. Martinique (French) is a West Indies island.

Marteena; Martine (French); Martinique (*mar-ten-NEEK*)

MARVELL: (*mar-VELL*) (Latin) "Wonderful, extraordinary."

Marvella, Marvela, Marvelyn, Marvadene, Marva

MARVINA: (*mar-VEEN-ah*) "Renowned friend." Feminine form of Marvin.

MARY: (English/Hebrew) "Bitter." Variant form of Miriam. Biblical; the virgin mother of Christ. Mary became the object of great veneration in the Catholic Church. Through the centuries, names like Dolores and Mercedes have been created to express aspects of Mary's life and worship. Mary is also frequently used in blends and compounded names. See also Maira, Malia, Mamie, Manon, Mara, Mari, Maria, Mariana, Maribel, Mariela, Marigold, Marilyn, Marisa, Marissa, Marjan, Maureen, May, Mayra, Mia, Mimi, Miriam, Mitzi, Moira and Molly.

Maryann, Maryanne, Maryanna, Marybel, Marybell, Marybeth, Maryjo, Marylou, Marylu, Marylee

MATILDA: (German) "Strength for battle." See also Maude.

Matilde (French/Spanish); Mattie

MATSUKO: (*MAHT-soo-koh*) (Japanese) "Pine tree child."

MAUDE: (French) Variant form of Matilda.

MAUREEN: (Irish) Variant form of Moira and Mary. Maurissa and Maurisa may also be feminine forms of Maurice. See also Mara, Moreen and Morisa.

Maura, Maurianne, Maurissa, Maurisa

MAVIS: (*MAY-viss*) (English/French) "Song-thrush."

MAXINE: (English) "The greatest." Feminine form of Max.

Maxi, Maxie, Maximina

MAY: (Latin) "Maia, the month of May." Also used as a short form of Mary. See also Mai.

Mayleen, Maylene

MAYA: (*MYE-yah*) (Spanish) Short form of Amalia; also a variant of Maia. See also Mai.

MAYDA: (English) "Maiden." See also Maida.

MAYRA: (Irish) Variant of Maire, a Gaelic form of Mary. See also Moira and Myra.

MAIRA, Mairi (Scottish); Maire (Irish)

Mc- names: (Scottish/Irish) Surnames occasionally used as given names for girls, especially names that sound like Michaela. See also Mackenzie, McKenzie and Michaela.

McCall, McKayla, McKay, McKell, McKella, McKenna

MCKENZIE: (Scottish/Gaelic) "The fair one." See also Mackenzie and Kenzie.

MEDINA: (Arabic) "City of the Prophet." The city where Mohammed began his campaign to establish Islam.

MEDORA: (English) A literary creation; Medora is a romantic heroine in Lord Byron's narrative poem *The Corsair*.

MEENA: (Sanskrit) "Fish." Astrological name, Pisces. Hindu mythology; a name of the wife of Shiva.

MEERA: (Israeli) "Light." See also Mira.
Meira

MEGAN: (*MEG-an, MEE-gan, MAY-gan*) (Welsh) Variant form of Margaret, based on the short form Meg. Phonetic spellings of Megan are used to ensure one of the three pronunciations.
MEGHAN, MEAGAN, Meaghan, Maygan, Maegan, Meeghan, Meggan; Meegan (Gaelic) "soft, gentle"

MELANIE: (*MEL-a-nee*) (French/Greek) "Dark."
Melanee, Melaina, Melaine; Melina, Melana, Melania (Latin)

MELIA: (*me-LEE-ah*) (Hawaiian) "Plumeria."

MELINDA: (English/Greek) Blend of Melissa and Linda.
Malinda, Melynda

MELISANDE: (*mel-a-sahnd*) (French/German) "Strength, determination." Variant of Millicent.
Melisandra (*mel-a-SAHN-drah*) (Spanish)

MELISSA: (Greek) "Bee." Mythology; the name of a princess of Crete who was changed into a bee after she learned how to collect honey.
Melisa (*ma-LEE-sah*), Meliza (*ma-LYE-zah*), Melise (*ma-LEESE*), Melisse, Melisha, Missy

MELITA: (*ma-LEE-tah*) (Spanish) Short form of Carmelita. Malita is a variant of Maria.
Malita

MELODY: (*MEL-a-dee*) (Greek) "Music, song."
Melodie, Melodi, Melodee

MELVA: (English) Feminine form of Melvin.
Melvina

MERALDA: (*mer-AHL-dah*) (Latin) "Emerald." Short form of Esmeralda.

MERCEDES: (*mer-SAY-dees*) (Latin) "Mercies." Used in

reference to Mary as "Our Lady of Mercies." See also
Mercy.

Mercedez

MERCER: (English/French) "Merchant." Rare.

MERCY: (English/Latin) "Compassion, forbearance." See
also Mercedes.

Mercie, Mercia, Mercina, Mercilla

MEREDITH: (Welsh) "Great lady." In America, Meredith
now is used almost entirely as a girl's name.

MERIEL: (English) Variant of Muriel. See also Mariela
and Muriel.

MERRY: (English) "Mirthful, joyous." Also a short form
of Meredith. Meri (Finnish) means "sea."

Merrie, Merri, Merrilee, Meridel, Meri

MERYL: (French) "Blackbird." Feminine form of Merle.

Merla, Merryl, Maryl, Mirla, Myrla, Merlyn

MIA: (*MEE-ah*) (Israeli) Feminine short form of Michal.
Also a Scandinavian short form of Maria. See also
Miya.

MICAH: (*MYE-cah*) (Hebrew) "Who is like Jah?" Biblical;
a prophet and writer of the Book of Micah.

Micaiah (*mee-KYE-ah*)

MICHAELA: (*mih-KAY-lah*) (English/Latin) Feminine form
of Michael. One of the most frequently misspelled
names. Care should be taken with phonetic spelling
variants. See also Mc- names, Michal and Michelle.

Micaela, Mikaela, Mikayla, Mychaela, Mikella, Mikelle

MICHAL: (*MYE-kal*) (Hebrew) "Who is like God?" Feminine form of Michael. Biblical; Michal was King Saul's
daughter, the first wife of David.

Mychal, Mical, Michaelyn, Michaeline, Micole

MICHELLE: (*mee-SHELL*) (French) Feminine form of Michael. See also Michaela and Michal.

MICHELE, Mychelle, Mychele, Michela, Michella

MICHIE: (*mee-chee-AY*) (Japanese) "Gateway; gracefully drooping flower."

Michiko (*MEE-chee-koh*) "Child of beauty"

MIDORI: (*mee-DOR-ee*) (Japanese) "Green."

MIKI: (*MEE-kee*) (Japanese) "Three trees together." Miki (Hawaiian) "quick, nimble." Mikki is sometimes used as a short form of names like Michaela.

Mika, Mikko, Mikki

MILDRED: (English) "Gentle strength."

MILIANI: (*mee-lee-AH-nee*) (Hawaiian) "Gentle caress." Miliana is a Latin feminine form of Emeliano.

Miliana; Milana (Czech)

MILLICENT: (French/German) "Strength, determination." See also Melisande.

Millie

MIMI: (*mee-mee*) (French) Pet name for Miriam or Marie. Also used as a Spanish pet name for Mira, Maria and Noemi.

MINA: (*MEE-nah*) (German) "Love." Name endings (mina and mena) used as independent names. Min and Meena are Irish Gaelic names meaning "smooth, fine, small." See also Meena.

Minna, Minnie, Minette, Minnette, Mena, Min, Meena

MINDY: (English) Short form of Melinda.

Mindi, Mindie, Mindee; Minda (Sanskrit)

MINERVA: (*mi-NER-vah*) (Latin) Mythology; name of the Roman goddess of wisdom.

MIRA: (Slavic) Variant of Myra and Miranda. See also Meera.

Miri, Miriana

MIRANDA: (Latin) "Worthy of admiration." In Shakespeare's *The Tempest*, Miranda is an innocent girl raised and educated on an isolated island by her magician father.

MIRELLA: (Latin) Feminine variant form of Mireya, from

the Hebrew male name Amariah meaning "Jehovah has said."

Mireille (French); Mirelle, Myrelle, Mireya

MIRIAM: (*MEER-ee-em*) (Hebrew) An older version of the name Mary. Biblical; the sister of Moses, who saved his life as a baby when she hid him in a basket among the rushes at the river's edge for Pharaoh's daughter to find.
Myriam

MISCHA: (*MEE-shah*) (Russian/Slavic) Nickname for Michael.
Miesha, Misha

MISTY: (Contemporary) Literally, "misty." A name from nature. See also Mystique.
Misti, Mistie, Mystee, Mysti

MITZI: (*MIT-see*) (German) Pet name for Mary and Marie. Mitsu is a Japanese surname meaning "shine, reflect."
Mitzy, Mitsu

MIYA: (*MEE-yah*) (Japanese) "Three arrows; temple." See also Mia.

MODESTY: (Latin) "Without conceit; modest."
Modesta, Modestine

MOHALA: (*mo-HAH-lah*) (Hawaiian) "Petals unfolding; shining forth."

MOIRA: (Scottish) Variant of the Irish Maire, from Mary; phonetic spelling is Moyra. See also Mayra and Myra.
Moyra

MOLLY: (English/Irish) From the Gaelic *Maili*, a pet form of Mary. In use since the late Middle Ages, recently revived in popular usage, probably in part due to actress Molly Ringwald.
Mollie, Mollee, Molli, Molley

MONA: (*MOH-nah*) (Irish) "Noble." Mona is also an Italian short form of Madonna. Famous name bearer: the "Mona Lisa," a portrait painted by Leonardo da Vinci, which has itself inspired name blends. See also Madonna and Monica.

Monisha, Monalisa, Monalissa

MONICA: (English/Latin) Variant of Mona.

MONIQUE (*moh-NEEK*) (French); Monika (German)

MONSERRAT: (*mohn-sir-AHT*) (Latin) "Jagged mountain." The name of a mountain in Spain (Montserrat), a monastery and a celebrated image of the Virgin Mary.

Montserrat

MONTANA: (*mon-TAN-nah*) (Latin) "Mountain." The name of the western state used as a given name.

Monteene, Montina

MOREEN: (Irish) "Great." See also Maureen.

Morella

MORENA: (*moh-RAY-nah*) (Spanish) "Brown, brown-haired."

MORGAN: (Welsh) "Bright sea." Usage for girls increased sharply during the Eighties, probably due in part to actress Morgan Fairchild. Morgaine and Morgayne are medieval Irish forms.

Morganne, Morgann, Morgana, Morgaine, Morgayne

MORIAH: (*moh-RYE-ah*) (Hebrew) Biblical; the name of the mount of the Temple of Solomon in Jerusalem. See MARIA for the similar-sounding name Mariah.

MORISA: (*mor-EES-ah*) (Spanish) Feminine form of Maurice. See also Maureen.

Morissa

MORNA: (Irish) "Affection." See also Myrna.

MORWENNA: (Welsh) "Ocean waves."

MURIEL: (Irish/Celtic) "Shining sea." See also Meriel and Marilla.

MYISHA: (*mye-EE-shah*) (Arabic) "Woman, life." Variant of Aisha.

Myesha, Myeisha, Myeshia, Myiesha

MYLA: (Contemporary) "Merciful." Feminine form of Myles.

Mylene, Myleen, Milena

MYRA: (English) Poetic invention, possibly a variant of Mayra. See also Moira.

Myrah, Myriah

MYRNA: (Aramaic/Arabic) "Myrrh; sweet oil." Also a Gaelic name meaning "beloved." See also Morna.

Mirna

MYRTA: (*MER-tah*) (Latin) Variant of Myrtle, a nature name based on the evergreen shrub that was sacred to Venus as a symbol of love. Myrtle is very rarely used today.

Myrtle

MYSTIQUE: (*miss-TEEK*) (French) "Air of mystery." The use of Mystique as a contemporary name for girls is probably an outgrowth of the popularity of the name Misty.

Mystica, Mistique

N

NA- names: (Contemporary) Blends of Na- plus various endings, with pronunciation emphasis on the second syllable.

Nakisha, Nakeisha, Nakia, Nakita, Nalani, Naquita, Nareesha, Natahnee, Natavia, Natisha, Notosha, Natoya

NADIA: (*NAH-d'yah*) (French/Slavic) "Hope." See also Nadine.

Nadja (German); Nadya (Russian); Nada (Arabic) "Dewy"

NADINE: (*nay-deen*) (French) Variant of Nadia.

Nadeen

NANA: (*NAH-nah*) (Hawaiian) Name of a spring month and the name of a star. The Spanish Nana is a pet form of Ana.

Nani (Hawaiian) "Beauty, splendor."

NANCY: (*NAN-cee*) (English/French) Variant of Anne.
Nanci, Nancey, Nancie, Nan, Nann

NANETTE: (French) "Favor, grace." Variant form of Anne.
Nannette, Nanine

NAOMI: (*nay-OH-mee*) (Hebrew) "Pleasantness." Biblical; an ancestress of Jesus and mother-in-law to Ruth.
NOEMI (*no-AY-mee*) (Spanish); Noemie (French); Neomi, Neoma

NARA: (Celtic) "Contented." Contemporary variants are probably based on Noreen.
Nareen, Nareena, Nareene

NARIKO: (*nah-REE-koh*) (Japanese) "Gentle child."

NATALIE: (*NAT-a-lee*) (French/Latin) "Birthday," especially referring to the birthday of Christ. The "h" is silent in the French form Nathalie; some American variants (like Nathalee) are phonetically spelled to retain the "h" sound. See also Natasha.
Natalia (Spanish); Natalya (Russian); Nathalie (French); Natalee, Nathaly, Nathalee, Nathalia

NATASHA: (*na-TAH-shah*) (Russian) Variant of Natalie. See also Tasha.
Natashia, Natasia, Natascha

NAZNEEN: (*nahz-NEEN*) (Farsi) "Exquisitely beautiful; charming." The name is meant to convey the superlative sense of the charm of a beloved woman or child.

NEDDA: (English) Feminine form of Ned, the equivalent of Edda. Nedra

NEEMA: (Swahili) "Born in prosperity."

NEILA: (*NEE-lah*) (English/Gaelic) Feminine form of Neil.
Neelie, Neely

NEIVA: (*NEE-vah*) (Spanish) "Snow." Feminine form of the Spanish word *nieve*. Neva is the name of a river in

Russia, and Neff is a related German surname in rare
use as a girl's name.

Neyva, Neva, Neff

NELLY: (English) Short form of Eleanor.

Nellie, Nell, Nella; Nelida (Spanish)

NEREIDA: (*ne-RAY-dah*) (Greek) "Sea nymph; daughter
of Nereus." Greek mythology; the Nereids were deities
of the seas, mermaids.

Nereyda, Nerida, Nerissa, Narissa

NETTIE: (English) Name ending used as an independent
name.

Netty, Netta

NIA: (*NEE-ah*) (Contemporary) Short form of names with
the "-nia" ending, used as an independent name after
the fashion of Mia.

NICHELLE: (*nee-SHEL*) (Contemporary) Blend of Nichole
and Michelle.

Nichele

NICOLE: (*ni-KOHL*) (French) Feminine form of Nicholas.
(See historical note in boy's Index.) During the Middle
Ages names that seem feminine today, like Nicolet and
Nicol, were actually male names. See also Colette and
Nikki.

NICHOLE, Nicholle, Nichol, Niccole; Nicola, Nicoletta
(Italian); Nicolette (French); Nickole, Nikole, Nikkole,
Nycole

NIDIA: (Latin) "Nest."

Nydia

NIKKI: (Contemporary) Short form of Nicole. Nic- and
Nik- variants are used in many cultures. Greek mythology; Nike (*NYE-kee*) was the name of the goddess of
victory. Nikki (*NEE-kee*) is also a Japanese surname
with the potential meaning "two trees."

Nikita (Russian); Nikia; Niki, Nike (Greek); Nikkie,
Nicki, Nickie; Nicci (Italian)

NINA: (*NEE-nah, NINE-ah*) (English/Russian) Diminutive name ending used as an independent name, especially in Russia.
Nena, Neena

NINON: (*nan-ahn*) (French) Variant of Anne. Ninon de Lenclos was a seventeenth-century aristocrat famous for her wit and beauty.
Ninette, Nynette

NISHA: (*NEE-shah*) (Contemporary) Name ending used as an independent name.
Niesha, Neesha, Nyssa (*NISS-ah*)

NITA: (*NEE-tah*) (Spanish) Diminutive ending used as an independent name.

NOELANI: (*no-ah-LAH-nee*) (Hawaiian) "Mist of heaven." Noe (*noh-AY*) "Mist, misty rain."

NOELLE: (*no-ELL*) (French) "Birth-day." Feminine form of Noel. Commonly used in reference to Christ's birth and the Christmas festival.
Noel, Noell, Noella, Noele

NOLA: (*NO-lah*) (English/Gaelic) Feminine form of Nolan or a variant short form of Fenella, from Fiona.
Nolene, Nolana

NONA: (Latin) "Nine."

NORA: (English) Short form of names like Eleanora and Honora.
Norah, Norabel, Norissa

NOREEN: (Irish) Variant of Nora, combining a diminutive with a diminutive (-nora plus -een).
Norene, Noreena, Norine

NORELL: (*no-RELL*) (Scandinavian) "From the north." Occasional usage of this surname as a given name may be due to the perfume. The variant Narelle is especially popular in Australia.
Narelle

NORIKO: (*noh-REE-koh*) (Japanese) "Child of ceremony"; "law, order."

NORMA: (English/Latin) Feminine form of Norman.

NOVA: (*NOH-vah*) (Latin) "New." Astronomy; a nova is a star that suddenly releases a tremendous burst of energy, increasing its brightness many thousandfold.

NURA: (*noor-ah*) (Arabic) "Light."

NYLA: (*NYE-lah*) (Contemporary) Feminine form of Nyles, from Neil.
Nila

O

OCEANA: (*oh-shee-AH-nah*) (Greek) "Ocean." Feminine form of Oceanus. Greek mythology; Oceanus was a Titan, the father of rivers and water nymphs.

OCTAVIA: (*ock-TAHV-yah*) (Latin) "Eighth." Feminine form of Octavius. A clan name of Roman emperors. See also Tavia.
Octaviana

ODELIA: (*oh-DEEL-yah*) (French) "Wealthy."
Odile (*oh-dyle*), Odilia, Odila, Odella, Odette, Ottilie

ODESSA: (*oh-DESS-ah*) (Latin/Greek) "Wandering; quest." Variant form of Odysseus.

OLA: (Hawaiian) "Life, well-being." Also (Nigerian) "precious."

OLETHA: (*oh-LEE-thah*) (English/Scandinavian) "Light, nimble."

OLEXA: (*oh-LEKS-ah*) (Czech) Feminine form of Alexander.

OLGA: (Russian/Scandinavian) "Blessed."

OLIDA: (*oh-LEE-dah*) (Latin) Variant form of Olivia.
Oleta

OLINA: (*oh-LEE-nah*) (Hawaiian) "Joyous."
Oleen, Oline

OLINDA: (Latin) A poetic name created in the sixteenth century.
Olynda

OLIVIA: (*oh-LIV-ee-ah*) (Latin) "The olive tree." Feminine form of Oliver. Biblical; the olive tree is a symbol of fruitfulness, beauty and dignity. Today "extending an olive branch" traditionally signifies an offer of peace. See also Olida.

OLYMPIA: (*oh-LIM-pee-ah*) (Greek) "From Olympus." One of the many saints' names with origins in mythology. Mount Olympus was the home of the ancient Greek gods.
Olimpia

OMEGA: (*oh-MAY-gah*) (Greek) "Large." The last letter in the Greek alphabet.

ONDREA: (Czech) Variant of Andrea.
Ondra

OONAGH: (*OO-nah*) (Irish) "Lamb." See also Una.
Oona

OPAL: (Sanskrit) "Gemstone, jewel." A uniquely colorful iridescent gemstone.

OPHELIA: (*oh-FEEL-yah*) (Greek) "Help." Name of the unfortunate maiden who loved Hamlet in Shakespeare's play *Hamlet*.
Ofelia (Spanish)

OPHRAH: (*OHF-rah*) (Hebrew) "Young deer" or "place of dust." A Biblical place name. Oprah Winfrey, actress and TV talk-show hostess, has made this very rare name familiar.
Ophra, Ofra (Israeli)

ORAH: (Israeli) "Light."
Oria

ORALIA: (*oh-RAYL-yah*) (Latin) "Golden." Variant form of Aurelia.
Orelia

ORIANA: (*or-ee-AHN-ah*) (Latin) "Dawning."
    Orianna (Italian); Oriane (*or-ee-AHN*) (French); Oreana
ORINDA: (Latin) A seventeenth-century poetic name.
ORLA: (Irish) "Golden lady."
OSANNA: (Latin) Short form of the Latin hosannah, a
    chanted prayer meaning "save, we pray."

P

PAGAN: (*PAY-gan*) (English/Latin) "Country dweller."
    Once a common medieval given name, Pagan fell out of
    favor when it became a term used for an irreligious per-
    son or someone who believed in more than one god.
PAIGE: (English/French) "Young attendant." A page in
    medieval households was usually a young boy whose
    service was the first step in his training as a knight.
    Page, Pagett
PAISLEY: (*PAYS-lee*) (Scottish) the name of a patterned
    fabric that was at one time the principle product manu-
    factured in Paisley, Scotland.
PALOMA: (*pa-LOH-mah*) (Spanish) "Dove."
PAMELA: (English/Greek) "Honey; all sweetness." A po-
    etic invention from the sixteenth century.
    Pam, Pamella
PANDORA: (Greek) "All gifted." Greek mythology; Pan-
    dora was gifted with powers and desirable attributes
    from all the gods, then given charge of a mysterious box
    she was forbidden to open. When she opened the box,
    every kind of mankind's ills flew out.
PARIS: (*PARE-iss*) The name of the French capital. My-
    thology; see boys' index.
    Parisa, Parris, Parrish
PATIENCE: (English) "Enduring, forbearing." Rare.
PATRICIA: (English/Latin) "Noble; a patrician." The Ro-
    mans once were divided socially and politically into two
    major classes, the plebeians and the patricians. To be

patrician meant one was highly ranked, an aristocrat. See also Trisha.

Patrice (French); Patrisha, Patrina, Patrisse, Patrizia, Patryce, Patty, Patsy, Patti, Patria

PAULA: (English/Latin) "Little." Feminine form of Paul.
Paulina, Pauline, Paulene, Pauletta; Paulette (French); Paola, Paolina (Spanish/Italian); Paulita (Spanish); Pavla, Pavlina (Czech/Russian); Pauli (German)

PAYTON: (*PAYT-on*) (Irish) Variant form of Patrick.
Peyton

PAZ: (*pahz*) (Spanish) "Peace," from the Latin word *pax*. In Catholic use, a reference to "Our Lady of Peace."

PEARL: (English) A jewel name.
Perla, Perlita (Spanish); Pearla, Pearlie, Pearlinda, Pearline, Perle

PEGGY: (English) Rhyming pet name from medieval times, based on Margaret (Meggy).

PENNY: (Greek) "Weaver's tool." Short form of Penelope. Mythology; Penelope, wife of Ulysses, fended off suitors by weaving during the day and unraveling at night a tapestry she said had to be completed before she would wed another husband. The name has come to signify a loyal, capable and clever woman.
Penelope (*pen-NELL-a-pee*), Pennie

PEONY: (*PAY-uh-nee*) (Greek) "Praisegiving." A flower name. As a Chinese name motif, the peony signifies riches and honor.

PERDITA: (*per-DEE-tah*, *PER-di-tah*) (English/Latin) "Lost." Shakespeare created this name for a young heroine in *The Winter's Tale*.

PERI: (Greek) In Greek mythology, an *oread*, nymph of mountains and caves. In Persian fable, a fallen angel. Pera and Perita are Spanish short forms of Esperanza. Perah is an Israeli name meaning "flower."

Pera, Perita, Perah

PERRI: (English) Feminine variant of Peter. See also Petra.
Perris, Perrianne, Perrine, Perrin

PERSIS: (*PER-sees, PER-siss*) (Greek) "Woman of Persia." Biblical; a first-century Christian woman commended by Paul.

PETRA: (*PEH-trah*) (English/Latin) Feminine variant form of Peter.
Petrina, Peta, Pier, Pierette, Petronella

PHAEDRA: (*FAY-drah*) (Greek) "Shining." Phaedra is derived from Phoebus, another name for Apollo.
Phedre, Phadra, Fedra

PHILIPPA: (English) "Fond of horses." Feminine form of Philip.
Philana, Philina, Pippa

PHOEBE: (*FEE-bee*) (Greek) "Bright, radiant." Biblical; a Christian woman who aided Paul and others. Greek mythology; a reference to Apollo, the god of light.
Phebe (Spanish)

PHYLICIA: (*fa-LEE-shah*) (Contemporary) Blend of Felicia and Phyllis, made familiar today by actress Phylicia Rashaad.
Philicia

PHYLLIS: (*FILL-iss*) (Greek) "Green branch."
Phillida, Phyliss

PIA: (*PEE-ah*) (Latin) "Pious, reverent."

PILAR: (*pee-LAR*) (Latin) "Pillar." In Catholic tradition, a reference to a marble pillar connected with an appearance of the Virgin Mary.

POLA: (Latin/Arabic) "Poppy." Short form of Amapola.

POLLY: (English/Irish) A medieval rhyming nickname based on Mary (Molly). See also Molly.

PORTIA: (*POR-shah*) (Latin) Feminine form of a Roman clan name. Portia was used by Shakespeare as the name of a clever, determined young heroine in *The Merchant of Venice*. Today, the similar sounding name Porsche is used almost as often, though probably more in reference to the sports car than to Portia.

Porsha, Porsche, Porcha, Porscha, Porschia

PRECIOUS: (English/French) "Of great value; highly esteemed." A name of endearment. In Catholic tradition, also a reference to the "precious blood of Christ."

Precia, Preciosa

PRIMA: (*PREE-mah*) (Latin) "First."

PRINCESS: (English) A title name.

Princesa (French); Princessa (Italian)

PRISCILLA: (*pris-SILL-ah*) (Latin) "Of ancient times." Biblical; a first-century Christian missionary. Priscilla was a favored name with the Puritans of England. Longfellow gave the name to the heroine of his poem, *The Courtship of Miles Standish*.

PRUDENCE: (English) "The exercise of caution and wisdom."

Prue

Q

QUEENA: (English) Variant of the title used as a given name.

Queenie, Queen, Quenna

QUERIDA: (*kare-EE-dah*) (Spanish) "Beloved, darling."

QUINN: (Gaelic) "Counsel." A Scottish and Irish surname occasionally used for girls.

R

RA- names: (Contemporary) Blends of Ra- plus various name endings, with pronunciation emphasis on the second syllable.

Ranelle, Ranessa, Ranisha, Rashanda

RACHEL: (*RAY-chel*) (Hebrew) "Ewe." Biblical; Jacob's wife, described as being "beautiful in form and countenance." Rachelle is a variant pronunciation. See also Raquel, Rochelle and Richelle.

RACHAEL, RACHELLE (*ra-SHELL*); Rachele (Italian); Rachell; Raechel, Raychel, Rashelle, Rachelann, Rachelanne

RAE: (English) Short form of Rachel or a feminine form of Ray. Also used as a prefix in contemporary names, following the Ra- name pattern. See also Ray- names.

Rae, Raeann, Raeanne, Raeanna, Raedell, Raedine, Raelee, Raelena, Raelyn, Raelynn, Raelynne, Raelene, Raeleen, Raelina, Raelani, Raenisha

RAFAELA: (*rah-fah-AY-lah*) (Spanish) Feminine form of Raphael.

Raphaella

RAINBOW: (English) The word used as a given name. See also Iris.

RAISA: (*RAY-sah, RAY-zah*) (Russian/Greek) "Rose."

Raiza, Raissa

RAMAH: (Israeli) "High."

RAMONA: (Spanish) "Guards wisely." Feminine form of Ramon, Raymond.

Ramie, Ramee

RANA: (*RAH-nah*) (Scandinavian) "Catcher." (Arabic) "Beautiful." Scandinavian mythology; Rana was goddess of the sea. Rani is a Hindu title meaning "royal, queen."

Rani, Ranae

RANDI: (Contemporary) Feminine form of Randy, or short form of Miranda.

Randee; Randa (Arabic) "Beautiful."

RAQUEL: (*rah-KELL*) (Spanish/Portuguese) Variant of Rachel.

Raquelle, Raquela, Racquel, Racquell, Roquel

RASHEEDA: (*ra-SHEE-dah*) (Swahili/Arabic) "Righteous."

Rasheedah, Rashida

RAYA: (Israeli) "Friend."

RAY- names: (Contemporary) Feminine variants using Ray as a prefix. See also Ra- names and Rae.

Rayann, Rayanna, Rayana, Rayleen, Raylene, Raylynn, Raynisha, Raynesha, Raynell, Rayeann, Raye, Raycine

RAYNA: (English/Scandinavian) "Counsel."

Raina (Slavic); Reyna, Rayne, Raine, Raynee, Rainey, Rainee

REANNA: (*ree-ANN-ah*) (Contemporary) Variant of Rhiannon.

Reanne, Reannon, Reannah, Reeanne

REBECCA: (English/Hebrew) "Tied, knotted." Biblical; Rebekah, noted in the Genesis account as a maiden of beauty, modesty and kindness, became the wife of Abraham's son Isaac. See also Becky and Riva.

REBEKAH (Hebrew); Rebeca (Spanish), Reba

REGAN: (*REE-gan, RAY-gan*) (English/Irish) "Reigning, kingly."

Reagan, Ragan

REGINA: (*re-JEEN-ah*) (Latin) "Queen."

Regine (French); Regeena, Regena

REIKO: (*RAY-koh*) (Japanese) "Pretty; lovely child."

Rei

RENA: (*REE-nah*) (English) Short form of Irene and Irena.

Reena, Reene, Rina

RENEE: (*ren-NAY*) (French) "Reborn." Phonetic spellings of Renee have resulted in a number of contemporary variants. Ren- is also used as a prefix with various endings to create new names.

Renae, Rene, Renaye, Renay, Renita; Renata (Latin); Renisha, Reneisha, Renne, Rennie

REXANNE: (Contemporary) Blend of Rex and Anne. These names are also used as feminine forms of Rex. Rexanna, Rexana, Rexine

REYNALDA: (Latin/German) "Counselor ruler." Feminine form of Reynold. See also Rayna.

RHEA: (*REE-ah*) (Greek) "Flowing stream." Mythology; Rhea was the mother of Zeus, Poseidon, Hera and Demeter. Rhea is also a Welsh name referring to a river in Wales.

Rhia, Rhaya, Rhae, Reya

RHIANNON: (*ree-ANN-an*) (Welsh) "Maiden." Mythology; name of the Welsh horse goddess described in legend as dressed in shining gold and riding a pale horse. See also Reanna and Riona.

Rhianna, Rheanna, Rheanne, Rhiann, Rhiannan, Rhianon, Rhiana, Rhyan, Riana, Rianna, Rianne, Riane, Riannon

RHODA: (*ROH-dah*) (Greek) "Rose." See also Rosa. Biblical; a servant girl who was one of the early Christian disciples.

RHONA: (Scottish) Variant form of Ronald.

Rona

RHONDA: (*RON-dah*) (Welsh) "Fierce waters."

Ronda, Rhonette

RIA: (English) Short form of Maria.

Rie

RICHELLE: (*ri-SHELL*) (Contemporary) Feminine blend of Richard and Rachelle. Also related feminine short forms based on Ricky, Rickie or Frederica.

Rikki, Ricki, Riki, Rikkie, Ricci, Ricca

RIMA: (*REE-mah*) (Spanish) "Rhyme, poetry." Literary; in Hudson's *Green Mansions*, Rima was an elusive maiden of the South American rain forest who spoke the language of animals and birds.

RINAH: (Israeli) "Joyful."

RIONA: (*ree-OH-nah*) (Irish) "Queenly."

RISA: (*REE-sah*) (Spanish) "Laugh, laughter."
Rise (*ri-ZAY*) (French); Reesa

RITA: (English/Spanish) Short form of Margarita, from Margaret.

RIVA: (*REE-vah*) (English/Hebrew) Short form of Rebecca.
Reva

ROBERTA: (English) "Famed; bright, shining." Feminine form of Robert. Robbie is used occasionally for boys. See also Robin and Bobbie.
Robertha, Robbie

ROBIN: (English) Variant of Robert, in popular use as a boy's name since the days of Robin Hood. Now used more for girls. See also Roberta.
ROBYN, Robynn, Robynne, Robena, Robina

ROCHELLE: (*roh-SHELL*) (French) Feminine variant of Rocco (Italian).
Rochele; Rochella (Italian); Roshelle

RODERICA: (English/German) "Famous ruler." Feminine form of Roderic.

ROLANDA: (English/Latin) "Renowned in the land." Feminine form of Roland.
Rolande (French)

ROMINA: (Latin) "Woman of Rome." Mythology; Roma was the daughter of Evander, who named Rome for her. Romi and Romy are German pet names.
Roma, Romana, Romalda, Romelia, Romi, Romy

RONNIE: (English) Short form of Veronica or feminine variants of Ron and Ronald. Roni (*ROH-nee*) is also an Israeli name meaning "song."
Ronni, Roni, Ronae, Ronay, Ronisha, Ronnette, Ronelle, Ronica, Ronika

ROSA: (Latin) "Rose." This most popular flower name for girls has many variants and compounds. Rosa is the Latin form, Rose is English, and both are well-used in English-speaking countries. See also Charo, Raisa, Rhoda, Rosalba, Rosalie, Rosalind, Rosamond, Rose, Roseanne, Rosemary and Roza.

Rosabelle; Rosella (Italian)

ROSALBA: (*rohs-AL-bah*) (Latin) "White rose." See also Rosa.

ROSALIE: (*ros-ah-lee*) (French) See also Rosa.

Rosalee, Rosalia, Roselia

ROSALIND: (Latin) A sixteenth-century poetic creation by Spenser, which has acquired the meaning "beautiful rose."

Rosalinda (Spanish); Rosalynd; Rosalinde (German); Rosalyn, Rosalin, Rosaline, Rosalina; Rosaleen (Irish); Roselyn, Roslynn, Roslyn

ROSAMOND: (Latin/French) "Rose of the world; rose of purity."

Rosamund, Rozamond, Rozamund

ROSE: (English) See also Rosa and Roza.

Rosie, Rosey, Rosy, Rosetta, Rosette, Rosio, Rosita, Rosina, Rosine

ROSEANNE: (English) Combination of Rose and Anne. Rossana may be intended as a feminine form of Ross. See also Rosa and Roza.

Roseanna, Roseann, Rosanne, Rosanna; Rosana, Rossana, Rossanna

ROSEMARY: (English) Blend of Rose and Mary. Also refers to the fragrant herb, which in folklore is the emblem of remembrance.

Rosemarie

ROSHAN: (*roh-shahn*) (Sanskrit) "Shining light."

Roshana, Roshawn, Roshawna, Roshaunda

ROWAN: (*ROH-an*) (Gaelic/Scandinavian) "Red-berry tree." Rowena was the name of one of the heroines in Sir Walter Scott's *Ivanhoe*.
Rowena *(roh-EEN-ah)*, Roanna, Roanne

ROXANNE: (Greek/Persian) "Dawn." Roxandra is a contemporary blend of Roxanne and Alexandra, appropriate since Roxanne was the Persian princess Alexander the Great married during his travels of conquest.
ROXANA (Spanish); Roxanna, Roxane (French); Roxann, Roxandra, Roxie, Roxy, Roxi, Roxene

ROYA: (Contemporary) Feminine name based on Roy.
Royalle, Royanna, Royleen, Roylene

ROZA: (*ROH-zah*) Variant of Rosa and Rose. The "z" spelling reflects French, Slavic or Yiddish influence. In contemporary usage, Roza is also a phonetic means of ensuring the stronger consonant pronunciation of *z* over the softer *s*. See also Rosa, Rosalie, Roseanne and Rosalind.
Rozalyn, Roz, Rozalee, Rozanna, Rozlyn, Rozana, Rozella, Rozelle, Rozetta

RUBY: (English) "Red." A jewel name.
Rubi, Rubie, Rubina, Rubena, Rubianne

RUDI: (German) Feminine form of Rudy, from Rudolf.
Rudie

RUE: (*roo*) (English) "Regret." The name of an herb used for cooking and in medicine. In Shakespeare's *Hamlet*, Ophelia called rue the "herb-grace o' Sundays." Actress Rue McClanahan has made this name familiar.

RUI: (*ROO-ee*) (Japanese) "Tears; affection."

RUSTI: (Contemporary) "Red." Feminine form of Rusty.

RUTH: (Hebrew) "Companion." Biblical; Ruth was the young Moabite widow who said to her Hebrew mother-in-law Naomi, "Where you go, there shall I go also; your people will be my people, your God my God."

Ruthie, Ruthanne, Ruthann, Ruthellen

RYANN: (Contemporary) Feminine form of Ryan.

Ryanne, Ryane, Ryana, Ryanna

RYLEE: (Contemporary) Variant of Riley, an Irish surname of uncertain origin. Ryley is also used for boys.

Ryley, Rylie, Rylina

S

SABELLE: (*sa-BELL*) (Latin) Short form of Isabel.

Sabella

SABINA: (*sa-BEE-nah*) (Latin) "Of the Sabines." A saint's name in use at least since the second century. See also Sabra.

SABLE: (*SAY-bel*) (Slavic) "Black." A highly prized fur, dark brown, almost black. Also used in French and English heraldry as a term for black.

SABRA: (*SAY-brah*) (Israeli/Arabic) "Thorny." A name signifying one who is native born, especially in Israel. Also a variant form of Sabina.

SABRINA: (*sa-BREE-nah*) (English) Meaning uncertain. Mythology; the name of a Celtic maiden in a Welsh tale. See also Breena and Brina.

Sabreena, Sabrena, Sabryna, Sabrinna, Sabreen, Sabrene

SACHI: (*SAH-chee*) (Japanese) "Benediction; fortunate." Sachiko (*SAH-chee-koh*) "Blessed child, fortunate child."

SADE: (*shah-DAY, shar-DAY*) Short form of Folasade (*fol-lah-shah-DAY*), a Yoruban/African name meaning "honor confers a crown." The West Indian singer Sade has greatly influenced popularity of the name and the *shar-DAY* pronunciation. Sadie is a short form of Sarah. Saida is a spelling variant of Zaida (Arabic) "huntress; fortunate." See also Sharde.

Sadie, Saida, Sada, Sayda, Sadee, Sadia, Sadina

SADIRA: (*sa-DEER-ah*) (Persian) "Lotus."

SAGE: (English/French) "Wise one."
Saige

SAHARA: (*sah-HAH-rah*) (Arabic) "Wilderness." See also Zahara.
Saharah, Sahra

SALLY: (English) Variant of Sarah. The variants of Salina are more derivative of Sally than of the similar sounding name Selene.
Sallie, Sallee, Salina, Salena, Saleena

SAMANTHA: (*sa-MAN-thah*) (English) Blend of Sam and Anthea. Samantha became very popular in the Sixties due to the TV show *Bewitched* and has kept a high ranking among name choices ever since.

SAMI: (Arabic) "Exalted." Sammie variants are short feminine forms of Samuel.
Sammie, Sammijo, Sammi, Samma, Samia, Samina; Samara, Samira (Arabic) "pleasant"

SANA: (*sa-NAH*) (Arabic) "Brilliant."

SANDRA: (*SAN-drah, SAHN-drah*) (English) "Helper of mankind." Short form of Alexandra.
SANDY, Sandi, Sandie, Sandee, Sanda, Sondra; Saundra (Scottish)

SAPPHIRE: (*saff-ire*) (Arabic) "Beautiful." From the Sanskrit "beloved of Saturn." A jewel and color name. Sapphira is very rarely used, probably because the Biblical Sapphira was a woman who was executed by God for lying. Safira (*sa-FEER-ah*) (Spanish) is based on Ceferino, from Zephyr, the name of a third-century pope.
Sapphira, Safira; Safiya (Arabic) "friend"

SARAH: (Hebrew) "Princess." Biblical; originally called Sarai, Sarah shared an adventurous nomadic life with her husband Abraham. She is described as being exceptionally beautiful even into her older years. See also Sade, Sahara, Sally, Sarina, Shari and Zaira.

SARA, Sarabeth, Sarajane, Sarajean, Saralee, Saralyn, Saralynn, Sarahlee, Sarahlynn, Saramae; Sarai (Hebrew); Saraya, Sarahi, Sariah (Arabic); Sari (Hungarian); Sarrah, Sarra (Russian); Saira, Sairah, Sayra, Saray; Sirke (*SEER-kah*) (Israeli/Finnish)

SARINA: (Latin) Variant of Sara.
   Sarena, Sarita (Spanish/Portuguese); Sareen (Irish); Sarene, Sareena, Sarinna

SASA: (*sah-sah*) (Japanese) "Help, aid."

SASHA: (*SAH-shah*) (Russian) Short form of Alexander.
   Sascha (German); Sacha (French); Sasheen (Irish)

SATIN: (French/English) The name of the luxury fabric used as a given name.
   Satina (sa-TEE-nah)

SAVANNAH: (Spanish) Literally, a grassland or treeless plain.
   Savanna, Savanah, Savana, Savonna

SCARLETT: (English/French) Surname referring to the bright-red color, brought into use as a given name primarily due to Margaret Mitchell's heroine in the novel *Gone With the Wind*.
   Scarlet, Scarlette

SEANA: (*SHAWN-ah*) (Irish) Feminine form of Sean. See also Shan, Shana, Siana and Shawna.
   Seanna

SELENA: (*sa-LEEN-ah*) (Greek) "Goddess of the moon." Mythology; Selena was sister to Helios, the sun. For Salina and variants, see Sally. See also Celina.
   Selina; Selene (French/Greek); Selenia (Latin); Selenne

SELMA: (English/German) "God's protection." Feminine short form of Anselmo.

SERAFINA: (*ser-ah-FEE-nah*) (Italian) A Latin saint's

name from the Hebrew word seraphim, "burning ones," referring to a class of angels.

Seraphina

SERENA: (Latin) "Serene, calm." When spelled Sirena, the name could be a reference to the Sirens, creatures of Greek mythology, who by their irresistible singing lured seamen to their doom. See also Sarina.

Serina, Sereena, Serene, Syrena, Sirena, Sirenia

SERENITY: (English/French) Refers to a calm and serene temperament.

SHA- names: (Contemporary) Blends of Sha- plus various name endings, with pronunciation emphasis on the second syllable. Of all the contemporary prefix names, names beginning with Sha- are the most popular. Some may be duplicates of existing names from African, Arabic, Israeli or other cultures. See also Cha- names, Charlene, Shadya, Shalisa, Shanay, Shantel, Shanice, Sharon, Shawna, Sioban, Shan- and She- names.

Shadira, Shadonna, Shakeena, Shakira, Shalaina, Shalaine, Shalana, Shalane, Shalaya, Shalee, Shaleena, Shalena, Shalene, Shalia, Shalina, Shalita, Shaliza, Shalonda, Shalynn, Shamaine, Shamara, Shameka, Shamika, Shanel, Shanelle, Shanell, Shannell, Shania, Shanae, Shanay, Shanea, Shanedra, Shanee, Shanessa, Shanetta, Shanika, Shaniqua, Shanique, Shanita, Shannae, Shaquise, Shaquita, Sharae, Sharaia, Sharana, Sharay, Sharaya, Sharayah, Sharaye, Sharice, Sharika, Sharina, Sharisa, Sharise, Sharissa, Sharita

SHADIYA: (Arabic) "Singer."

Shadya, Shadia

SHAHNAZ: (*shah-nahz*) (Farsi) "King's glory."

SHAINA: (*SHAY-nah*) (Israeli) "Beautiful." Shaina and its variants may also be contemporary feminine forms of Shane.

Shayna, Shayne, Shaena, Shainah

SHALIMAR: (Persian) The rare use of Shalimar as a given name for girls today is probably due to the perfume Shalimar. Chanel, Norell, Dior, Ciara and Aviance are other perfume names used for girls.

SHALISA: (*shah-LEE-sah*) (Hebrew) Variant of Shalishah, a Biblical place name.

Shalise, Shalishah

SHAN- names: (Contemporary) Blends of Shan- and various name endings, with pronunciation emphasis on the second syllable. See also Shandra, Shanice, Shantay, Shantel, Sha- and She- names.

Shandelle, Shandel, Shandell, Shandon, Shantoya, Shantrice

SHANA: (*SHAH-nah*) (Irish) "Old, wise." Also a variant of Sean. Shana has been made familiar today by journalist Shana Alexander. See also Seana, Shawna and Siana.

Shanna, Shannah; Shani (Swahili) "marvel, marvelous," Shan, Shanda, Shandi

SHANAY: (*sha-NAY*) (Contemporary) Possibly a phonetic variant name inspired by Sinead, an Irish form of Jane. See also Sinead, Sha- and Shan- names.

Shanae, Shanay, Shanea, Shannea

SHANDRA: (*SHAHN-drah*) (Contemporary) May be a short form of the Irish name Killashandra or a variant of Chandra. See also Killashandra.

SHANI: (*SHAH-nee*) (Swahili) "A marvel; wondrous."

SHANICE: (*sha-NEESE*) (Contemporary) An especially favored Sha- name, rhyming with the variants of Janise.

Shaniece, Shaneice, Shanise, Shanese, Shannice

SHANNON: (Irish) "Wise."

Shannan, Shannen

SHANTAY: (Contemporary) Variant of Shante, a Sanskrit name meaning "peaceful."

Shantae, Shantai, Shante, Shantee

SHANTEL: (Contemporary) "Singer." Variant of Chantel, following the "Shan-" name pattern. See also Chantel.
Shantell, Shantelle, Shantal

SHARDE: (*shar-DAY*) (Yoruban/African) "Honor confers a crown." Phonetic variant of Sade.
Shadae, Shardae, Sharday, Shardai, Shardei

SHARI: (English) Variant of Sarah or phonetic form of Sherry.
Shara, Sharee, Sharae

SHARIK: (*sha-REEK*) (African) "God's child; one on whom the sun shines."

SHARLENE: (English) Variant of Charlene and Charla.
Sharla, Sharlee, Sharly, Sharleen, Sharlyn, Sharlynne, Sharlina, Sharlana, Sharlaine, Sharlane, Sharlan, Sharlisa, Sharletta, Sharlamaine

SHARMAINE: (Contemporary) See Charmaine.

SHARMILA: (*shar-mee-lah*) (Sanskrit) "Modest."

SHARON: (English/Hebrew) "The plain of Sharon." Biblical place name; the Song of Solomon describes the beloved Shulamite woman as a flower of Sharon.
Sharron, Sharyn, Sherron, Sharona, Sharonda, Sharonna, Shareen, Shareena, Sharena, Sharene

SHASTA: (American Indian) Tribal name, the name of a mountain in California and the name of the Shasta daisy.
Shastina

SHAVONNE: (Contemporary) See Siobhan.

SHAWNA: (English/Irish) Feminine variant of Shawn. See also Seana, Siana and Shana.
Shauna, Shawnna, Shawnice, Shawniece, Shawnda, Shawndelle, Shawnee, Shawni, Shawneen, Shawntae, Shawnte, Shawntay, Shaunna, Shaunte, Shauntay, Shaunice, Shaunda, Shaundee, Shaunelle

SHE- names: (Contemporary) Blends of She- plus various name endings, with pronunciation emphasis on the second syllable. See also Sherisa, Sha- and Shan- names.
Shelanna, Shelisa, Shelonda, Shenelle, Sherae, Sheraya, Shevonda

SHEA: (*shay*) (Irish) "Courteous." Shai is an Israeli name meaning "gift," and Shaya is an Israeli diminutive of Isaiah. Some of the variants may be based on Sheila.
Shay, Shae, Shaye, Shai, Shaya, Shayla, Shaylah, Shaela, Shaila, Shaylene, Shayleen, Shaylynn, Shaylynne, Shaylyn, Shealynn, Shailyn, Shayda, Shayana, Shaelee

SHEBA: (*SHEE-bah*) (Hebrew) The name of a kingdom in southern Arabia, noted for its great wealth. Biblical; the queen of Sheba journeyed to Jerusalem to see for herself if accounts about Solomon's great wisdom and wealth were true.

SHEENA: (Scottish/Gaelic) Variant of Jean. Increased interest in this name is probably due to singer Sheena Easton.
Sheenah

SHEILA: (*SHEE-lah*) (English/Irish) Variant of an Irish form of Celia.
Sheela, Sheilah, Sheelagh, Shelagh

SHELBY: (English/Scandinavian) "Willow farm." English surname used as a given name for girls and occasionally for boys.
Shelbi, Shelbie

SHELLEY: (English) Surname used as a given name for girls and as a short form of names like Michelle, Rochelle and Shirley.
Shelly, Shelli, Shellee

SHERIDAN: (English/Gaelic) "Bright." Surname in rare use as a given name for boys and girls.

SHERISA: (*she-REE-sah*) (Contemporary) Variant based on Cherise or Sherry. See also She- names.
Sherise, Sherissa, Sherita, Sherrina, Sherronda

SHERRY: (English) Short form of Sharon and the many names beginning with Sher-. Sherry also may be used in reference to the wine, after the fashion of Brandy. See also Cherie.
Sheri, Sherri, Sherree, Sherrie, Shereen, Sherae, Sheray

SHERYL: (*SHAR-el*) (English) Variant of Cheryl. The Sheryl spelling ensures the soft "sh" pronunciation. Sherilyn is a blend of Sheryl and Marilyn, and some of the names listed here also could be considered as variant forms of Shirley. See also Cheryl and Sha- names.
Sherril, Sherrill, Sherill, Sharell, Sharelle, Sharrell, Sherell, Sherelle, Sherrell, Sherrelle, Sherelene, Sherilyn, Sherylann, Sherylayne, Sherlynn, Sherlene

SHILOH: (*SHY-loh*) (Hebrew) "The one to whom it belongs." See historical note in boys' index.
Shyla, Shylah, Shilo, Shyloh

SHIRAE: (*shee-rah-EH*) (Japanese) "White bay"; "white creek."

SHIRLEY: (English) "Bright meadow." See also Sheryl.
Shirleen, Shirlee, Shireen, Shirell, Shirelle (*she-RELL*)

SIANA: (*SHAWN-ah*) (English/Welsh) Variant of Sian (*shon*), a Welsh form of Jane. See also Seana, Shanay, Shawna and Shana.
Sian, Sianna

SIBYL: (Greek) "Prophetess, oracle." See also Sybil and Cybil.

SIDNEY: (English) See Sydney.

SIDONIA: (*sih-DOHN-yah*) (Latin) "From Sidon."

SIENNA: (*see-EN-ah*) (Latin) "From Siena." The city of Siena in Italy; also a brownish-red color.

SIERRA: (*see-ERR-ah*) (Latin) "Mountains, mountainous." A name associated with environmental concerns due to the Sierra Club. See also Ciara.

SIGRID: (Scandinavian) "Beautiful; victorious."

SILVANA: (*sil-VAHN-ah*) (Italian) "Woodland; forest." Feminine form of Silvanus.
Silvanna (*sil-VAN-ah*)

SILVIA: (Latin) "Wood, forest." Literary, Shakespeare used Silvia for a heroine's name in *Two Gentlemen of Verona*. See also Sylvia.

SIMONE: (*see-mohn, see-mun*) (French) Feminine form of Simon.
Simona, Symone, Simonne

SINEAD: (*sha-NADE*) (Irish/Gaelic) Variant of Jane or Janet. Sinead has been made familiar to Americans today by rock singer Sinead O'Connor.

SIOBHAN: (*sha-VAHN*) (Irish/Gaelic) Variant of Joan. The unusual spelling of Siobhan is used less frequently than its phonetic variants.
Shavaugn, Shavon, Shavonna, Shavonne, Shavona, Shavonda

SIRENA: (Greek) see Serena.

SIRI: (Scandinavian) Variant of Sigrid.
Siriana

SKYE: (English) Skye and Sky are used as nicknames for Skyler and Skylar, as nature names, and possibly in reference to the Isle of Skye in Scotland. See also Schuyler in the boys' index.
Sky, Skyla, Skylar, Skyler

SKYLAR: (English/Dutch) Phonetic form of the Dutch surname Schuyler.
Skyler

SLOANE: (Scottish) "Fighter, warrior." Surname. Sloan is the preferred form for boys.

SOLANA: (*soh-LAH-nah*) (Latin) "Eastern wind." A saint's name.

SOLANGE: (*soh-LANZH*) (French) "Solemn, dignified." A saint's name. A fanciful meaning for the name is "angel of the sun."

SONIA: (*SOHN-yah*) (English) Variant of Sophia.
Sonya (Russian); Sonja (Scandinavian); Sonni

SOPHIA: (*soh-FEE-ah*) (Latin/Greek) "Wisdom."
Sofia (Spanish/Scandinavian); Sofie (Scandinavian); Sophie (French); Sophy, Sofiah; Safiya (Swahili) "pure"

SORRELL: (English/French) "Reddish brown."
Sorelle (French)

STACY: (English) As a boy's name, a short form of Eustace. Now primarily used for girls, Stacy and Stacey are generally considered to be short forms of Anastacia, after the fashion of Stasia and Stasha.
STACEY, Stacie, Staci, Stacee, Stacia, Stasia, Stasha

STARLA: (Contemporary) Astronomical name based on "Star."
Starr, Star, Starlene, Starlena, Starlette, Starleena, Starlyn, Starlynn

STELLA: (English/Latin) "Star." See also Estella.

STEPHANIE: (*STEFF-a-nee*) (English/French/Greek) Feminine form of Stephen. The name of the first Christian martyr was a favored name choice from the earliest centuries of the Christian era. Stephania, a Latin form of the name, was used for girls. The French form Stephanie became popular early in the twentieth century.
STEFANIE, STEPHANY; Stefani (Italian); Stephani; Stefana, Stephania (Latin); Stefania (Slavic); Stephaine, Stephine, Steffi, Stevana, Stevie

STORMY: (English) Name from nature based on the vocabulary word and surname Storm.
Stormie, Stormi

SUMIKO: (*soo-MEE-koh*) (Japanese) "Child of goodness"; "beautiful child."

SUMMER: (English) Nature name; the season used as a girl's name.

SUNNY: (English) Nature name.
Sunnie, Sunni; Sunita (Sanskrit) "Well-behaved"

SUSAN: (English/Hebrew) "Lily." Short form of Susannah. In the apocryphal Book of Tobit, Susannah was a woman of courage who defended herself against wrongful accusation. See also Xuxa and Zsa Zsa.
SUZANNE, Susanne, Susette, Suzette (French); SUSANA (Spanish); Suzan, Suzana (Slavic); Susanna (Italian); Susannah, Suzanna, Suzannah, Susie, Susy, Suzie, Suzy, Suzi, Sue, Sueann, Sueanne, Sueanna, Suellen, Suelyn

SUZU: (*soo-zoo*) (Japanese) "Long-lived"; "crane."
Suzuko (*soo-ZOO-koh*) "Spring, autumn child"

SYBIL: (Greek) "Prophetess, oracle." See also Sibyl and Cybil.
Sybille

SYDNEY: (English/French) "From St. Denis." Sidney is favored as a name for boys, and Sydney is almost entirely used for girls. See also Cydney.
Sydnee

SYLVIA: (English) See also Silvia.
Sylvie, Sylvina, Sylvana, Sylvonna

T

TA- names: (Contemporary) Blends of Ta- and various name endings, with pronunciation emphasis on the second syllable. See also Tanisha and Te- names.
Talani, Talanna, Talea, Taleah, Taleen, Talena, Talene, Talona, Talyssa, Talicia, Talina, Talisa, Talisha, Tamika, Tamica, Tameika, Tamiko, Tamisha, Tanaia, Taneece,

Tanelle, Tanika, Tarina, Tashina, Tasheena, Tashana, Tashara, Tasharra, Tawana

TABITHA: (*TAB-i-thah*) (Aramaic) "Gazelle." Biblical; the Aramaic name of Dorcas, a kindly woman, noted for her good works, who was resurrected by Peter. See also Dorcas.

TACY: (*TAY-cee*) (English/Latin) "Silence." May also be intended as a short of Anastacia.

TAJA: (*TAH-zha, TAY-zhah*) (Sanskrit) "Crown." A feminine form of Taj. Taji (*TAH-jee*) is a Japanese surname with the meaning "silver and yellow color."
Taisha, Taija, Tajia, Tajah, Taji, Tajiana

TALIA: (*TAL-yah*) (Hebrew) "Lamb, lambkin." From Taliah. Talia is also a short form of Natalia.
Talya, Tahlia, Taliah

TALITHA: (*ta-LEE-thah, TAL-a-thah*) (Hebrew) "Child." Biblical; a reference to the resurrection of Jairus's daughter when Jesus said, "Child, arise."

TALLIS: (English/French) "Woodland." Rare.

TAMA: (*tah-mah*) (Japanese) "Well-polished"; "globe, ball."
Tamae (*tah-mah-EH*) "Ball, bell"

TAMARA: (*TAM-a-rah*) (Russian/Hebrew) "Palm tree." Variant form of Tamar. Biblical; a daughter of King David and sister to Absalom. See also Tammy, Tara and Mara.
Tamar (*TAY-mar*) (Hebrew); Tamra, Tamarah, Tamryn

TAMI: (*TAH-mee*) (Japanese) "Let people see benefit."
Tamiko (*tah-MEE-koh*) "Child born in spring"

TAMMY: (English) Short form of Thomasina and Tamara.
Tammi, Tammie, Tam, Tami, Tammiejo, Tamlyn, Tamilyn

TANI: (*TAH-nee*) (Spanish/Slavic) Spanish short form of Estanislao, "make famous," from the name borne by several Slavic kings and three saints.

Tanis

TANISHA: (*ta-NEE-shah*) (African) "Born on Monday."
Tanesha, Taniesha, Tanishia

TANYA: (Russian) Short form of Tatiana or Titania. See also Tawny and Tonya.
TANIA (English/Spanish); Tahnee, Tahni, Tahna, Tahnia; Tana (African); Taina (Scandinavian); Tanee, Tanamarie

TARA: (*TAH-rah*) (Irish) "High hill." Ancient Tara was the site of the "stone of destiny" on which Irish kings were crowned. Hindu mythology: Tara (Sanskrit), "shining," is one of the names of the wife of Shiva. See also Terra.
Tarah, Tarrah, Tarra, Taralynn, Taralyn

TAREE: (*tah-ree-EH*) (Japanese) "Bending branch."

TARYN: (Contemporary) Blend of Tara and Erin.
Tarin, Tarryn, Tarynn

TASHA: (English/Russian) Short form of Natasha, the Russian form of Natalie. See also Latasha.
Tashia, Tashi, Tassa, Tassie, Tosha, Toshiana

TASIA: (*TAH-zha, TAY-zhah*) (Contemporary) Short form of Anastasia. See also Taja.
Tazia (Italian); Tasya (Russian); Tashia

TATE: (Scandinavian) "Cheerful." (Irish) "Measure of land."
Tatum

TATIANA: (*tah-sh'AHN-ah*) (Russian) Feminine form of Tatius, a Roman family clan name. A saint's name. See also Tiana and Tanya.
Tatianna

TAURA: (*TAW-rah*) (English) An astrological name, the feminine form of Taurus. See boys' index. Taura (*tah-OO-rah*) (Japanese) can mean "many lakes" or "many rivers."
Taurina

TAVIA: (*TAY-vee-ah*) (Latin) Short form of Octavia.
Tava

TAWNY: (Irish) "A green field." Also an English surname. Contemporary variants probably are intended as forms of Tanya or they refer to the literal meaning of tawny, the warm sandy color of a lion's coat.
Tawni, Tawnya, Tawnee, Tawney, Tawnie, Tawnia, Tawna

TAYA: (*tye-AH*) (Japanese) "Valley field."

TAYLOR: (English) "Tailor."

TE- names: (Contemporary) Blends of Te- plus various name endings, with pronunciation emphasis on the second syllable. See also Ta- names, Tanisha and Tiana.
Teanna, Teana, Telayna, Telisa, Telisha, Tenisha, Tenesha, Teona, Teonna, Tenaya

TEAGAN: (*TEE-gan*) (English/Irish) "Good-looking." Surname.
Tegan, Teige (*teezh, tayzh*)

TEAL: (English) A name from nature; the bird or the blue-green color.
Teela

TEDDI: (English) Short form of Theodora.

TEMPEST: (English) "Turbulent, stormy." Child actress Tempestt Bledsoe has brought attention to the name in recent years.

TEMPLE: (English/Latin) The surname refers to the medieval priories and settlements of the Knights Templars, a military religious order. Rare.

TERESA: (*te-REE-sah, te-RAY-sah*) (Spanish/Italian) Variant of Theresa. The popularity of two saints, Teresa of Avila and Therese of Lisieux, has resulted in the creation of many variants. See also Theresa, Terri and Tessa.
Teresita (Spanish); Teresina (Italian); Terez, Terezia, (Slavic); Terese (Scandinavian); Tresa (German); Teressa, Tressa

TERRA: (*TARE-ah*) (Latin) "The planet earth." Mythology; the Roman earth goddess, equivalent to the Greek Gaia. See also Tierra.
Terrah, Teralyn

TERRI: (English) Short form of Teresa. Variants are contemporary blends based on Teresa. Terry is used more for boys. See boys' index for historical note.
Teri, Terry, Terrie, Terika, Terilynn, Teriann, Teriana, Teryn, Terrin, Terryn

TESSA: (English) Short form of Teresa.
Tess, Tessia, Tessie

THALIA: (*THAYL-yah*) (Greek) "Flowering." Mythology; Thalia was the Muse of comedy and one of the Three Graces, goddesses who were the embodiment of beauty and charm.

THEA: (Greek) "Goddess, godly." Short form of names like Althea and Dorothea. Mythology; the Greek goddess of light, mother of the sun, moon and dawn.
Tia, Tiah, Teah

THELMA: (Greek) "Will, wilful." A literary creation from the nineteenth century.
Telma (Spanish)

THEODORA: (Latin/Greek) "God given." Feminine form of Theodore.
Teodora (Spanish); Theadora

THERESA: (*the-REE-sah, ter-REE-sah*) (Greek) Meaning uncertain; possibly a Greek place name. See also Teresa.
Therese (French); Theressa

THOMASINA: (English) "Twin." Feminine form of Thomas.
Tommie, Tommi, Tomasina, Tamsen, Tamsin

TIANA: (*tee-AHN-ah*) (Contemporary) Short form of Tatiana. See also Tatiana and Te- names.
Tianna, Tiani, Tiahna, Tiandra, Tiane, Tianne, Tiauna, Tiona, Tionna

TIARA: *(tee-ARH-ah)* (Latin) "Headdress." A tiara is a jeweled headpiece or demi crown. Tierra is the Spanish word meaning "earth."
Tierra, Tiarra

TIFFANY: (English/French) Variant of the Greek Theophania, a name referring to the Epiphany, the manifestation of divinity.
Tiffanie, Tiffani, Tiffney

TINA: *(TEE-nah)* (English/Latin/Slavic) Name ending used as an independent name and in combination with other names.
Teena, Tinamarie

TIPPER: (Irish) Nickname and variant of Tabar, an Irish name meaning "a well."

TISHA: *(TEE-shah)* (Contemporary) Short form of Leticia or Latisha.
Tiesha

TOMIKO: *(toh-MEE-koh)* (Japanese) "Happiness child."

TONI: (English) Short form of Antonia and Antoinette, with contemporary variants based on Toni. See also Tonya.
Tonette, Tonia, Tonell, Tonisha, Toniesha

TONYA: (Russian) "Praiseworthy." Short form of Antonina. See also Tanya and Tawny.

TORI: (Scottish/English) Tori short forms and independent names are mostly derived from Victoria, but may also be the feminine use of surnames. See Tory in boys' index. Tori (Japanese) means "bird."
Tory, Torrey, Torri, Torrie, Torey, Torry, Torree, Toriana

TOSHI: *(TOH-shee)* (Japanese) "Mirror reflection."

TOYA: *(TOY-ah)* (Spanish) Short form of Victoria, also a Japanese surname meaning "house door," or "door into the valley." See also LaToya.
Toyana

TRACY: (English/French) "From Thracia." Surname dating from before the Norman conquest. Occasionally used for boys.

Tracey, Traci, Tracie, Tracee

TRINA: (*TREEN-nah*) (English/Scandinavian) Short form of names with the -trina ending. Trena is a Latin term meaning "triple" and sometimes is used in reference to the Trinity.

Treena, Treen (Irish); Trena, Trinadette, Trini

TRISHA: (English) Short form of Patricia. See also Teresa for similar sounding variants.

Tricia, Trish, Trissa, Trisa, Trishana

TRISTA: (*TRISS-tah*) (Contemporary) Feminine form of Tristan and/or a rhyming variant of Christa. The spelling of Trysta suggests the English word *tryst*, usually taken to mean a romantic appointment to meet. Tristan is used more for boys than for girls; Tristan variants serve as alternatives to names like Kristin and Christine.

Tristan, Tristen, Tristin, Tristina; Tristyn, Trystin (Welsh); Trysta

TRIXIE: (English) "Brings joy." Short form of Beatrix.

TRUDY: (*TROO-dee*) (German) "Strength." Short form of names like Gertrude.

TWYLA: (*TWYE-lah*) (English) Usage is probably due to dancer/choreographer Twyla Tharp and to a character in a novel by Zenna Henderson.

Twylla, Twila

TYRA: (*TEER-ah, TYE-rah*) (Scandinavian) "Of Tyr, god of battle."

Tyla, Tylena

U

ULA: (*OO-lah*) (Spanish) Short form of Eulalie; (Scandinavian) "Wealthy." See also Eulalie.

UNA: (*OO-nah*) (English/Latin) "One."
Oona, Oonagh (Irish) "lamb"
UNIQUE: (*you-NEEK*) (Latin) "Only one." Use of the English word as a given name may be influenced by its similarity to Monique.
URSULA: (*UR-soo-lah*) (Latin/Scandinavian) "She-bear." A medieval saint's name.
USHA: (*oo-shah*) (Sanskrit) "Dawn." Mythology; daughter of heaven, sister of night.

V

VALENCIA: (*vah-LEN-cee-ah*) (Latin) "Strong." From Valentinus, a saint's name.
VALENTINA: (Latin) "Strong." Feminine form of Valentinus.
Valen, Valyn, Valene
VALERIE: (English/French) "Strong, valiant." Feminine form of Valerius, a Roman family clan name.
Valeria (Italian/Spanish); Valarie, Valaree
VAN: (Dutch) "Of." The Dutch equivalent of "de" in French names. When some early immigrants to America dropped this prefix from their surnames, they converted it to a given name.
VANESSA: (English) An early eighteenth-century literary name created by Jonathan Swift. See also Venicia.
Vanesa (Spanish)
VANNA: (Contemporary) Short form of Ivana, the Russian feminine form of John or a variant of Vanessa. Vanda is a Czech form of Wanda.
Vanda, Vanetta
VELMA: (English) Variant of Wilma or Wilhemina.
Valma (Finnish)
VELVET: (English) The name of the soft-napped fabric used as a given name for girls.

VENECIA: (*ve-NEE-shah*) (Contemporary) Variant of Venetia, the Latin form of Venice.
Venice, Venitia, Venicia, Venita

VENUS: (*VEE-nus*) (Latin) Roman mythology; the goddess of beauty and love, equivalent to the Greek Aphrodite.

VERA: (Latin) "Truth." (Russian) "Faith."
Verla, Verena

VERITY: (*VER-i-tee*) (English/Latin) "Truthfulness."

VERNA: (English) Short form of Laverne or a feminine form of Vernon.
Vernisha, Vernita, Verena

VERONICA: (*ver-RON-ni-kah*) (Latin) "True image." Vernice and Verenice are variant spellings of Bernice. See also Ronnie.
Veronika (Czech/Scandinavian); Veronique (French); Vernice, Verenice, Verenise, Verona

VIANNA: (*vee-ANN-ah*) (Contemporary) Variant of Viviana. Vianca is a Spanish variant of Bianca. See also Vivian.
Viana (Portuguese); Vianca, Viona, Vina

VICTORIA: (English/Latin) "Conqueror." Feminine form of Victor. See also Latoya, Tori and Toya.
Viktoria (Scandinavian); Vittoria (Italian); Vicky, Vicki, Vickie, Vikki, Viki

VIDA: (*VEE-dah, VYE-dah*) (Latin) Short form of Davida. Vida is also the Spanish word for "life." Veda may be used in reference to the Hindu Veda (Sanskrit), "knowledge."
Veda

VIENNA: (*vee-EN-ah*) (Latin) The name of the Austrian city, used as a given name.

VIOLET: (English) One of the earliest flower names. Shakespeare used the Latin form Viola for the enterprising heroine in *Twelfth Night*.

Violeta (Spanish); Violetta (Italian); Violette (French); Viola

VIRGINIA: (English/Latin) "Chaste, virginal." See also Ginger and Ginny.

Virgina, Virgena, Virgene *(ver-JEEN)*

VIRIDIANA: *(ver-REE-dee-AHN-ah)* (Latin) "Green." An Italian saint's name.

VIVIAN: (English/Latin) An ancient personal name. In Malory's *Mort d'Arthur*, Vivien was the Lady of the Lake, also the enchantress of Merlin. See also Vianna.

Viviana, Vivianna, Vivianne; Viviane, Vivien, Vivienne (French)

VONDRA: (Czech) "Womanly, brave." Variant of Andrea.

W

WANDA: (English/German) "Traveler." See also Vanna.

WAVA: *(WAY-vah)* (English/Slavic) "Stranger." Pet name formed from Varvara, the Russian form of Barbara.

WENDY: (English) Literary; a created name that first appeared in James Barrie's *Peter Pan*.

Wendi

WESLEE: (English) Feminine form of Wesley.

Weslia

WHITLEY: (English) "White meadow." Occasional use is probably influenced by its similarity to Whitney, and to the character Whitley on the TV show *A Different World*.

WHITNEY: (English) "Fair island."

WILLA: (English) "Resolute protector." Feminine form of William.

Wilma, Wilhelmina (Dutch/German)

WILLOW: (English) Literally, the willow tree, noted for its slender, graceful branches and leaves.

WINIFRED: (Welsh) "Reconciled, blessed." Winifred, a

martyred Welsh princess, traditionally is called the patron saint of virgins.

Winnie

X

XANDRA: (*ZAN-drah*) (Greek) Variant of Alexandra. See also Zandra.

XANTHE: (*ZAN-thah*) (Greek) "Yellow, blond."

XAVIERA: (*ecks-say-vee-EHR-ah*) (Spanish/Arabic) "Bright, splendid." Feminine form of Xavier.

XENIA: (*ZAYN-yah*) (Greek) "Welcoming, hospitable." See also Zenia.

Xena (*ZAY-nah*), Xia

XUXA: (*SHOO-shah*) (Latin) Nickname for Susana used by the hostess of a very popular children's TV show in Brazil.

Y

YASMIN: (*yahz-meen*) (Arabic) "Jasmine flower." See also Jasmine.

Yasmine, Yasmina, Yazmin, Yasmeen

YESENIA: (*yeh-SEE-nee-ah*) (Spanish) Probably a created name made popular by the Gypsy title character of a Spanish soap opera prominent in the seventies. See also Jessenia and LLessenia.

YNES: (French) "Chaste." Variant of Agnes. See also Inez.

Ynez

YOLANDA: (Spanish) Variant of Yolande, a French form of Violet.

Yolonda, Yolande

YSABEL: (French) Medieval form of Isabel.

YUMIKO: (*you-MEE-koh*) (Japanese) "Arrow child."

YURIKO: (*you-REE-koh*) (Japanese) "Lily child" or "village of birth."

YVETTE: (French) Feminine form of Yves. See also Ivette.

YVONNE: (French) Feminine variant of Yves. See also Evonne and Ivonne.
Yvonna

Z

ZAHARA: (Arabic) "Flowering." See also Sahara, Zara and Zohra.
Zahra (Swahili)

ZAIDA: (Arabic) "Huntress" or "fortunate." See also Sade.
Zayda, Zada

ZALIKA: (Swahili) "Well-born."
Zuleika (Arabic)

ZANDRA: (Spanish) Variant of Alexandra. See also Xandra.

ZANETA: (*zah-NEE-tah*) (Spanish) A saint's name; variants also may be used as feminine forms of Zane.
Zanita, Zanetta

ZARA: (Arabic) "Dawning." See also Zahara.
Zaira (Italian); Zayra, Zarah; Zareena, Zarina "golden"

ZELDA: (English/Latin) Short form of Grizelda. The similar sounding Zelde is a Yiddish name meaning "happiness."
Zelde

ZELMA: (English) Variant form of Selma.

ZENIA: (English/Greek) "Welcoming." Variant of Xenia. Zena is a short form of Zenobia.
Zina, Zena

ZENOBIA: (*ze-NOH-bee-ah*) (Latin) Queen Zenobia (third century B.C.) was ruler of the wealthy city of Palmyra in the Arabian desert.

ZIA: (*zee-ah*) (Arabic) "Light, splendor."

ZITA: (*ZEE-tah*) (Hungarian/Slavic) Short form.

ZIVAH: (Israeli) "Radiant."

ZOE: (*ZOH-ee*) (Greek) "Life."
Zoey

ZOHRA: (Arabic) "Blossom." Biblical; the name of a city
in Judah where Samson was born. See also Zahra.
Zora (Slavic) "dawn."

ZSA ZSA: (*zhah-zhah*) (Hungarian) Pet name for Susan.

ZULEMA: (*zoo-LEE-mah*) (Arabic/Hebrew) "Peace." Variant form of Salome or Solomon.
Zulima

BOYS' INDEX

A

AARON: (Hebrew) "Lofty, inspired." Biblical; Moses' brother Aaron was the first high priest of Israel.
Aron (French/Slavic/Scandinavian); Arron, Aaren; Aren (Nigerian) "eagle"

ABDULLAH: (Arabic) "Servant of God."
Abdul, Abdulla; Abdalla (Swahili)

ABEL: (Hebrew) "Exhalation of breath." Biblical; the second named son of Adam. The variant form Able is an English surname.
Abell, Able

ABNER: (Hebrew) "Father of light." Biblical; King Saul of Israel's army chief by this name was a valiant warrior and clever strategist.

ABRAHAM: (Hebrew) "Father of multitudes." Biblical; Abraham, celebrated for his great faith, was the ancestor-father of Israel and some of the Arabic peoples. See also Ibrahim.
Abe

ABRAM: (*AY-bram*) (Hebrew) "Exalted father." Biblical; the patriarch Abraham's name before God changed it.
Abran (Spanish)

ABSALOM: (Hebrew) "Father of peace." Biblical;

Absalom, son of King David, was renowned for his handsome appearance and ability to win the loyalty and allegiance of others.

ACE: (English) A nickname given to one who excels. It's also an English surname meaning "noble."

ACHILLES: (*a-KILL-eez*) (Greek) The mythological hero of the Trojan War famous for his valor and manly beauty.

ADAIR: (Scottish) "From the oak tree ford." Used for boys and girls.

ADAM: (Hebrew) "Earthling man; from the red earth." Biblical; in the Genesis account, man was created from the red earth of Eden.
Addam, Adamson; Adan (Spanish)

ADDISON: (English) "Son of Adam."

ADIN: (*AY-den*) (Hebrew) "Pleasure given." Biblical; an exile who returned to Israel from Babylon.

ADLAI: (*AD-lay*) (Hebrew) "My ornament." A Biblical name made noteworthy in the twentieth century by the presidential candidate Adlai Stevenson.

ADLER: (German) "An eagle."

ADNAN: (Arabic) "Pleasure."

ADOLFO: (German/Latin) "Noble wolf."
Adolph, Adolphus

ADONIS: (Greek) "Handsome; a lord." Greek mythology; a youth beloved of Aphrodite.

ADRIAN: (English/Latin) "From Adria." (The Adriatic sea region.)
Adrien (French); Adriano (Spanish); Adrion, Adron

ADRIEL: (*AY-dree-el*) (Hebrew) "Of God's flock." A Biblical name.

AHMED: (*AH-med*) (Arabic) "Much praised." One of the many names of the prophet Muhammad.
Ahmad, Amad, Amadi

AIDAN: (*AY-den*) (Irish/Gaelic) "Fiery."

Aiden

AKENO: (*ah-KAY-noh*) (Japanese) "In the morning"; "bright shining field."

AL: (English) A short form of names beginning with "Al-."

ALAN: (English/Celtic) "Fair, handsome." See also Allen.

ALARIC: (*AL-a-rik*) (German) "Rules all." Historical; the Gothic king who plundered Rome in A.D. 410.

Alric, Alrick

ALASDAIR: *(AL-as-dare)* (Scottish/Gaelic) Variant of Alexander.

Alastair, Alistair, Alistaire, Allister, Alister

ALBERT: (English/German) "Noble, bright." One of the most famous Alberts was Prince Albert, consort of Queen Victoria, who was noted for his enthusiastic support of the application of science to the modern industrial age. Albert Einstein devised the Theory of Relativity when still a young man.

Alberto (Spanish); Adelbert (German)

ALBIN: (English) "White." Alban and Albin are English surnames probably based on Alba, a Spanish and Italian place-name.

ALBION: (*AL-bee-an*) (Latin/Celtic) "White cliffs." Albion is an ancient poetic name for Britain.

ALDEN: (English) "Wise/old, friendly."

Aldrin, Aldric: "old/wise ruler."

ALDO: (Italian/German) "Old one, elder."

ALEX: English short form of Alexander.

ALEC, Aleck (Scottish); Alek (Russian); Aleko (Greek)

ALEXANDER: (Greek) "Defender of mankind." Alexander the Great (356–323 B.C.) conquered and ruled the greater part of the known world before his death at the age of thirty-three. History describes him as a man of high physical courage, impulsive energy and fervid imagination. See also Alasdair, Alex, Lex, Sandy and Zander.

ALEJANDRO, Alexandro (Spanish); Alexandre, Alixandre (French); Alessandro (Italian); Alexis, Alexei (Russian); Alexi, Alexio

ALFONSO: (*al-FON-so*) (Spanish/German) "Ready, eager." Alfonso has been favored by Spanish royalty.

Alfonse, Alfonzo, Alphonse (French); Alphonso

ALFORD: (English) "The old ford."

ALFRED: (English) "Elf-wise counselor."

ALFREDO, Alf, Alfie

ALGERNON: (*AL-jer-non*) (French) "Bearded."

ALI: (Arabic) "The greatest." Variant of Allah, title of the Supreme Being in the Muslim faith. The homonym Allie is most often a short form of names beginning with "Al-."

Aly, Allie

ALLARD: (English/French) "Noble, brave."

ALLEN: (English/Scottish) Variant of Alan.

ALLAN (Scottish); Alain (al-LAYNE) (French); Allain Allyn, Alun (Welsh); Alon, Allon (Hebrew) "Great tree"

ALONZO: (*a-LON-so*) Spanish/Italian form of Alphonse; see Alfonso.

Alanzo, Alonso

ALTON: (English) "From the old town." See also Elton.

ALVA: (Arabic/Hebrew) "Sublime." Biblical; Alvah was a place and tribal name.

Alvah, Alvan

ALVARO: (*AL-vah-roh*) (Spanish/German) "Truth-speaker" or "guardian."

Alvar

ALVERN: (Latin) "Spring, greening." See also Elvern.

ALVIN: (English) "Wise friend."

Alvyn, Alwin, Alwyn; Alvino (Spanish) "White, fair."

ALVIS: (*AL-viss*) (English) "All-knowing."

AMADEUS: (*ah-ma-DAY-us*) (Latin) "Loves God."
  Amadeo (Spanish)
AMBROSE: (Greek) "Immortal."
AMES: (French) "Friend." Rare.
AMIR: (*a-MEER*) (Arabic) "Prince."
AMON: (*AY-mon*) (Hebrew) "Trustworthy, faithful." Biblical. Also the name of one of the gods of Thebes in Egypt.
AMORY: (*AM-er-ee*) (English/German) "Brave, powerful." See also Emory.
  Amery (Irish) "Ridge, long hill"
AMOS: (*AYM-ess*) (Hebrew) "Bearer of burdens." Biblical; the prophet who wrote the Book of Amos.
ANDREW: (English/Scottish/Greek) "Manly, brave." Biblical; the first chosen of the twelve apostles; Andrew is called the patron saint of Scotland and Russia. See also Jedrick and Kendrick.
  ANDY; ANDRE (French/Portuguese); ANDRES, Andreo (Spanish); Andreus, Andreas (Greek); Andrei, Andrik (Slavic); Andino (Italian); Andras (Welsh); Aundre, Andric, Andrian, Andriel (Contemporary); Anders, Anderson (Scandinavian)
ANGEL: (*AHN-hail, AIN-jel*) (Latin/Greek) "Messenger." Biblical; name for the spirit creatures sent by God to men as His messengers. Latin male usage is dominant for this cross-gender name.
  ANGELO, Angelino (Italian/Portuguese/Spanish)
ANGUS: (Scottish/Gaelic) "Singular, choice."
ANSELL: (English/German) "God's protection."
  Ansel, Anselmo
ANSON: (English) "Anne's son." A surname.
ANTARES: (*an-TARE-ees, an-TAHR-ees*) (Greek) The name of a giant red star, the brightest in the constellation Scorpio.
ANTHONY: (English/Latin) "Highly praiseworthy." Mark

Antony (82–30 B.C.), Roman triumvir and general, shared a throne and a tempestuous political career with Queen Cleopatra of Egypt. St. Anthony founded the first Christian monastic order and is traditionally renowned for his resistance to temptation by the Devil. See also Tony.

ANTONIO (Spanish/Italian); Antonino, Antony (Italian); ANTOINE (AN-twan) (French); Anton (Slavic); Antone (*AN-tone*)

APOLLO: (Greek) "Destroyer." Mythology; the Greek and Roman god of light, music and poetry. The name comes from Appollyon, Greek translation of the Hebrew word abaddon, meaning "destroyer." Biblical; Apollo was one of the early Christian disciples.

ARAM: (*AIR-am*) (Assyrian) "High, exalted."

ARAMIS: (*AIR-a-miss*) In fiction, the famous swordsman from Alexander Dumas's *Three Musketeers*, notable for his ambition and religious aspirations.

ARCHER: (English/French) "A bowman." An English surname.

ARCHIBALD: (English) "Valuable, bold."
Archie

ARDELL: (*ar-DELL*) (Latin) "Eager, industrious." Rare.

ARDEN: (Celtic) "Lofty, eager." Rare.
Ardon (Hebrew) "Bronze." A Biblical name.

ARI: (Hebrew) "Lion;" (Norse) "eagle."

ARIC: (English/Norse) "Rule with mercy." See also Eric.
Aaric, Arick, Arik, Arrick

ARIEL: (Hebrew) "Lion of God." Biblical; a name for Jerusalem. Shakespeare gave this name to a prankish spirit in *The Tempest*.

ARION: The name of a Greek poet and musician. Mythology; the name of the mythological magic horse born to Poseidon and Demeter.
Arian (Welsh), Arien

ARLEN: (Hebrew) "Pledge."
Arlin, Arlan, Arland, Arlando
ARLEY: (English) Variant of Harley.
Arlie, Arleigh
ARLO: (Latin) "Strong, manly." Italian variant of Charles.
ARMANDO: (Spanish/German) "Army man." Variant of Herman.
Armand (French); Arman (Russian); Armond, Armondo (Italian)
ARMON: (Hebrew) "High place."
Armen, Armin
ARNAN: (Hebrew) "Quick, joyful." A Biblical name.
Arnon "torrent valley"
ARNOLD: (English/German) "The eagle rules."
Arnoldo (Spanish); Arno (Italian); Arnie, Arnel, Arnell, Arnett; Arne, Arni (Scandinavian)
ARSENIO: (*ar-SEE-nee-oh*) (Greek) "Virile, masculine." St. Arsenius the Great tutored the sons of the Roman emperor Theodosius. The actor/television personality Arsenio Hall has brought the name into prominence.
Arcenio
ARTHUR: (English/Celtic) "Noble, courageous." King Arthur of Britain (sixth century) and his Round Table of knights have become legendary figures.
ARTURO (Spanish); Artur (Portuguese); Artie, Art
ARVIN: (English) "The people's friend."
Arwin, Arwyn, Arvie, Arvis, Arvon
ASA: (*AY-sah*) (Hebrew) "Healer, physician." Biblical; name of the third king of Judah.
Ase (Scandinavian)
ASH: (English) "Ash tree." Ashton is used about equally for boys and girls.
Ashford, Ashton, Ashtin, Ashley
ASHER: (Hebrew) "Happy; happiness." Biblical; Asher,

the eighth son of Jacob, was promised a life blessed
with abundance.

AUBREY: (*AW-bree*) (English, French) "Rules with elf-
wisdom."
Aubry

AUDEN: (English) "Old friend."
Audie, Audel, Audley

AUDRIC: (English) "Old/wise ruler."

AUGUST: (Latin) "Majestic dignity; grandeur." St. Augustine was the first Archbishop of Canterbury.
Agustin (Spanish); Agustine, Augustine, Augustus (German)

AURELIO: (*aw-REE-lee-oh*) (Latin) "Golden." Spanish
form of Aurelius.
Aurelius, Aureliano (Spanish)

AUSTIN: (English/French) Variant of Augustine. Austen is
occasionally used for girls.
Austen, Austyn

AVERY: (*AY-vree*) (English/French) "Rules with elf-
wisdom."

AXEL: (Scandinavian) Variant of Absalom.

AYERS: (English) "Heir to a fortune."

B

BAILEY: (English/French) Comes from the word meaning
steward or public official; man in charge.
Bayley

BANNER: (English/Scottish) "Flag; ensign bearer."

BARAK: (*ba-RAHK, BARE-ek*) (Hebrew) "Flash of lightning." Biblical; a valiant fighting man who cooperated
with the prophetess Deborah to win victory in a battle
against overwhelming odds. See also Barric.
Barrak, Baruch ("Blessed")

BARAN: (Russian) "The ram; forceful, virile." See also
Baron.

BARCLAY: (English/Scottish) "The birch tree meadow."
See also Berkley.
Bartley

BARD: (English/Celtic) "Minstrel; a singer-poet."
Baird, Barden, Bardon

BARNABAS: (Hebrew) "Son of comfort." Biblical; a first-century missionary companion of Paul.
Barnaby (English); Bernabe (Spanish); Barney

BARNETT: (English) "Of honorable birth."
Barnet

BARON: (English/French) A title of nobility used as a given name. Also the Hebrew phrase Bar Aaron, "son of Aaron."
Barron, Barr

BARRETT: (English) Variant of Barnett.
Barret

BARRIC: (English) "Grain farm." A place name. See also Barak.
Barrick, Beric

BARRY: (English/Irish) "Fair-haired."
Barrie, Barrington

BARTHOLOMEW: (Hebrew) "The son of Tolmai (the farmer)." Biblical; one of the twelve apostles, known as the patron saint of tanners and vintners. Variants listed here are related English surnames.
Bart, Barton, Bates, Bardo, Bartel, Barth

BARTRAM: (English/German) "Glorious raven." The raven was consecrated to Odin, the Norse god of war, and was the emblem of the Danish royal standard. See also Bertram.

BASIL: (*BAZZ-el*) (English/Greek) "Royal, kingly."

BAXTER: (English) "Baker." An occupational name.

BAYARD: (*BAY-erd*) (English/French) "Auburn-haired." The name of a sixteenth-century French knight and national hero renowned for his valor and purity of heart.

Bay, Baylen

BEALE: (English/French) "Handsome."

Beal, Beall

BEAU: (French) "Handsome."

BEN: (English) Short form of names like Benjamin and Benedict.

Benny, Bennie, Benji, Benjy; Benn (English surname)

BENEDICT: (Latin) "Blessed." A name used by 15 popes and a monastical order, the Benedictines. Shakespeare's Benedick in *Much Ado About Nothing* is a self-assured, witty bachelor.

Benedick; Benedetto, Benito (Italian)

BENJAMIN: (Hebrew) "Son of the right hand." Biblical; the twelfth and most beloved son of the patriarch Jacob.

BENJIRO: (*ben-jee-ROH*) (Japanese) "Enjoy peace."

BENNETT: (English) Variant of Benedict.

Bennet, Benson

BENTLEY: (English) "Grassy meadow."

BENTON: (English) "Settlement in a grassy place."

BERKLEY: (English/Irish) "The birch tree meadow." Also see Barclay and Burke.

Berke, Berkeley, Berk

BERLYN: (*BER-lin*) (German) "Son of Berl." See also Burl.

Berl, Berle, Burlin

BERNARD: (English/German) "Strong as a bear." See also Bjorn.

Bernardo (Spanish/Portuguese); Bernie, Bern (Scandinavian); Berne, Bernelle, Burnard, Burnell, Barnard

BERT: (English) "Illustrious."

Bertie, Berton, Bertin

BERTRAM: (English/German) "Glorious raven." See also Bartram.

Bertrand (French)

BEVAN: (Welsh) "Son of Evan."

BILLY: (English) Nickname for William, now often used as an independent name. Billie is frequently used for girls.
Bill, Billie

BIRCH: (English) "Bright, shining; the birch tree." A nature name and surname.

BJORN: (*bee-YORN*) (Scandinavian) "Bear." Famous name bearer: the Swedish tennis champion, Bjorn Borg. See also Bernard.

BLADE: (English) "Knife, sword." This surname has been in use since medieval times.

BLAINE: (Scottish/English) Surname meaning uncertain. Rare.
Blayne, Blane, Blaney

BLAIR: (Scottish) "Field, plain." Used somewhat more for girls than for boys.

BLAISE: (French/Latin) "Lisp, stutter." The homonym Blaze means "fire." Blaise Pascal was a brilliant seventeenth-century child prodigy, mathematician, scientist and philosopher; he invented the calculating machine and hydraulic press before he died at age thirty-nine.
Blaize, Blayze, Blaze, Blase, Blais, Blaisdell

BLAKE: (English/Scottish) "Dark, dark-haired." Can also mean the reverse: "fair, pale."
Blakeman, Blakely

BO: (Scandinavian) Nickname and short form occasionally used for boys and, due to actress Bo Derek, for girls. See also Beau.

BOBBY: (English) Short form of Robert. Bobbie is more frequently used for girls.
Bob, Bobbie

BODEN: (Scandinavian) "A shelter."
Bodin, Bodie, Bodine, Beaudean

BOONE: (English/French) "Good; a blessing." Daniel Boone, the American frontier hero, has influenced the use of the surname as a given name.

BORAK: (Arabic) "The lightning." According to legend, Al Borak was the name of the magical horse that bore Muhammad from earth to the seventh heaven.

BORG: (Scandinavian) "Castle."

BORIS: (Russian) "Fighter." St. Boris is known as the patron saint of Moscow.

BOWEN: (Welsh) "Son of Owen."

Bohannon (Irish)

BOYCE: (English/French) "Lives near the wood."

BOYD: (Scottish) "Blonde, fair-haired."

BRAD: (English) "Broad, wide."

Bradd, Braddock "broad-spreading oak."

BRADEN: (English/Irish) "Broad hillside."

Bradon, Braddon, Braeden, Braedon, Brayden, Braydon

BRADLEY: (English) "Broad clearing in the wood." Also related English surnames.

Bradlee, Bradford, Bradshaw

BRADY: (Irish/English) "Broad."

BRAM: (English/Scottish) "Bramble; a thicket of wild gorse." Short form of Abraham, Abram. A noted name bearer was Bram Stoker, author of *Dracula*.

BRAND: (English/German) "Fiery torch, beacon." May also derive from Brandon.

Brandt (German); Brando (Italian); Brandell

BRANDON: (English) "Beacon on the hill" or "gorse-covered hill."

BRANDEN, Brandin, Brandan, Brandyn

BRANNON: (Irish) Variant of Brandon.

Brannan, Brannen, Branson

BRANT: (English) Variant of Brand. Joseph Brant, a Mohawk Indian, was a renowned strategist who fought on the British side during the American Revolution. He was also a devout scholar who translated Christian religious works into his native Indian tongue.

Brantley, Branton, Brantson

BRECK: (Gaelic) "Freckled."
Brexton

BRENDAN: (Irish) "Prince." Brendan Behan was a noted Irish playwright and wit.
BRENDON, Brenden

BRENNAN: (Irish) Variant form of Brendan.
Brennen, Brennon, Brenn

BRENT: (English/Celtic) "Hilltop."
Brenton, Brenten, Brendt, Brentley, Brently

BRETT: (English) "Brit." A native of Brittany (France), or Britain (England). Rare usage of Britt.
BRET, Britton, Brittan, Brittain (English); Bretton (Scottish); Britt (Dutch)

BREWSTER: (English) "One who brews ale." See also Webster.

BRIAN: (Celtic) "He ascends." Brian Boru (tenth century) was a high king of Ireland and one of its greatest national heroes. See also Bryan.
Brien, Brion, Briant, Bryant (French)

BRICE: (English/French) A given name of medieval origin. See also Bryce.

BRICK: (English) "Bridge."
Brickman, Brigham, Brik

BROCK: (English/German) Variant form of Brook. The related surnames are English and German/Jewish variants of names like Baruch.
Brockman, Brockton, Broxton

BRODERICK: (Scottish/Scandinavian) "Brother."
Broderic, Brodrick, Brodric

BRODIE: (Scottish) Place name. There is a Castle Brodie in Scotland.
Brody, Broden

BRONSON: (English/German) "Brown's son."
Bron

BROOK: (English) "Water, stream."

Brooks, Brooke

BRUCE: (English/Scottish) Surname used since medieval times, now a common given name, especially in Scotland. The tale of "the Bruce," (Robert, King of Scotland in the fourteenth century) who watched and learned the value of perseverance from a spider spinning a web, has become a part of the world's folklore.

BRUNO: (German) "Brown."

BRYAN: (English) Very popular variant form of Brian.

BRYANT, Bryon

BRYCE: (Scottish) Surname form of Brice.

Brycen, Bryson, Bryceton, Bryston

BUCK: (English) The word for a male goat or deer, used as a given name or nickname. Also an English slang word used to describe a sportsman, a dandy.

Buckley

BUD: (English) "Brother." Nickname used since medieval times.

BUELL: (*BEW-el*) (German) "Hill dweller." Use of surnames like Buell, Buford and Beauregard as given names stems from the custom of naming sons after commanding officers during and after the Civil War. In the North, names like Grant and Scott became popular choices.

BURDETT: (*ber-DETT*) (English/French) Surname used as a given name.

Burdette

BURKE: (English) "Fortified hill." See also Berkley.

Bourke

BURL: (English) "Fortified." See also Berlyn.

Burle, Burleigh, Burrell

BURNE: (English/Irish) "Bear, brown."

Burnell, Burnette, Burney, Byrne

BURT: (English) "Fortified."

Burton

BYRON: (*BYE-ron*) (English) Surname often used as a given name. The variant form Biron was the name of a character in Shakespeare's *Love's Labours Lost*.
Biron

C

CABLE: (English) "Ropemaker." An English surname.
Cabe

CADELL: (*kay-DELL*) (Welsh) "Spirit of battle." See also Kade.
Cade, Caden

CAELAN: (*KAY-lan*) (Gaelic) Meaning uncertain; possibly a contemporary variant of Cailean (Scottish).
Calan, Cailin, Cailean, Caley

CAESAR: (*SEE-zar*) (Latin) Caesar was the title of the Roman emperors after Augustus Caesar. Czar (Russian) and Kaiser (German) are variant forms. See also Cesar.

CAIN: (Hebrew) "Something produced." Biblical; Cain, the firstborn son of Adam, killed his brother in jealous anger and spent the rest of his life as a wanderer in exile.

CAINE: (English/French) Place name and surname. No connection to the Biblical Cain. See also Kane.

CAL: (English) Short form of names beginning with "Cal-".

CALDER: (English/Scottish) "Rough waters."

CALE: (English) Surname derived from Charles.

CALEB: (*KAY-leb*) (Hebrew) "Dog; tenacious and aggressive." Biblical; Caleb, a companion of Moses and Joshua, was noted for his astute powers of observation and fearlessness in the face of overwhelming odds.

CALLUM: (Gaelic) "Dove."
Calum

CALVERT: (English) "Cowherd, cowboy."
Calbert

CALVIN: (Latin) "Bald." A Roman family clan name.

CAMDEN: (Scottish) "Winding valley."

CAMERON: (Scottish) "Bent nose." This nickname of an especially valorous ancestor became the surname of one of the oldest clans in Scotland.
Camron, Cam

CAMILO: (*ka-MEE-lo*) (Latin) "Free-born child; noble." Masculine form of Camille.
Camillo

CARDELL: (English/French) Surname, meaning uncertain.

CAREY: (Welsh/Irish) "Of the dark ones." See also Cary.

CARL: (German) Variant of Charles. See also Karl.
CARLOS (Spanish); Carlo (Italian); Carlin (German)

CARLTON: (English) "Free men's town."
Carleton, Carlson, Charlton, Carlisle, Carlyle

CARMELO: (Hebrew) "Fruitful orchard." Refers to Mount Carmel in Palestine.

CARNE: (*karn*) (Welsh/Gaelic) Variant of English surname Cairn, meaning a landmark or memorial made of piled-up stones.

CARNELL: (English) "Defender of the castle."

CARRICK: (Irish) "Rock."

CARRINGTON: (English/Celtic) Place name and surname.

CARSON: (Scottish) Surname, meaning uncertain.

CARTER: (English) "One who transports goods."

CARY: (Welsh) "Loving." See also Carey.

CASEY: (Irish) "Alert, vigorous." See also Kasey.
Case, Cace, Cacey

CASIMIR: (*KAH-zee-meer*) (Slavic) "Enforces peace." See also Kasimir.

CASPAR: (Persian) "Keeper of the treasure." In medieval tradition, Caspar was one of the Three Magi who traveled from afar to find the baby Jesus.
Casper

CASSIDY: (Irish/Welsh) "Curly-headed."

Cass, Cassian

CASSIUS: (*KASH-us*) (Latin) Roman family clan name. Shakespeare's *Julius Caesar* depicts Caius Cassius as politically ambitious. In modern times, Cassius Clay was the birth name of the heavyweight boxing champion Muhammad Ali.

CECIL: (*SESS-ul*) (Latin) "Blind." Also an English/Welsh surname.

CEDRIC: (Welsh) "Gift of splendor." Cedro and Cidro are Spanish short forms of Isadoro. See also Kedrick.
Cedrick, Cedrik; Cedro, Cidro (*SEE-dro*)

CESAR: (Latin) Spanish variant form of Caesar.
Cezar (Slavic); Cesario (Spanish/Italian); Cesare (*CHEZ-a-ray*) (Italian)

CHAD: (English) A medieval given name of uncertain meaning. Also a short form of various surnames.
Chadd, Chadwick, Chadwell, Chadric, Chadrick

CHAN: (Spanish) Nickname for John. Chano and Chayo are similar Spanish short forms for names ending in "-ano" and "-rio." Chan is also a Chinese family name. The Sanskrit name Chan means "shining."
Chano, Chayo

CHANCE: (English/French) Variant form of Chauncey, often used in the sense of "fortune; a gamble."
Chauncey, Chauncy, Chaunce, Choncey

CHANDLER: (English/French) "Candlemaker."

CHANNING: (English/Irish) "Young wolf."
Chann, Channe, Channon

CHARLES: (English/French/German) "A man." French variant form of Carl, adopted by the English especially since the seventeenth-century reigns of King Charles I and II. Charles and its variant forms have been favored by the royalty of several countries, including the present Prince of Wales. Charlie and Charly are occasionally used for girls. See also Arlo, Carl and Karl.

Charlie, Charley, Charly, Charlton, Charleston, Charleson, Chaz, Chas, Chuck, Chick

CHARRO: (Spanish) Nickname for a cowboy, especially in Argentina.

CHASE: (English) "Huntsman."
Chace, Chayce, Chasen

CHE: (*chay*) (Spanish) Short form of José, made familiar as a given name by the Latin-American revolutionary Che Guevara.

CHEROKEE: (American Indian) "People of a different speech." The name of one of the largest tribes, used as a given name.

CHESTER: (English) "Camp of the soldiers."
Chet, Chess, Cheston

CHEVY: (French) "Horseman, knight." A short form of Chevalier. Chevy Chase, the actor-comedian, has brought the name into modern notice.
Chevell (*sha-VELL*), Cheval (*she-VALL*), Chevalier

CHEYNE: (French) "Oak-hearted."
Chayne, Chane, Chaney, Cheney

CHICO: (*CHEE-koh*) (Spanish) "Boy, lad." Also a Spanish short form of Ezekiel.
Chiko (Japanese) "Arrow" or "pledge"

CHRIS: (English) Short form of Christopher and Christian.
Cris (Spanish)

CHRISTIAN: (Greek) "Follower of Christ, the Anointed." The "Cr-" spellings are Spanish forms. Occasionally used for girls.
CRISTIAN, Cristos, Criston, Christan, Christos

CHRISTOPHER: (Latin) "With Christ inside."
Christofer, Christoffer (German); Christophe, Christofor (French); Cristofer, Cristofor, Cristoval (Spanish)

CISCO: (*SISS-co*) (Spanish) Diminutive of Francisco.

CLANCY: (Irish) "Redheaded fighter."

CLARENCE: (Latin) "Bright, shining, gentle."

CLARK: (English) "Cleric, secretary."
Clarke

CLAUDE: (English/Latin) "Lame."
Claudio, Claud, Claudius

CLAYTON: (English) Place-name and surname derived from Clay.
Clay, Clayborne, Clayburn, Claiborne

CLEAVON: (*KLEE-von*) (English) "Cliff."

CLEMENT: (Latin) "Clemency, mercy." A name borne by 14 popes.
Clemens (Danish); Clem

CLETUS: (*KLEE-tus, KLAY-tus*) (Greek) "Illustrious."
Cleytus, Cleo, Cleon

CLEVELAND: (English) "Land of cliffs."
Cleve

CLIFFORD: (English) "Cliff-side ford."
CLIFTON "town by the cliff," Cliff, Clyford

CLINTON: (English) "Hillside town."
Clint, Clintwood

CLIVE: (*kleeve, klyve*) (English) "Cliff."

CLOVIS: (Latin/German) "Renowned fighter." Variant form of Louis.

CLYDE: (Scottish) Refers to the Clyde river in Scotland.

COBURN: (Scottish/English) Surname and place name.
Coby

COCHISE: (*ko-CHEECE*) (American Indian) The name of a renowned warrior, chief of the Chiricahua Apache. Rare.

CODY: (Irish/English) "Helpful."
Codie, Codey, Codell

COLBY: (English) "Dark; dark-haired."
Colbey, Colbert (French)

COLE: (English) A short form of Nicholas.
Coleman, Coley, Colman, Colson

COLIN: (*KOH-lin*) (English/French) Short form of Nicholas.

COLLIN (*KAH-lin*), Collins, Colan, Colyn

COLLIER: (English) "Coal miner."

COLT: (English) "Young horse; frisky." Variants are English surnames used as given names.

Colter, Coulter, Coltrane

COLTON: (English) "Coal town."

Colten

CONAN: (*KOH-nan*) (Irish/Celtic) "Hound."

CONNAL: (Irish/Celtic) "High, mighty."

Connell, Conal, Conall, Conn

CONNOR: (Irish) "Hound-lover."

Conor, Conner

CONRAD: (German/Slavic) "Brave, wise." See also Konrad.

CONROY: (Irish) "Wise adviser."

CONSTANTINE: (Latin) "Constant, steadfast." Most notable name bearer was Constantine the Great, the fourth-century emperor who made Christianity the official state religion of the Roman Empire.

CONWAY: (Welsh) Place-name and surname.

COOPER: (English) "Barrelmaker." May also be the English form of a German surname meaning "coppersmith."

CORBETT: (English/French) "Raven."

CORBIN: (English/French) "Raven-haired." Variants are English surnames used as given names.

Corben, Corbyn, Corvin, Corby

CORDELL: (English) "Cordmaker."

Cord, Cordale, Corday, Cordell

COREY: (English/Irish) "Hill hollow." See also Cory.

Correy, Corry, Corrick, Corley, Corky

CORMAC: (*KOR-mak*) (Irish) "Raven's son." Historical;

the third-century Irish king who founded schools of military science, law and literature at Tara.

Cormack, Cormick

CORNELIUS: (*kor-NEEL-yus*) (Latin) "Horn, hornblower." Biblical; Cornelius was a Roman centurion who was baptized by Peter.

Cornell, Cornel

CORRIN: (Irish) "Spear-bearer."

Corin, Corran, Corren, Corlan

CORT: (English/French) "Courtier; court attendant." Today Courtney is primarily used for girls. See also Curt and Kurt.

Court, Cortland, Courtland, Courtney, Courtenay

CORTEZ: (*kor-TEZ*) (Spanish) "Courteous." Variant of Curtis. Surname of the Spanish explorer and adventurer who with a small expeditionary force conquered the Aztec civilization of Mexico.

CORWIN: (Gaelic) "From beyond the hill."

Corwyn

CORY: (English/Irish) Surname. See also Corey.

COYAN: (*KOY-an*) (French) "Modest."

Coyne

COYLE: (Irish) "Leader in battle."

CRAIG: (Scottish) "Rock, rocky."

CREED: (English/Latin) "Belief; guiding principle." Creedon is an Irish surname.

Creedon

CREIGHTON: (Scottish) "Border dweller."

Crayton

CRISPIN: (English/Latin) "Curly-haired." St. Crispin was a third-century martyr now known as the patron of shoemakers.

Crespin

CROYDON: (English) Surname and place-name.

Croy

CRUZ: (*krooz*) (Spanish/Portuguese) "Cross."
CULLEN: (Irish/Gaelic) "Good-looking lad."
  Cullin, Cullan
CURRAN: (Gaelic) "Dagger."
  Curry, Currie
CURT: (English) Short form of Curtis. See also Cort and Kurt.
CURTIS: (English/French) "Courteous." See also Curt, Kort and Kurtis.
  Curtiss
CYD: (Contemporary) Variant short form of Sydney.
  Cydney
CYRANO: (*SEER-ah-no*) (French) Cyrano de Bergerac was a seventeenth-century soldier/science-fiction writer. His talents and his extraordinary nose provided the inspiration for Rostand's *Cyrano de Bergerac*.
CYRIL: (*SEER-el*) (English/Greek) "Master, lord."
  Cyrill, Cy; Ciro (Spanish)
CYRUS: (Greek/Persian) "Enthroned." Historical; Cyrus the Great conquered Babylon at the height of its powers and founded the Persian Empire.
CZAR: (*zar*) (Russian) "Caesar, emperor." See also Cesar.

D

DA- and D'- names: (Contemporary) Blends of Da- plus various endings, with pronunciation emphasis on the second syllable. Names beginning with D'- (meaning "of") follow an Italian style of surnames. See also Damario and De- names.
  DaJon, DaJohn, DaJuan, D'Angelo, DaMar, Damarco, Damarko, D'Amico, D'Amante, Damont, DaMonte, DaSean, DaShae, DaShaun, DaShawn, DaShonn, DaVar, Davaughn, DaVon, DaWayne
DACE: (*dayce*) (English/French) "Of the nobility." Dacio is a Spanish name meaning "from Dacia."

Dacey, Dacian, Dacio

DAEGAN: (*DAY-gan*) (Irish/Gaelic) "Black-haired." Variant form of Deegan.

Dagen, Daeg, Deegan; Dag (*dahg*) (Scandinavian) "Day"

DAI: (*dah-EE*) (Japanese) "Large," "generation." Also a Welsh short form of David.

DAKOTA: (*da-KOH-tah*) (American Indian) "Friend, ally." Tribal name.

Dakotah

DALE: (English) "Valley."

Dael

DALLAS: (Scottish) "From the dales, the valley meadows." Name of the Texas city and surname used as a given name.

DALLIN: (Irish) "Blind." A saint's name.

Dallon, Dallen, Dalan, Dalon, Dal

DALTON: (*DOLL-ton*) (English) "From the valley town."

DAMARIO: (*da-MAH-ree-oh*) (Spanish) Masculine form of Damaris (Greek) "gentle."

Demario

DAMIAN: (*DAY-mee-en*) (Greek) Variant of Damon. The Belgian priest, Father Damien, is honored as the man who gave his life helping the lepers of Molokai in Hawaii. St. Damian (third century) is known as the patron of physicians.

DAMIEN (French); Damion; Damiano (Italian)

DAMON: (*DAY-mon*) (Greek) "One who tames, subdues." Daman (Irish); Damone (*da-MONE*), Daymon

DAN: (Hebrew) "Judge." Biblical; Dan was the fifth son of Jacob and founder of one of the twelve tribes of Israel. While Dan is an independent name, it's also used as a short form of Daniel.

Dann

DANA: (*DAY-na*) Variant of Daniel or Dane.

DANE: (English) "From Denmark." Variant Daine and Dayne are English/French surnames occasionally used as given names.

Daine, Dayne, Dain, Dayner, Danon

DANIEL: (Hebrew) "God is my Judge." Biblical; the prophet and writer of the Book of Daniel was a teenager when he was taken to Babylon after the destruction of Jerusalem in 607 B.C. He survived two death sentences, first in a lions' den, then in a fiery furnace. Many prominent men have had the name since, among them Daniel Webster the statesman and Daniel Boone the frontiersman.

DANNY, Dannie; Danilo (Spanish); Danell, Dantrell

DANNO: (*DAH-noh*) (Japanese) "Field gathering." Surname.

DANTE: (*DAHN-tay*) (Spanish/Italian) "Enduring." Historical; Dante Alighieri, considered one of the greatest poets of all time, wrote *The Divine Comedy*, notable for the graphic description of the medieval version of Hell known as "Dante's Inferno."

Dantae, Daunte, Dantel

DANTON: (*dan-TONE* or *dan-TAHN*) (French) Variant of Anthony.

D'Anton

DARBY: (English/Irish) "Without envy."

DARCEL: (*dar-SELL*) (French) "Dark." Variant of the surnames Darcy or D'Arcy; "dark." The Darcy variants are used more for girls than for boys.

Darcell, Darcio, Darcy, D'Arcy

DARENCE: (Contemporary) Blend of Darell and Clarence.

Darrence, Darrance, Derrance

DARIN: (English) Meaning uncertain. Variants are surnames. See also Darren.

Daron, Daren, Daran; Daryn (Welsh); Darrin, Darron, Darryn, Derrin, Derren, Derrian

DARIO: (*DAR-ee-oh*) (Latin) Variant of Darius.

DARION: (Greek) "Gift." Possibly a variant of Darin. Of unknown origin, Darien has poetic significance; John Keats described the moment of discovery when explorers stood "silent, upon a peak in Darien."
Darien, Darian, Darrien, Darrian, Darrion

DARIUS: (*da-RYE-us, DARE-ee-us*) (Medo-Persian) Possibly a royal title, like Caesar. Historical; Darius the Mede assumed the kingship of Babylon after its conquest by Cyrus. See also Dario.
Darrius

DARNELL: (English) "Hidden." Place-name and surname.
Darnel, Darneil

DAROLD: (Contemporary) Blend of Daryl and Harold or Gerald.
Darrold, Derrold, Derald

DARRELL: (*DARE-el*) (English/French) "Open." A surname and given name that dates from at least the eleventh century. See also Darryl.
Darel, Dareau (*da-ROW*) (French); Dariel, Dariell, Darroll, Derrall, Derrell, Derrill, Derell

DARREN: (English) Origin uncertain. See also Darin.

DARROCH: (Irish/Gaelic) "Strong, oak-hearted." See also Derek.
Darrick, Darick, Daric, Darrock

DARRYL: (English) Variant of Darrell. Daryl is occasionally used for girls. See also Darrell.
DARYL, Daryll, Daryle, Darryll, Darrel, Derryl

DARTAGNAN: (*dar-TAN-yan*) (French) Dumas's swashbuckling tale *The Three Musketeers* was based on the real D'artagnan's memoirs.

DARVELL: (English/French) "Town of eagles."

DARVIN: (Contemporary) Blend of Daryl and Marvin.
Dervin

DARWIN: (English) "Dear friend." Historical; Charles

Darwin, nineteenth-century naturalist, was the first major exponent of human evolution.

Darwyn

DAVID: (Hebrew) "Beloved." Biblical; one of the most remarkable personalities in the Scriptures. David was a shepherd, musician, poet, soldier, statesman, prophet and king. He wrote about half of the Psalms and very likely composed music for them as well. He is the only David mentioned in the Bible; his name occurs there more than a thousand times. Today there are variants of the name in almost every language group. See also Davis.

Dave; Davin (French); Davyn (Welsh); Davey, Davie (Irish); Davy, Davion, Davian, Daveon, Daviel, Daviot

DAVIS: (English) Surname. Variant of David.

Davies (Welsh); Davison, Davidson, Dawson, Dayson, Dayton

DAX: (French) Place-name; a town in southwestern France that dates from before the days of the Roman occupation.

Daxton, Dack (English)

DAYLAN: (Contemporary) Daylan and its variants probably are rhyming variants of the name Waylon.

Daylen, Daylin, Daylon, Deylin, Daelan, Dalen, Dalyn

DE- names: (Contemporary) Blend of De- plus various endings, with pronunciation emphasis on the second syllable. These given names follow the French style of aristocratic surnames using the prefix "de." Capitalizing the second syllable is optional and often appears both ways in contemporary usage. See also DeAndre, DeShawn and Da- names.

DeAnthony, Deonte, Deante, DeAngelo, DeJohn, DeJon, DeJuan, DeLeon, Delon, Deloran, Delorean, DeMar, DeMario, DeMauri, DeMarco, DeMarcus, Demarcos, DeMarr, Demond, Demonte, Deondre, Deontae, Derelle,

DeRoyce, DeShay, DeVal, DeVell, DeVane, DeVaughn, DeVaun, DeVonn, Devonte, DeWayne

DEACON: (*DEE-ken*) (English/Greek) "Dusty one; servant."

Deakin, Deke, Dekle, Dekel

DEAN: (*deen*) (English) "From the valley." Dean is a surname and a "title" name, signifying a church official or the head of a school.

Deane, Dene

DEANDRE: (*dee-AHN-dray, dee-ahn-DRAY*) (Contemporary) An especially popular De- name.

DeAndre, Deandrae, D'Andre

DECLAN: (*DECK-lan*) (Irish) The name of an Irish saint. Decker and Dekker are similar-sounding Dutch and German surnames in rare use as given names.

Decker, Dekker

DEDRICK: (*DEE-drick*) (English/Dutch) "Gifted ruler." Variant form of Diederick.

Dedric, Diedrick, Dietrich, Dieter (German)

DEL: (French) Surname prefix meaning "of the." Used today as an independent name and as a short form of names beginning with Del-.

DELANEY: (*de-LANE-ee*) (Irish/French) "From the elder tree grove."

Delane, Delaine, Delancy, Delano (*DELL-a-no*)

DELBERT: (English) "Noble, bright."

Dalbert

DELMAR: (French) "Of the sea."

Delmer, Delmore

DELMON: (English/French) "Of the mountain." The English surname Delman means "man from the valley."

Delman, Delmont

DELROY: (French) "Of the King."

Delray, Delrick, Delrico, Delron

DELTON: (English) "From the town in the valley."

DELVIN: (English) "Godly friend."
Delvon; Delwin, Delwyn (Welsh)

DEMETRIUS: (Latin/Greek) "Of Demeter." Mythology;
Demeter is the Greek goddess of corn and harvest. Her
withdrawal for the part of the year that her daughter
Persephone must spend with the god of the underworld
is the reason for winter. See also Dimitri.
Demitrius; Demetrio (Spanish); Demetri, Demitri

DENNIS: (English/Greek) Variant of Dionysius. Mythology; Dionysius is the Greek god of wine, responsible
for the growth of the vines in spring and the originator
of winemaking; he is equivalent to the Roman god Bac-
chus. Biblical; a judge of Athens who was converted to
Christianity by the apostle Paul.
Denny, Dennie, Denney, Dennison; Denis, Denys
(French)

DENVER: (English/French) Possibly a variant of the
English/French surname Danvers, meaning "from
Anvers." Contemporary use probably refers to the name
of the capital city of Colorado.

DENZEL: (English) A place-name in Cornwall.
Denzell, Denzil

DEREK: (English/German) "Gifted ruler." From
Theodoric. See also Darrick and Dirk.
DERRICK, DERICK, Dereck, Derrek, Derrik, Derik,
Deryk, Darek, Deryck

DERRY: (Irish/Gaelic) "Oak grove." Surname.

DERWIN: (English) "Gifted friend." Derwent is a similar-
sounding English surname referring to the Derwent
River in England.
Derwyn, Durwin, Derwent, Dervin, Dervon

DES: (*dez*) (English) Short form of names beginning with
Des-, occasionally used as an independent name.

DESHAWN: (Contemporary) DeShawn is an especially
popular prefix name. See also De- and Da- names.

DeSean, Deshaun, Deshon, DeShonn, Deshane

DESI: (*DEZ-ee*) (Latin) "Yearning, sorrow." Short form of Desiderus.

Dezi

DESMOND: (Gaelic) "From South Munster." An Irish surname referring to Munster, one of the five regions of ancient Ireland.

Desmund, Dezmond

DESTIN: (*DESS-tin, dess-TEEN*) (French) "Destiny." The French surname Destan means "by the still waters."

Deston, Destan

DESTRY: (*DESS-tree*) (English/French) Variant of a French surname. Destry has the flavor of the American west due to the classic western film, *Destry Rides Again*.

Destrie, Destrey

DEV: (English) Short form of names beginning with Dev-. Also a Sanskrit title name meaning "divine, god."

DEVEREL: (*DEV-er-al*) (English/French) Place-name.

Deverell, Deveral, Devereau, Devereaux (surnames); Devere, Devery, Devry, Deverick

DEVIN: (French/Latin) "Divine, perfect." See also Devon.

DEVLIN: (Irish) "Misfortune."

Devlyn, Devlon, Devland

DEVON: (English) Name of the county in England, noted for its beautiful farmland. See also Devin.

Devan, Deven, Devyn, Devion, Deveon, Devron, Deavon, Devonn

DEWEY: (*DOO-ee*) (English) Place-name and surname; possibly a Welsh form of David.

DEXTER: (Latin) "Right-handed."

Dex, Dexton

DICK: (English) One of the rhyming nicknames from medieval times. Richard was shortened to Rick, then rhymed to Dick, and variants like Dickson and Dix (which is also the French word meaning "ten") followed. Today Dick is rarely used as an independent name. See also Richard.

Dickson, Dixon, Dix

DIEGO: (*dee-AY-go*) (Spanish) Variant of James.

DILLON: (Irish/French) "Like a lion." See also Dylan.

Dillen, Dilan

DIMITRI: (*de-MEE-tri*) (Slavic) Variant of Demetrius. In Catholic tradition, Dimas was the name of the compassionate thief who died with Jesus at Calgary.

Dimetrius, Dimitrios, Dimas (*DEE-mas*)

DINO: (*DEE-no*) (Italian/Spanish) Short form ending of names like Bernardino.

DION: (*DYE-on*) (English/French) Short form of Dionysius. Diandre and Diondre are blends of Dion and Andre.

Deon, Dionte, Diondre, Diandre, Dondre

DIRK: (Dutch/German) "Wealthy." Variant of Derek and Dietrich.

See also Dedrick.

DOLAN: (Irish) "Dark, bold."

DOLPHUS: (German) Short form of Adolphus.

DOMINIC (Latin) "Of the Lord." The French spelling of Dominique is used more for girls than for boys.

DOMINIQUE, DOMINICK, Dominic, Dominik; Domingo, Domenico (Spanish); Dominico

DON: (English) Short form of names beginning with Don-. Mythology; the Irish Donn was known as king of the underworld. Use of the Welsh Gaelic surname Donne as a given name may be in honor of John Donne, the seventeenth-century poet.

Donn, Donne, Donnie, Donny

DONALD: (Scottish) "Great chief." Donald is one of the clan names of Scotland. See also Donnell.

DONATO: (*doh-NAH-toh*) (Spanish/Italian) "Gift from God." A short form of Donatello.

Donatello, Donzel

DONNELL: (*DON-el, don-NEL*) (Scottish/Irish) Variant of Donald.

Donal, Donell, Donnel

DONOVAN: (Irish) "Brown-haired chieftain."

Donavon, Donavan

DONTE: (*don-TEE, don-TAY, DON-tee*) (Contemporary) Phonetic variant of Dante. See also Dante.

Dontae, Dontay, Dontaye, Dontell, Dontrell

DORIAN: (English/Greek) "Descendant of Dorus." Literary; in Oscar Wilde's novel *The Picture of Dorian Gray*, Dorian was granted the wish that a portrait of himself would change to show the ravages of time while he himself would retain perpetual youth and beauty.

Dorion, Dorien

DORRAN: (Contemporary) (Irish/English) Contemporary usage of Dorran and other related surnames as given names listed here as variants is probably influenced by the rhyming patterns of favored names like Darren, Torrance and Darryl. Doron is an Israeli name meaning "dweller."

Dorren, Doran, Doron, Dorrin, Dorrance, Dorrell, Dorrel

DOUGLAS: (Scottish) "From the dark river." Historical; there were two branches of this powerful Scottish clan and family, the Black Douglases and the Red Douglases. The lords of these clans are key figures in Sir Walter Scott's novels.

Douglass, Doug

DOV: (Hebrew) "Bear."

DOVER: (Welsh) "Water." Name of the British seaport on the English channel. Rare.

DOYLE: (Irish/Gaelic) "Dark stranger."

DRAKE: (English/Greek) "Dragon."
  Drago (*DRAY-go*) (Italian/French); Draco (Latin); Draken, Drakon (Greek); Dracon, Drayce (Contemporary)

DREW: (English) Short form of Andrew.
  Dru (French); Drue

DUANE: (*d'wain*) (Irish) "Dark." See also Dwayne. (Historical note: Many Irish and Scottish names have the meaning "dark" or "black." Most Gaels had brown hair and darker skin coloring that contrasted with the fair hair and pale skins of Norwegian and Swedish invaders.)
  Duayne, Duwayne, Duante (*d'wan-TAY*) (Contemporary)

DUARTE: (*d'-WAR-tay*) (Spanish) "Prosperous guardian." Variant of Edward.
  Duardo

DUGAN: (*DOO-gen*) (Gaelic) "Dark."

DUKE: (English) Title used as a nickname or given name. Duke is also a short form of Marmaduke.

DUMONT: (French) "Of the mountain."

DUNCAN: (Scottish/Gaelic) "Brown-haired."

DUNSTAN: (English) "Hill stone."

DURAND: (English/French) "Firm, enduring."
  Duran, Durant, Durante, Durrant

DURBIN: (Latin/German) "City-dweller."

DUREAU: (*dur-ROW*) (French) "Strong."
  Durrell, Durell (English); Duron, Durango

DUSTIN: (English) "A fighter." The exposure given to this name by actor Dustin Hoffman has been a major influence on contemporary usage. Popularity is also influenced by the rhyming similarity to another favored name, Justin.
  Dustan, Dustyn, Duston, Dusty

DUVAL: (*doo-VAL*) (French) "Of the valley."

DWADE: (Contemporary) This blend of Dwayne and Wade could be given the combined meaning "dark traveler."

DWAYNE: (Irish) "Dark." See also Duane.

   Dwain, Dwaine, Dwane, Dawayne, Dewayne, DeWayne

DWIGHT: (English) Surname, meaning uncertain.

DYLAN: (Welsh) "From the sea." See also Dillon.

   Dyllon, Dyllan

E

EAGAN: (Irish) "Fiery, forceful."

   Egan, Egon

EAMON: (*EE-mon, AY-mon*) (Irish) "Prosperous protector." Variant of Edmund.

   Eames

EARL: (English) "Nobleman." Name based on the English title.

   Earle, Erle

EASTON: (English) "From East town."

   Eston

EBEN: (*EBB-an, EE-ben*) (Hebrew) "Stone." Biblical; a memorial stone erected by the prophet Samuel to mark a critical defeat and a victory in Jewish history.

EDDIE: (English) Short form of names beginning with "Ed-."

   Eddy, Ed, Edlin (German)

EDER: (*EE-der*) (Hebrew) "Flock." Biblical; the tower of Eder near Hebron was built as a watchtower from which shepherds could watch their flocks. The name became a symbol of God's watchfulness over His people.

EDGAR: (English) "Fortunate and powerful."

   Edgardo (Spanish); Edgard (French)

EDISON: (English) "Son of the fortunate warrior."

   Edson

EDMUND: (English/French) "Prosperous protector." See also Eamon.

Edmond, Edmundo, Edmon

EDRIC: (English) "Power and good fortune."

Eddrick, Edrick, Edrik

EDSEL: (German) "Noble, bright."

EDWARD: (English) "Prosperous guardian." A favorite name of British royalty. See also Eddie and Ned.

EDUARDO, Edwardo (Spanish/Portuguese); Eduard (French)

EDWIN: (English) "Rich in friendship."

Edwyn

EINAR: (*EYE-ner*) (Scandinavian) "Warrior chief."

EKON: (Nigerian) "Strong."

ELAM: (*EE-lam*) (Hebrew) Biblical; one of the five sons of Noah's son Shem.

ELBERT: (German) "Bright, famous."

ELDRED: (English) "Old/wise ruler."

Eldrian, Eldrick, Eldridge, Elder, Eldwin

ELEAZAR: (*el-ee-AY-zor*) (Hebrew) "God has helped." Biblical; the son of Aaron and later his successor as High Priest of Israel.

Eliezer, Eliazar (Spanish)

ELGIN: (English/Celtic) "Noble, white."

Eljin, Elgine (*el-GEEN*)

ELI: (*EE-lye*) (Hebrew) "Ascended" or "my God." Biblical; Eli was a high priest who judged Israel for 40 years and instructed the boy Samuel.

Ely.

ELIHU: (*ee-LYE-hoo, ee-LYE-hew*) "My God is He." Biblical; a young man whose fiery defense of God's righteousness is recounted in the Book of Job.

ELIJAH: (ee-LYE-jah) (Hebrew) "My God is Jehovah." Biblical; Elijah, one of the foremost prophets of Israel.

The Book of Kings recounts many miracles performed for and by him. See also Elliot, Ellis and Ilya.

ELIAS (Spanish); Elia, Elija

ELISHA: (*ee-LYE-shah*) (Hebrew) "God is salvation." Biblical; faithful attendant and successor to the prophet Elijah. Sometimes used for girls as a variant of Elise.

ELLERY: (English/Greek) "Joyful, happy."

ELLIOT: (English) Variant of Elijah.

ELLIOTT, Eliot, Eliott

ELLIS: (English) Variant of Elias, from Elijah.

Ellison, Elliston, Elson, Elston

ELMER: (English) "Famed, noble." Elmo is a short form of Erasmus, the name of a noted Dutch scholar.

Elmo, Elmore

ELOY: (Latin) "Chosen one." Short form of Eligius, the name of a French saint.

ELROY: (English/Latin) "The king." Also an Irish name meaning "red-haired youth."

Elric, Elrick, Elrod

ELTON: (English) "From the old town."

Elston, Elson, Eldon, Elden, Elder

ELVIN: (English) "Elf-wise friend." Variant of Alvin.

Elwin, Elwyn, Elvyn, Elvern

ELVIS: (English) Variant of Elvin. Brought into prominence by singer/actor Elvis Presley, the name continues to be quietly but steadily used.

ELWOOD: (English) "Forest dweller."

EMERSON: (English/German) "Brave, powerful."

EMILIO: (*eh-MEEL-ee-oh*) (Latin) Spanish form of Emil, from a Roman clan name with the possible meaning "industrious." The German/English form Emil (*AY-mul*) is in rare use today.

Emiliano (Italian); Emil, Emile (French) (*ay-MEEL*); Emlyn (Welsh); Emlen (*EMM-lin*)

EMMANUEL: (*ee-MAN-yoo-ul*) (Latin) "With us is God."

Variant of the Hebrew name Immanuel. Biblical; a name-title applied to the Messiah. See also Manuel.

EMANUEL (Spanish); Emanuele (Italian)

EMMETT: (English) Male variant of Emma, a girl's given name from premedieval times.

EMORY: (English/German) "Brave, powerful." Variant of Amory.

Emery

ENOCH: (*EE-nok*) (Hebrew) "Trained and dedicated." Biblical; Enoch was the father of Methuselah, the oldest living man named in the Bible.

ENRIQUE: (*en-REE-kay*) (Spanish) "Rules his household." Variant of Henry.

Enrico (Italian); Enzo

EPHRAIM: (*EFF-ram*) (Hebrew) "Doubly fruitful." Biblical; one of Joseph's two sons by his Egyptian wife Asenath. Efron is a Hebrew name meaning "young stag."

EFRAIN (Spanish); Efren, Efrem, Ephron, Efran, Ephrem, Efraim

ERIC: (Scandinavian) "Ever kingly." Scandinavian legend relates that the Viking sea rover Ericson (son of Eric the Red) landed on the shores of America 500 years before Christopher Columbus. Today actor Eriq La Salle has generated interest in the French spelling, Eriq. See also Aric.

ERIK, ERICK; Erich (German); Eriq (French); Erickson, Ericksen, Ericson, Erikson (Scandinavian); Eryk, Erix

ERIN: (Gaelic) Poetic name for Ireland. Rare. Eron is a Spanish variant of Aaron.

Eran (Hebrew) "Roused, awakened," Eron, Eri

ERNEST: (English/German) "Serious, determined."

ERNESTO (Spanish); Ernie, Earnest

ERROL: (Scottish/German) "Earl, nobleman."

Erroll

ERSKINE: (*ERS-kin*) (Scottish) "Ascending."

ERVIN: (English) "Friend." Variant of Irving. See also Irvin.

Earvin, Erwin, Erving, Ervine

ESAU: (*EE-sah*) (Hebrew) "Hairy." Biblical; Esau, the older twin brother of Jacob, was a skilled and adventurous hunter.

ESMOND: (English) "Protector."

Esmund

ESTEBAN: (*ess-TAY-ban*) (Spanish) Variant of Stephen.

Estevan, Estevon

ETHAN: (*EE-than*) (Hebrew) "Enduring, overflowing." Biblical; a man of Israel noted for his wisdom.

ETIENNE: (*eh-T'YIN*) (French) Variant of Stephen.

EUGENE: (Greek) "Wellborn." See also Gene.

Eugenio (Spanish/Italian)

EUSTACE: (*YOOS-tiss*) (Greek) "Productive."

Eustis, Estes

EVAN: (Welsh) Variant of a Gaelic name anglicized as John.

Evann, Evin, Evon, Evyn

EVERARD: (English/German) "Hardy, brave."

Everardo, Evarado (Spanish); Ewart (German)

EVERETT: (English) "Hardy, brave." Variant form of Everard.

Evert (German); Everet, Everton

EVIAN: (*EV-ee-an*) (Contemporary) Usage may be as a variant of Evan, influenced by the town in France famous for Evian springwater. If considered a blended name (Evan and Ian), Evian could take on the meaning "John-John."

EWEN: (*YOU-en*) (Irish) Possibly a variant form of John. See also Keon.

Ewan, Euan

EZEKIEL: (*ee-ZEE-k'yul*) (Hebrew) "God strengthens." Biblical; Ezekiel was a prophet who was among the captives taken to Babylon at the first fall of Jerusalem; he wrote the Book of Ezekiel while in captivity. See also Zeke.
Ezequiel, Esequiel (Spanish)

EZRA: (Hebrew) "Help." Biblical; a fifth-century B.C. Jewish priest, scholar, copyist and historian who wrote the two Chronicles and the Book of Ezra and began the compiling and cataloging of the other books that formed the Hebrew Scriptures, the Old Testament.
Esra, Ezrah

F

FABIAN: (*FAY-bee-en*) (English/Latin) From Fabius, a Roman clan name, the name of several Roman emperors and 16 saints.
Fabien (French); Favian, Fabion; Fabiano, Fabio (Italian); Favio, Faber

FAINE: (English) "Good-natured."
Fane (Welsh)

FALCO: (Latin) Surname having to do with falconry. See also Hawk.
Falcon (English); Falken, Falk, Falke (German)

FARAJI: (*fah-rah-jee*) (Swahili) "Consolation."

FARID: (*fah-REED*) (Arabic) "Exceptional, unequaled."

FARLEY: (English) "Fair meadow." Surname.
Farleigh, Farlow

FARRAN: (*FARE-en*) (Irish) "The land." Similar sounding variants: Farren (English) "adventurous," Ferron "ironworker," Faron (Spanish) "pharoah." Faro is a Spanish short form that also may be used in reference to the card game. Farran, Farren and Farrin are also used for girls.
Farren, Farrin, Faron, Faro, Farron, Ferron, Ferrin

FARRELL: (*FARE-el*) (Irish) "Brave."

Farrel, Ferrell

FARRIS: (English) "Iron strong."
Faris, Ferris

FELIPE: (*feh-LEE-pay*) (Spanish) Variant of Philip.
Felippe

FELIX: (Latin) "Happy." Biblical; Roman procurator of Judea during Paul's time; a wily politician.
Feliciano (Spanish/Italian)

FERGUS: (Scottish) "Man of strength."
Ferguson

FERNANDO: (Spanish) "Adventurer." See also Hernando.
Ferdinand (Spanish/German); Fernand (French)

FIDEL: (*fee-DELL*) (Latin) "Faithful."
Fidal, Fidello

FINN: (Irish) "Fair." Mythology; Finn Mac Cumhail was a legendary Irish third-century hero somewhat like the English Robin Hood. His warrior-followers were called Finians.
Finnegan, Finian

FITZ: (English/French) Surname prefix meaning "son of."
Fitzgerald, Fitzhugh, Fitzpatrick, etc.

FLETCHER: (English/French) "Arrowmaker."

FLINT: (English) Place-name and surname. Also a name from nature, referring to the hard quartz that produces a spark of fire when struck by steel.

FLORIAN: (Slavic/Latin) "Flower." Masculine form of Flora, from a Roman clan name.

FLOYD: (English) Variant form of Lloyd.

FLYNN: (Irish) "Son of a red-haired man."
Flinn, Flyn

FONSO: (Latin/German) Short form of Alfonso.
Fonzo, Fonzie, Fonsie, Fonzell

FONTAINE: (*fahnn-TANE*) (French) "Fountain; water source."
Fontayne, Fonteyne, Fontane; Fontana (Italian)

FORD: (English) Literally, a shallow place used to cross a river or stream. Surname.
Forde

FORREST: (English) "Woodland."
Forest; Forrester, Forester, Foster "forest-ranger"

FORTINO: (*for-TEEN-oh*) (Latin) "Strong; fortunate."
Fortunato

FRANCIS: (Latin) "From France."

FRANCISCO: (*frahn-CEES-koh*) (Spanish) Variant of Frank.
Francesco (Italian); Frisco

FRANK: (English/French) "Free; a free man." Frankie is occasionally used for girls. See also Francisco.
Frankie, Franky; Franco (Italian); Frantz, Franz (German); Francois (French)

FRANKLIN: (English) "Free man, landholder."
Franklyn

FRASER: (*FRAY-zer*) (Scottish) "Of the forest men." One of the major clans of Scotland.
Frazer, Frazier, Frasier

FREDERICK: (German) "Peaceful ruler."
FREDDY, Freddie, Fred; Fredrick, Fredric, Fredrik, Frederik (Scandinavian); Frederic (French); Frederico, Federico (Spanish/Italian); Friedrick, Fritz (nickname)

FREEMAN: (English) Surname used as a given name. Literally, a free man, one freed from bound servitude to an overlord.
Freman, Fremont (French)

G

GABRIEL: (Hebrew) "God's able-bodied one." Biblical; the Archangel Gabriel is the only angel besides Michael named in the canonical Scriptures.
Gabe, Gabrian; Gavriel (Jewish)

GAGE: (French) "Pledge."

GALEN: (*GAY-lan*) (Greek) "Tranquil." The name of a second-century physician whose research provided a basis for accepted medical practices for 1,500 years.
Gaelan, Galan, Galyn; Galeno (Spanish)

GALVIN: (Irish) "Sparrow."

GANNON: (Irish/Gaelic) "Fair."

GARDNER: (English/French) "Keeper of the garden."
Gard, Gardiner

GARETH: (Welsh) "Gentle." Sir Gareth, noted for his modesty and bravery, was a knight of King Arthur's Round Table.
Garreth

GARLAND: (French) "Wreath; prize."
Garlan, Garlen, Garlyn

GARNET: (*GAR-net, gar-NET*) (English/French) "Keeper of grain." Surname. Rare.
Garnell, Garnett, Garner

GARRAD: (*GARE-ad*) (English) Variant of Garret, from Gerald.
Garred, Gared; Gerred (*JARE-ad*)

GARRETT: (English) Variant of Gerald.
Garret, Garett; Garritt, Gerrit, Gerritt (Dutch)

GARRICK: (English/German) "Rules by the spear."

GARRISON: (English/German) "Spear-fortified town."
Garson

GARRON: (French/German) "Guards, guardian."
Garran (Irish); Garren, Garrin, Garan, Garin, Garon, Geron, Garen, Garion

GARTH: (English/Scandinavian) "Garden."

GARVYN: (English/German) "Spear friend; ally."
Garvin, Garve (Irish) "Rough, rugged."

GARY: (English/German) "Spear."
Garry, Garey, Garrey

GAVIN: (Scottish/Welsh) "White hawk." A form of the medieval name Gawain. See also Gwayne.

Gavino (Italian); Gavan, Gavyn

GENE: (English) Short form of Eugene.

GEOFFREY: (*JEF-ree*) (English/French) "Peaceful." See also Jeffrey.

Geffrey, Geoff (*jef*)

GEOMAR: (*joe-MAR*) (German/Italian) "Famous in battle." Joemar is a blend of Joseph and Mary.

Giomar, Joemar

GEORGE: (English/Greek) "Farmer." St. George, a knight who became the patron saint of England, achieved legendary status through the medieval depiction of his struggle with a fire-breathing dragon, symbolic of the Devil. See also Joren, Jorge, Keoki and Yuri.

Georgio, Giorgio (Italian); Geordie

GERALD: (English/German) "Rules by the spear." See also Garrad, Garrett, Jarrett, Jarrod and Jerald.

Geraldo (Spanish); Gerrald, Gerold, Gerrell, Gere

GERARD: (*je-RARD*) (French/German) "Spear strong." See also Jerard.

Gerardo (Spanish); Gerrard; Gerhard (*GARE-hard*) (German)

GERMAIN: (French/Latin) "Brotherly." See also Jermaine.

GERONIMO: (*hare-ON-ee-mo, jer-ON-ee-moh*) (Spanish/Greek) "Sacred name." Variant of Jerome, a saint's name. The American Indian Geronimo (nineteenth century) was one of the last of the renowned Apache warrior chiefs.

GERRY: (English) Short form of names beginning with "Ger-." See also Jerry.

GIACOMO: (*JOCK-a-moh*) (Italian) Variant of James and Jacob.

GIAN: (*jon*) (Italian) Short form of John, often used in combination with other names. Gianni is equivalent to Johnny.

Gianni, Giancarlo, Gianfranco, Gianluca, etc.

GIDEON: (*GIH-dee-on*) (Hebrew) "One who cuts down."
Biblical; a judge of Israel who won battles through skillful planning and faith rather than strength of arms alone.

GILBERT: (English/French/German) "Bright lad."
Gilberto (Spanish)

GILES: (*jiles*) (Greek) "Young shield." Gil is also an Israeli name meaning "joy."
Gil (Spanish)

GILMORE: (Scottish) "Sword bearer."
Gilmer, Gilmar

GILROY: (Scottish/Gaelic) "Serves the king."

GINO: (*GEE-no*) (Italian) Short form of names like Gian
and Giovanni.
Geno (Spanish)

GIOVANNI: (*joe-VAHN-ee*) (Italian) Variant of John. See
also Jovan.
Geovanni, Giovani, Giovanny, Giovany, Giovonni,
Geovanny, Geovani, Geovany

GIULIANO: (*joo-lee-AHN-oh*) (Italian) Variant of Julian,
Julio.
Giulio (*JOO-lee-oh*)

GIUSEPPE: (*jeh-SEP-ee*) (Italian) Variant of Joseph.

GLENN: (Gaelic) "Valley."
GLEN, Glendale, Glendon, Glendyn, Glynn

GODFREY: (English/German) "God's peace."

GORDON: (English/Scottish) "From the marshes." Name
of one of the great Scottish clans.

GRADY: (Irish) "Man of rank."

GRAHAM: (*GRAY-em*) (Scottish/English) "Farm home."
Graeme

GRANT: (English/Scottish) "Bestow" or "great, tall."
Grantland

GRAYSON: (English) "Gray-haired; son of the Gray family; son of Gregory."
Greyson, Gray, Grey, Graden, Gradon, Graysen

GREG: (English) Short form of Gregory. The double consonant ending on a short form usually indicates an English surname, as in Gregg.
Gregg, Gregson

GREGORY: (English/Greek) "On the watch." The first of the 16 popes to bear the name was called Gregory the Great. He founded monasteries, reorganized papal administration and fostered the development of the Gregorian chants. See also Greg.
Gregorio (Italian/Spanish/Portuguese); Grigor (Welsh/Russian); Gregor (Scottish/German); Gregori (Russian)

GRIFFIN: (Welsh) "Fighting chief; fierce." Mythology; in Greek mythology and medieval legend, the Gryphon was a fierce creature with the foreparts of an eagle and the hindquarters of a lion.
Griffen, Griffith, Griff, Gryphon

GROVER: (English) "Grove dweller."

GUILLERMO: (*gui-YARE-mo*) (Spanish) Variant of William.
Guillaume (gui-AHM) (French); Gillermo

GUNTHER: (German) "Battler, warrior."
Gunnar (Scandinavian)

GUSTAV: (French/German) "Royal staff."
Gustave; Gustavo (Spanish); Gus, Gustaf (Swedish)

GUY: (Latin) "Lively." See also Wyatt.
Guido (Italian); Guyon (English), Guyton

GWAYNE: (Welsh) "White hawk." Variant of the medieval name Gawain.

H

HADRIEN: (*HAY-dree-an*) (Latin) "Dark." Variant form of Adrian. The Roman Emperor Hadrian (second century A.D.) was a gifted writer and architect; he caused the Hadrian wall to be built in Britain.
Hadrian

HAKIM: (*hah-KEEM*) (Arabic) "Wise."
Hakeem

HAKON: (Scandinavian) "High-born."
Haakon, Hakan

HAL: (English) A nickname for Henry.

HALDEN: (English) "From Denmark."
Haldane

HALEN: (*HAY-len*) (Swedish) "Hall."
Hale, Hallen, Haylan

HALIM: (*ha-LEEM*) (Arabic) "Gentle."

HAMID: (Arabic) "Thankful to god." A variant of Muhammad.

HAMILTON: (Scottish) Place-name and surname of one of the great noble families of Scotland.

HAMPTON: (English) Place-name and surname.

HANK: (English) Nickname for Henry.

HANS: (Scandinavian/German/Dutch) Variant of John.
Hanson, Hansen (Dutch/Scandinavian); Han (Czech)

HARI: (*HAH-ree*) (Sanskrit) "Lion." Mythology; one of the names of Vishnu.

HARLEY: (English) "Meadow of the hares." Variants listed are related surnames.
Harlan, Harland, Harlen, Harlon, Harlow

HARMAN: (French) Variant of Herman. Harmon (Hebrew) "palace" is a biblical place-name.
Harmen, Harmon

HAROLD: (English/Teutonic) "Army commander." Herald is also literally "one who proclaims."
Herald, Heraldo; Harald (Scandinavian); Harrell

HARPER: (English) "Harpist, minstrel."

HARRY: (English) The English version of the French pronunciation of Henri. It's used as a nickname of Henry as well as of variants like Harrison and Harris.
HARRISON, Harris, Harriman

HART: (English) "Strong, brave."

Harte, Hartford, Hartley, Hartman

HARVEY: (English/Celtic) "Eager for battle."

HASSAN: (*hah-SAHN*) (Arabic) "Good-looking."
Hasan, Hassain, Hasani (Swahili) "Handsome"

HAVEN: (*HAY-ven*) (English) "A place of safety; shelter."

HAYDEN: (English) "The hill meadow."
Hayden, Haydon, Hayes

HEATH: (*heeth*) (English) Surname and place-name. Heath is a word for untended land where certain flowering shrubs grow.

HEBER: (*HEE-ber*) (Hebrew) "Partner." Biblical; an ancestor of Abraham. Also an Irish name of uncertain meaning.

HECTOR: (Greek) "Steadfast." In Homer's *Iliad*, Hector was a prince of Troy.

HENRY: (English/German) "Rules his household." A favored royal name of England and France. The second son of the current Prince of Wales is named Henry. See also Enrique, Hal, Hank and Harry.
Henri (French); Heinrich (German); Henrick, Henrik, Hendrick (Scandinavian); Henryk (Polish); Henrique

HERBERT: (French/German) "Illustrious warrior."

HERCULES: (*HERK-yoo-lees*) (Greek) "In Hera's service." Mythology; the Greek Hercules was a son of Zeus who possessed extraordinary strength.

HERMAN: (German) "Soldier." See also Harmon.

HERMES: (*HER-mees*) (Greek) "Messenger." Mythology; Hermes was messenger for the gods on Olympus and was himself the god of eloquence. He was called Mercury by the Romans.

HERNANDO: (*her-NAHN-do*) (Spanish) "Adventurous." Variant of Ferdinand.
Hernan (*her-NAHN*), Hernandez

HERSCHEL: (Yiddish) "Deer."
Hershel, Hirsch

HILARIO: (*hi-LAH-ree-oh*) (Spanish) Variant of Hilary;
(Greek) "Joyful, glad." The name of more than 30
saints.

HIRAM: (*HIGH-ram*) (Hebrew) "My brother is exalted."
Biblical; the King of Tyre, friendly to King David and
King Solomon.

HOLDEN: (English) "Sheltered valley."
Holman "man from the valley."

HOLLIS: (*HAH-liss*) (English) "The holly tree."

HOLMES: (English/Scandinavian) "Home by the river."

HOLT: (English) "By the forest."

HOMER: (Greek) "Given as hostage; promised." Two of
the greatest works of Greek epic poetry, the *Iliad* and
the *Odyssey*, are attributed to Homer.
Homar

HORACE: (Latin) From Horatius, a Roman family clan
name.
Horacio, Horatio, Horatius

HOUSTON: (*HEW-ston*) (Scottish) Place-name and surname. The name's association with the American West
is due to the Texan general Sam Houston and the city in
Texas given his name.

HOWARD: (English/Scandinavian) "Noble watchman."
Surname of one of the great houses of English nobility.
Howie

HUBERT: (*HEW-bert*) (German) "Bright, intelligent."

HUGO: (Latin/German) Variant form of Hugh; "a thinker."
See also Keegan.
Hugh, Hughie, Huey, Huw (Welsh)

HUMBERTO: (*oom-BARE-toh*) (Spanish/German) "Big,
bright."

HUMPHREY: (*HUM-free*) (German) "Peace, strength."

HUNTER: (English) "Pursuer."
Hunt, Huntington, Huntley

HUSSAIN: (*hoo-SAIN*) (Arabic) "Good." Hussein was the name of the founder of Shiite Islam.
Husain, Hussein, Husayn

HYATT: (English) Surname used as a given name.

I

IAN: (*EE-an*) Scottish form of John.
Iain

IBRAHIM: (Arabic) Variant of Abraham.

IGNACIO (*eeg-NAH-see-oh*) (Latin) "Fiery." St. Ignacius of Loyola was the founder of the Catholic Jesuit order.
Inigo

IGOR: (*EE-gor, EYE-gor*) (Russian/Scandinavian) "Warrior of peace."

ILYA: (*ILL-yah*) (Russian) Short form of Elijah.

IMMANUEL: (German) Variant form of Emanuel.

INGRAM: (Scandinavian) "Raven of peace."

IRA: (*EYE-rah*) (Hebrew) "Full-grown." Biblical; name of a priest or chief minister to King David.

IRVING: (English) "Friend." See also Ervin.
IRVIN, Irwin, Irvine, Irvyn, Irven

ISAAC: (Hebrew) "Laughter." Biblical; the only son of Abraham by his wife Sarah. Famous name bearer: Itzhak Perlman, one of the world's greatest violinists.
Issac, Izaac (Dutch); Izaak (German); Itzhak (Israeli); Ike

ISAIAH: (*eye-ZAY-ah*) (Hebrew) "Salvation of Jehovah." Biblical; one of the major prophets and writer of the Book of Isaiah.
Isaias (Spanish)

ISMAEL: (*EES-mah-el*) (Spanish/Hebrew) "God listens." Variant form of Ishmael. Biblical; the son of Abraham by Sarah's Egyptian slave woman Hagar.
Ishmael

ISRAEL: (*izz-rah-el*) (Hebrew) "God perseveres, contends." Biblical; when Jacob was in his nineties, God changed his name to Israel as a token of blessing.

IVAN: (*ee-VAHN, EYE-van*) (Russian/Slavic) Variant of John. Ivanhoe is a medieval variant Sir Walter Scott used for the Saxon hero of *Ivanhoe.*
Ivanhoe, Ivano

IVES: (English/Teutonic) "Archer's bow." Variant of Yves, from Ivar. See also Yves.
Ivar, Ivo, Ivon, Ivor

J

JA- names: (Contemporary) Blends of Ja- plus various endings, with pronunciation emphasis on the second syllable. See also Je- names.
Jamar, Jamarr, Jamari, Jamelle, Jamaine, Jamon, Jamond, Jaray, JaRonn, JaVaughn, Javon, Javan, Jayvon

JABARI: (Swahili) "Valiant."

JABIN: (*JAY-bin*) (Hebrew) "God has built." A Biblical name.

JACAN: (*JAY-kin*) (Hebrew) "Trouble." A Biblical name.
Jachin

JACINTO: (*ha-CEEN-toh*) (Spanish) Masculine form of the Greek name Hyacinth, meaning "alas."
Jax; Jacek (Polish)

JACK: (English) Name based on John or Jacques, the French form of Jacob. Jackie is used more for girls than for boys.
JACKSON, Jackie, Jacky; Jock (Scottish); Jaxon, Jax

JACOB: (Hebrew) "Supplanter." Biblical; the son of Isaac and Rebekah and twin brother of Esau. Jacob fathered 12 sons and a daughter who became the ancestors of the nation of Israel. See also Giacomo, Jack, Jake and James.
Jakob (Scandinavian/German); Jacobo (Spanish); Jacques (French); Jacobus (Latin); Yakov (Russian)

JADON: (*JAY-don*) (Hebrew) "Jehovah has heard." A Biblical name.
Jaydon, Jaedon, Jaden, Jader

JADRIEN: (*JAY-dree-en*) (Contemporary) Blend of Jay or Jade and Adrien.

JAEGAR: (*JAY-ger*) (German) "Hunter." The similar sounding Jagur, a Biblical place-name, is an Aramaic name meaning "heap of stones; marker."
Jagur

JAGO: (*JAY-goh*) (English) Variant of James used in Cornwall.

JAIRO: (*HYE-roh*) (Spanish) Variant of Jairus, a Hebrew name meaning "Jehovah enlightens."
Jairus (*JARE-us*), Jarius

JAKE: (English) Short form of Jacob.

JAKEEM: (*ya-keem*) (Hebrew/Arabic) "Raised up."

JAMAL: (*ja-MAL*) (Arabic) "Handsome."
Jamaal, Jamahl, Jamall, Jahmal, Jamael, Jamel, Jamil, Jameel, Jamile, Jamiel

JAMES: (English) Variant of Jacob. Biblical; one of the 12 apostles of Jesus, who possibly was also a cousin of Jesus. Spanish pronunciation of Jaime: *HYE-may*. Scottish: *JAY-mee*. See also Diego, Jacob, Jago, Kimo and Santiago.
JAIME, JAMIE, Jamieson (Scottish); Jimmy, Jim, Jimmie, Jem, Jameson, Jamison, Jaymes, Jayme

JAMIN: (*JAY-min*) (Hebrew) "Right hand of favor." A Biblical name.
Jamian, Jamiel, Jamon, Jaymin

JAN: (Dutch/Slavic) Variant of John.
Janek (Czech/Polish); Jansen (Scandinavian) Janse

JAPHETH: (*JAY-feth*) (Hebrew) "May He grant ample room." Biblical; the oldest of Noah's three sons.

JARAH: (*JAY-rah*) (Hebrew) "He gives sweetness; honey." Biblical; a descendant of Jonathan. See also Jerah.

Jarrah (Arabic) "vessel."

JARED: (*JARE-ed*) (Hebrew) "Descending." A pre-flood Biblical name. Popularity of Jared may have started due to the character Jared on the late Sixties TV western *The Big Valley*. Many variants with the same sound have come into use. See also Jarrod and Jerrod.

Jerad (Hebrew); Jarod, Jarad, Jaryd

JAREK: (Polish) "January child." See also Jerrick.

JARELL: (*JARE-el, ja-RELL*) (Contemporary) Blend of Jar- and Darell. See also Jerrell.

Jarrell, Jarrel, Jarel, Jaryl, Jarryl

JARETH: (*JARE-eth*) (Contemporary) Bled of Jar- or Jer- and Gareth.

Jarreth, Jereth

JARL: (Scandinavian) Roughly equivalent to the English title of Earl.

JARON: (*JARE-on*) (Israeli) "Cry of rejoicing." Some of the many contemporary names similar to Jaron may be based on a blend of the sound of Jared or Jerry and Darren.

Jarron, Jaren, Jaran, Jarin, Jarren, Jarran, Jaryn, Jerron, Jerren, Jerrin, Jeran, Jeren

JARRETT: (English) "Spear strong." Surname, variant of Garrett.

Jarett, Jarret, Jerrett, Jerett

JARROD: (English) Variant and surname form of Garrett, from Gerald. See also Jared and Jerrod.

JARRED; Jarrad, Jarryd

JARVIS: (English) Variant of the French name Gervaise, meaning "spearman."

Jervis

JASON: (Greek) "A healing." Biblical; an early Christian contemporary of Paul. Greek mythology; Jason was leader of a group of warrior heroes called the Argonauts.

JAYSON, Jasen, Jase, Jaison, Jaysen, Jaycen, Jace, Jayce

JASPER: (Arabic) Variant form of Caspar or Gaspar. Jasper is also a semiprecious gemstone, red or reddish brown. Jaspar

JAVIER: (*HAH-vee-air*) (Spanish/Portuguese) "Bright." Variant of Xavier.

JAY: (English) Short form of names like Jason and Jacob. Jay and Jai are also Sanskrit names meaning "victorious." Mythology; Jay is the name of various deities in Hindu classical writings.
Jaye, Jae, Jai, Jayron, Jayronn

JAYCEE: (Contemporary) Phonetic name based on initials.
Jayar, Jayvee, Jaydee

JE- names: (Contemporary) Blend of Je- plus various endings, with pronunciation emphasis on the second syllable. See also Ja- names.
JeMar, JeMario, Jerae, Jeron, Jerone, Jevan, Jevon, Jerell, Jerelle

JEAN: (*jeen, zhahn*) (French) Variant of John. Jean is sometimes hyphenated with a second name, and the French pronunciation (*zhahn*) may be used.
Jeanpierre, Jean-Luc, Jean-Paul, Jean-Carlo

JEDIAH: (*je-DYE-ah*) (Hebrew) "Jehovah knows." A Biblical name.
Jedaiah

JEDIDIAH: (*jed-ah-DYE-ah*) (Hebrew) "Beloved of Jehovah." Biblical; a "blessing" name given in infancy to King Solomon, David's second son by Bathsheba.
Jed, Jedd, Jedediah, Jedadiah

JEDREK: (*JEDD-rick*) (Polish) "A strong man." Variant of Andrew.
Jedrick

JEFFORD: (*JEFF-erd*) (English) Surname and place-name.

JEFFREY: (*JEFF-free*) (English) "Peaceful." Variant of

Geoffrey. The three-syllable spelling alternate Jeffery has been used since medieval times. See also Geoffrey.

JEFFERY *(JEFF-er-ee)*, Jeff, Jefferson, Jeffry

JEHU: *(JAY-hew)* (Hebrew) "Jehovah is He." Biblical; Jehu was a military commander of Israel, later king, who was noted for his pell-mell style of chariot driving.

JEMAL: *(je-MAHL)* (Arabic) "Handsome." Variant of Jamal.

JERALD: (English) Variant and surname form of Gerald. Jerold, Jerrold, Jerrald; Jeraldo (Spanish)

JERARD: *(je-RARD)* (French) Variant of Gerard. Jerrard is also an English surname.
Jerrard; Jerardo (Spanish)

JEREMIAH: *(jare-ah-MYE-ah)* (Hebrew) "Jehovah exalts." Biblical; one of the major prophets, a scholar. Besides writing the Book of Jeremiah and Lamentations, Jeremiah compiled and wrote the histories of first and second Kings. See also Jeremy.
Jeremias (Spanish)

JEREMY: *(JARE-a-mee)* (English) Variant of Jeremiah. In use since the Middle Ages.
Jeramy, Jeremie, Jeramie

JERIAH: *(jer-RYE-ah)* (Hebrew) "Jehovah has seen." A Biblical name. Jerah is the name of a Hebrew lunar month, also a given name. See also Jarah.
Jerah, Jerrah

JERICHO: *(JARE-a-koh)* (Arabic) "City of the moon." Biblical; a city in Canaan destroyed when its walls fell down.
Jerico (Spanish)

JERMAINE: *(jer-MAIN)* (English/Latin) "Brotherly." Variant of Germaine. Made popular in modern times by Jermaine Jackson, the singer.
Jermain, Jermane, Jermayne

JEROME: (*jer-ROME*) (Greek) "Sacred name." See also Geronimo.

Jeronimo (Spanish)

JERRELL: (Contemporary) "Strong, open-minded." Blend of Jerold and Darell. See also Jarell.

Jerel, Jerrel, Jerrall, Jerryl, Jeryl, Jeriel, Jerriel

JERRICK: (Contemporary) "Strong, gifted ruler." Variant based on a blend of Jer- and Derrick. See also Jarek.

Jeric, Jerick, Jerric

JERROD: (Contemporary) Variant of Garrett. See also Jared and Jarrod.

Jered, Jerad, Jerod, Jerrad, Jerred, Jerryd, Jerande

JERRY: (English) Used as an independent name, Jerry is also a short form of names beginning with Jer-. See also Gerry.

JESSE: (Hebrew) "Jehovah exists." Biblical; the shepherd father of King David. Jessie is also used for girls. The similar sounding Jesiah is a variant form of Joshua.

JESSIE, Jessy, Jess, Jessey, Jesiah

JESTIN: (*JESS-tin*) (Welsh) Variant of Justin.

Jesstin, Jeston

JESUS: (Latin/Hebrew) Short form of Joshua, from the Hebrew name Jehoshua, meaning "Jehovah is salvation." The name of the Biblical Christ is very frequently used as a given name in Spanish-speaking families. Spanish/Portuguese pronunciation is *hay-SOOS*.

JETHRO: (*JETH-roh*) (Hebrew) "Overflowing, abundance." Biblical; Moses' father-in-law, a priest of Midian.

Jett

JIRO: (*jee-roh*) (Japanese) "Second son."

JOAQUIN: (*wah-KEEN*) (Spanish) Short form of the Hebrew name Jehoichin, meaning "Jehovah has established." Joaquin Miller was a noted and colorful nineteenth-century poet-adventurer of the American west.

JOB: (*jobe*) (Hebrew) "Persecuted." Biblical; a man called by God "blameless and upright." Job is proverbial as an example of patience under trial.

Jobe, Joby

JOBEN: (*JOE-ben*) (Japanese) "Enjoy cleanness."

JODY: (*JO-dee*) (English) Nickname for Joseph and Jude.

JOE: (English) Short form of Joseph.

JOEY (*JO-ee*)

JOED: (*JO-ed*) (Hebrew) "Jehovah is witness." A Biblical name.

JOEL: (*JO-el*) (Hebrew) "Jehovah is God." Biblical; a prophet and writer of the Book of Joel.

JOHN: (Hebrew) "Jehovah has been gracious; has shown favor." Biblical; the name of the longest-lived of the 12 apostles, who was especially loved by Christ. Also the name of John the Baptist, who baptized Christ in the Jordan river. Dozens of variant forms, given names and surnames, male and female, have been created in almost every language. See also Evan, Evian, Ewen, Gian, Giovanni, Hans, Ian, Ivan, Jack, Jan, Jean, Jon, Jonathan, Jonte, Juan, Keon, Keoni, Sean, Shane and Shawn. JOHNNY, Johnnie, Johnson, John-Paul, Johnn; Jan (Dutch/Slavic); Janos (Czech); Jansen (German/Dutch); Johan, Johann, Johannes, (German); Jantzen (Danish); Jensen, Jenson (Scandinavian); Joao (Portuguese); Jhan, Jhanick, Jhon (Contemporary)

JOMEI: (*joe-MAY*) (Japanese) "Spread light."

JON: (English) Variant of John or short form of Jonathan. Jon is sometimes used in the French fashion, hyphenated with a second name. See also Jean.

Jon-Carlo, Jon-Paul, Johnny, Jonn, Jonnie

JONAH: (*JOE-nah*) (Hebrew) "Dove." Biblical; because Jonah was on board a ship when God caused it to sink, sailors have traditionally used the name to personify someone who brings bad luck.

Jonas (Spanish)

JONATHAN: (Hebrew) "Jehovah has given." Biblical; the son of King Saul, Jonathan was noted for his manliness, generosity and unselfishness. He saved David's life when Saul would have killed him.

JOHNATHAN, JONATHON, JOHNATHON

JONTE: (*jahn-TAY*) (Contemporary) Variant of Jon combined with the favored end-sound of Dante.

Jontae, Johntay, Johnte, Jontell, Jontez

JORAH: (*JOR-ah*) (Hebrew) "He has reproached." Biblical.

JORAM: (*JOR-am*) (Hebrew) "Jehovah is exalted." Jorim was an ancestor of Mary.

Jorim

JORDAN: (*JOR-dan*) (Hebrew) "Down flowing." Name of the major river in Palestine, used as a given name since the Crusades. The short form Jordi is also a Catalan variant form of George.

Jordon, Jorden, Jourdan (*jor-DAN*) (French); Jourdon, Jordain (*jor-DAIN*), Jourdaine, Jordell, Jordy, Jordi

JORELL: (*jor-ELL*) (Contemporary) Usage possibly inspired by the fictional character Jor-el, father of Superman.

Joran, Jorian, Joran, Jorian, Jorel, Jorrel, Jorrell

JOREN: (*JOR-en*) (Scandinavian) Variant of George.

Joran, Jorian, Joron, Jorn, Jory, Jorry, Jorey

JORGE: (*HOR-hay*) (Spanish/Portuguese) Variant of George.

Jorje

JOSEPH: (Hebrew) "May Jah give increase." Biblical; the son of Jacob who, sold by his brothers into slavery, rose to become a supreme power in Egypt. Also, Jesus' legal father, a carpenter. See also Giuseppe, Jody and Joe.

JOSE (Spanish/Portuguese); Joselito (Span); Josef (German/Czech); Josephus (Latin); Jomar (combination of Joseph and Mary)

JOSHUA: (Hebrew) "Jehovah is salvation." Short form of Jehoshua. Biblical; Joshua was an attendant and helper to Moses during the Israelites' 40-year trek through the Sinai wilderness. He was appointed by God to lead the Israelites after the death of Moses.

JOSUE (Span); Josh, Joss

JOSIAH: (*jo-SYE-ah*) (Hebrew) "Jehovah has healed." Biblical; king of Judah at age eight after his father was assassinated, Josiah ruled ably and well for 31 years.

Josias (Spanish), Joziah

JOTHAM: (*JO-tham*) (Hebrew) "May Jehovah complete." Biblical; a king of Judah during a time of military strife.

JOVAN: (*jo-VAHN*) (Latin) "Father of the sky." Variant form of Jove, from Jupiter. Mythology; Jupiter was the supreme deity of Roman mythology, corresponding to the Greek Zeus. Some 20 saints have used the Latin form of the name, Jovanus. The Jovani variants may also be phonetic forms of Giovanni.

Jovin, Jovon, Jovi, Jovito, Jovani, Jovany, Jovann, Jovanni, Jovanny, Jeovany, Jeovani, Jeovanni

JUAN: (*wahn*) (Spanish) Variant form of John, often used in combination with other names.

Juancarlos, Juanito "little John," Juanluis, Juanpablo

JUBAL: (*JOO-bal*) (Hebrew) "The ram." Biblical; Jubal was the inventor of the harp and the pipes, and the founder of music making.

JUDAH: (*JOO-dah*) (Hebrew) "The praised one." Biblical; Judah was the fourth of Jacob's 12 sons. Judas, the Greek form of Judah, is very rarely used, due to the infamy of Judas Iscariot. See also Jody.

Jude, Judd, Judson

JULIAN: (*JOO-lee-en*) (English/Latin) "Jove's child." Variant of Julius, the family clan name of several of the most powerful Roman emperors. Biblical; Julius, a Roman centurion, saved Paul's life during a hazardous voyage. See also Giuliano.

JULIO, (*HOO-lee-oh*) Juliano, (Spanish); Julius; Julien, Jules (French)

JURO: (*joo-ROH*) (Japanese) "Tenth son"; "best wishes"; "longevity."

JUSTIN: (English/Latin) "Just, upright, righteous." Variant of Justus. Justus is a New Testament Biblical name. The soundalike Justice is a virtue name. See also Jestin.

Justan, Justyn; Justino (Spanish/Portuguese); Justain (*juss-TAYN*), Justus, Justis, Justice.

K

KACEY: (*KAY-see*) (Contemporary) Variant of Casey or a creation based on the initials K. C. Rare. See also Casey and Kasey.

Kacy, K.C.

KADE: (Scottish/Gaelic) "From the wetlands." See also Cadell.

Kaden, Kadon, Kadrick

KADIR: (*kah-DEER*) (Arabic) "Spring greening."

KAELAN: (*KAY-lan*) (Gaelic) "Slender, fair." Variant of Caelan. See also Kellen.

Kael, Kaelin, Kalen, Kalin, Kalan, Kaley

KAEMON: (*kah-AY-mon*) (Japanese) "Joyful"; "right-handed." Old samurai name.

KAHLIL: (*kah-LEEL*) (Arabic) "Friend."

Kahleil, Kalil

KAI: (*kye*) (Welsh) "Keeper of the keys." Variant of Kay. Kai is also a Hawaiian name meaning "the sea." Kaimi is a Hawaiian name meaning "the seeker."

Kaimi (*kye-EE-mee*)

KALANI: (*kah-LAH-nee*) (Hawaiian) "The sky; chieftain."

KALEB: See also Caleb.

KALVIN: See also Calvin.
Kalvyn

KAMDEN: "Winding Valley." See also Camden.

KAMERON: See also Cameron.
Kamron, Kam

KANA: (*KAH-nah*) (Hawaiian) Mythology; a Maui demi-god who could take the form of a rope and stretch from Molokai to Hawaii. Kano (Japanese) "One's masculine power, capability."
Kano (*kah-noh*)

KANE: (Irish) "Fighter." Kane (*kah-NAY*) is also a Japanese surname meaning "putting together"; "money." See also Caine.
Kaine, Kain, Kayne

KANNON: (Japanese) Variant of Kuan-yin, the Chinese Buddhist deity of mercy. Kannan (Sanskrit) is a variant of Krishna.
Kannan, Kannen

KANOA: (*kah-NO-ah*) (Hawaiian) "The free one."

KAORI: (*kah-oh-ree*) (Japanese) "Add a man's strength."

KARIM: (*kah-REEM*) (Arabic) "Generous; a friend." The Koran lists generosity as one of the 99 qualities of God.
Kareem, Kharim

KARL: (Scandinavian/German) "Man, manly." See also Carl.
Karle, Karlo, Karlos, Karson, Karlin, Karlton, Karel

KASEY: (Irish) "Alert, vigorous." Variant of Casey. See also Kacey.

KASIMIR: (*KAZ-e-meer*) (Slavic) "Enforces peace." The name of the patron saint of Poland; also a favored name of Polish royalty. See also Casimir.
Kazimir, Kaz

KASPAR: (Polish) "Keeper of the treasure." Variant of Caspar.

KASSIDY: See also Cassidy.

KASSIM: (*kah-seem*) (Arabic) "Divided."
Kaseem, Kasim

KEANE: (*keen*) (English/Irish) "Ancient." Keandre (*kee-AHN-dray*) is a contemporary blend of "Ke-" and Andre.
Keene, Keandre, Keannen

KEARN: (Irish) "Dark."
Kearne, Kearney

KEATON: (*KEE-ton*) (English) "Place of the hawks."

KEDRICK: (English) "Gift of splendor." Variant of Cedric.
Keddrick, Kedric

KEEFE: (Irish) "Noble, gentle."

KEEGAN: (Irish) "A thinker; fiery." Variant of Hugh.
Kegan, Keagan, Kagan, Kagen

KEENAN: (Irish) Surname.
Kenan, Keenon

KEIJI: (*KAY-jee*) (Japanese) "Govern with discretion."

KEIR: (*KEE-er*) (Irish/Gaelic) "Dusky; dark-haired." A name made familiar by the actor Keir Dullea.

KEITARO: (*kay-tah-ROH*) (Japanese) "Blessed."

KEITH: (Scottish) "Woodland." Surname and place-name.

KELBY: (Gaelic/Scandinavian) "Place by the fountain; spring."

KELLEN: (Gaelic) "Slender, fair." See also Kaelan.
Kellan, Keelan, Keilan, Keillan, Kelle, Kelden

KELLY: (Irish) "Lively; aggressive."

KELVIN: (English/Celtic) "River man."
Kelvan, Kelven

KEN: (English) Short form of names beginning with "Ken-." Ken is also a Japanese name meaning "strong, physically healthy." Kenn is an English surname.
Kenn, Kennan

KENDALL: (English) "Royal valley." Surname referring to Kent, England.

Kendell, Kendal, Kendel, Kendale

KENDREW: (Scottish) "Manly, brave." Variant of Andrew.

KENDRICK: (Welsh/Scottish) "Royal chieftain." Surname.

Kendrik, Kendric, Kendrix, Kenrick, Kenrik

KENJI: (*KEN-jee*) (Japanese) "Intelligent second son, strong and vigorous." Kenjiro (*ken-jee-ROH*) "Second son who sees with insight; longsighted."

KENNARD: (Gaelic) "Brave chieftain."

Kenner, Kendon

KENNETH: (English/Scottish) "Good-looking, fair." See also Kenny.

KENNY: (Scottish) Surname and short form of Kenneth.

Kenney, Kennan, Kinney, Kennon

KENT: (English) "Royal chieftain."

Kenton, Kentrell

KENTARO: (*ken-tah-ROH*) (Japanese) "Sharp, big boy."

KEOKI: (*kee-OH-kee*) (Hawaiian) Variant of George.

KEON: (*KEE-an*) (Irish) Variant of Ewan, from John. See also Ewan.

Kian (Gaelic) "ancient"; Keondre

KEONI: (*kee-OH-nee*) (Hawaiian) Variant of John.

KERRICK: (English) "King's rule." English surname.

KERRY: (Irish/Gaelic) "Dusky, dark." Surname and name of the county in Ireland. Kerrigan is an Irish surname with the same meaning.

Kerrigan

KERWIN: (Irish) "Little dark one."

KEVIN: (Irish) "Handsome child." Name of a famous Irish hermit-saint. There are many spelling variants, but Kevin is by far the most popular.

Keven, Kevan, Kevyn, Kevon, Kevinn, Keveon, Kevion, Kevis, Kevron

KHANH: (*kahn*) (Turkish/Arabic) "Prince." Title used by central Asian tribal chieftains or ruling princes.

KIEFER: (*KEE-fer*) (German) "Barrelmaker." Variant form of Cooper.
Keifer, Keefer

KIERON: (*KEER-en*) (Irish/Gaelic) "Dusky, dark-haired."
Keiran, Kyran; Kiran (Sanskrit) "Beam of light"

KILIAN: (*KIL-ee-an*) (Irish) "Small, fierce."
Killian

KIM: (English) Short form of Kimball or Kimberly. Kim is also a Vietnamese name meaning "precious metal; gold."

KIMBALL: (English) "Bold kin." The related name Kimberly is almost entirely used for girls today.

KIMO: (*KEE-moh*) (Hawaiian) Variant of James and Jim.

KINGSLEY: (English) "King's field." King is one of several titles occasionally used as given names. Other male title-names are Prince, Duke, Earl, Count, Marquis, Caesar, Czar and Khanh.
King, Kingston, Kinsley

KIRBY: (English) "Church farm."

KIRK: (Scottish/Scandinavian) "Church." In Scotland, kirk is still used as a word meaning "church."
Kirkland, Kirklin, Kirklyn, Kerk, Kyrk, Kyrksen

KIT: (English) Nickname for Christopher. Notable name bearer, frontiersman Kit Carson.

KNUTE: (*k'NOOT*) (Scandinavian) "Knot." Variant form of Canute, the name of an eleventh-century king of Denmark and England.

KODY: "Helpful." See also Cody.
Kodey, Kodie

KOI: (*KO-ee*) (Hawaiian) "Urge, implore." Also the Hawaiian equivalent of Troy.

KOLBY: "Dark, dark-haired." Koby is a German/Polish short form of Jacob. See also Colby.

Kelby, Koby

KOLTON: "Coal town." See also Colton.

Kolt, Koltin, Kolten

KONNOR: "Desiring." See also Connor.

KONRAD: (Polish/German) "Bold adviser." See also Conrad.

KORBIN: "Raven-haired." See also Corbin.

KORDELL: "Cordmaker." See also Cordell.

Kord, Kordale

KORRIGAN: "Spearman." See also Corrigan.

KORT: (German/Dutch) Variant of Cort.

KORY: See also Cory.

Korey, Korry, Korrey

KRAIG: "Rock; rocky." See also Craig.

KRIS: (Scandinavian) Short form of names beginning with "Kris-."

KRISTIAN: (Scandinavian) Variant of Christian.

KRISTOPHER: (Scandinavian) Variant of Christopher.

Kristofer, Kristoffer, Krystopher, Khristopher; Kristoff, Kristof, Krystof (Czech)

KRUZ: "Cross." See also Cruz.

KURT: (German) "Brave, wise."

KURTIS: "Courtier." See also Curtis.

Kurtiss

KYLE: (Irish/Gaelic) Possibly a place-name referring to "the narrows," "a wood" or "a church."

Kile, Kiley, Kyler, Kylan, Kylar, Kylen, Kye, Kyrell

L

LA- names: (Contemporary) Blends of La- plus various endings, with pronunciation emphasis on the second syllable. Second syllable might or might not begin with a capital. See also Lamar, Lamont and Le- names.

Ladale, Ladell, Lajon, Lamarcus, LaMario, LaRay, Larenzo, LaRico, Larell, Larenzo, Laron, LaRon, Laroy,

Laroyce, LaSean, LaShawn, Laval, Lavante, LaVar, Lavaughn, Lavell, Lavelle, Lavon, Lavonte

LACHLAN: (*LOCK-lin*) (Scottish) "From the land of lakes."

LAFAYETTE: (*lah-fay-ett*) (French) Surname. Historical; the Marquis de Lafayette, a French nobleman, was only twenty when he came to serve four years in the American Revolutionary cause.

LAIRD: (Scottish) "Lord." Scottish landholder's title.

LAMAR: (French) "Of the sea." Surname.

LaMarr, Lamarr

LAMONT: (Scandinavian/Gaelic) "Man of law." Lamond is a Scottish clan name.

Lamonte, Lamond

LANCE: (French) "Lance, lancer." Mythology; in the tales of King Arthur, Sir Lancelot was the most renowned Knight of the Round Table. Lantz is a Yiddish name meaning "lancet." See also Lanzo.

Lancelot, Lantz, Launcelot

LANDON: (English) "Landowner."

LANE: (English) "Path, roadway."

Layne

LANGDON: (English) "From the long hill slope." Related English surnames: Langley "long meadow"; Langston "long stone."

Langley, Langston

LANNY: (English) Short form of names like Roland and Lanzo.

Lannie

LANZO: (*LAHN-zo*) (Italian) Variant form of Lance. See also Lonzo.

Lanza

LARAMIE: (*LARE-a-mee*) (French) Surname with western associations because of Laramie, Wyoming, a town on the Overland Trail, route of the Pony Express.

LARNELL: (*lar-NELL*) (Contemporary) Blend of Larry and Darnell.

LARRY: (English) Short form of Lawrence and Laurence, often used as an independent name.

LARS: (Scandinavian) Variant of Lawrence.
Larsen, Larson

LASALLE: (*la-SAL*) (French) "The hall."

LATHAN: (Contemporary) Rhyming variant of Nathan.

LAUREAN: (Contemporary) Variant of Lauren, from Laurence.
Laurian, Laureano, Lauriano

LAWRENCE: (English/Latin) "From the place of the laurel trees." Lawrence, a later English form of Laurence, is the preferred form of the name in America. See also Lars, Laurean, Loren, Lorenzo, Lorne and Renzo.
Laurence; Lauro (Italian); Laurent (French); Laurenz (German); Laurens (Dutch); Lorence, Lorance, Lawson, Lawton

LE- names: (Contemporary) Blend of Le- plus various endings, with pronunciation emphasis on the second syllable. See also La- names.
Ledell, Lemar, Leondre, LeRon, Lerone, LeSean, LeShawn, Latroy, Levell, Levelle, Levon, LeWayne

LEANDRO: (Latin/Greek) "Lionlike man." Variant of Leander. Leandre (French); Leander (English); Leandrew (Contemporary)

LEE: (English) Surname frequently used in the American south as a given name in honor of the Confederate general Robert E. Lee.

LEIF: (*life*) (Scandinavian) "Son, descendant." According to Norse legend, the Viking Leif Eriksson landed his longboat on American shores some 500 years before Columbus arrived.

LEIGHTON: (*LAY-ton*) (English) "Meadow town."
Layton

LELAND: (English) "Pasture ground."
Leeland

LEMUEL: (*LEM-you-el*) (Hebrew) "Belonging to God."
Biblical; a king mentioned in Proverbs 31 who was
given a detailed description of the value and capabilities
of a good wife.

LENNOX: (Scottish) Surname and clan name. Lennox, a
Scottish nobleman, appears in Shakespeare's *Macbeth*.

LENNY: (English) Short form of Leonard.
Len, Lenn, Lennie, Lennell

LEO: (English/Latin) "Lion."

LEON: (English/French/German) "Lion." The lion is a
central figure in the art and religious symbolism of
many different cultures, usually meaning kingliness,
grandeur and courage. See also Lionel.
Lion, Lyon

LEONARD: (*LEN-ard*) (French/German) "Lion-bold." Notable name bearer of Leonardo is Leonardo da Vinci,
considered to be one of the most brilliant and creative
men who ever lived. See also Lenny.
LEONARDO (Italian/Spanish/Portuguese); Lenard,
Lennard

LEOPOLD: (English/German) "A bold man."
Leopoldo (Spanish/Italian/Portuguese)

LERON: (*le-RON*) (French) "The circle." Also an Israeli
name meaning "my song."

LEROUX: (*la-ROO*) (French) "The red-haired one."
Larue

LEROY: (French) "The king."
LeeRoy, Leroi, LeRoy

LESLIE: (*LEZ-lee*) (Scottish) The name of a prominent
Scottish clan.
Les

LESTER: (English) "Fortified place."

LEVI: (*LEE-vye*) (Hebrew) "Joined." Biblical; Levi, third

of Jacob's 12 sons, became father of the tribe that was later assigned priestly duties.

LEWIS: (English) "Renowned fighter." Variant of Louis. See also Louis and Luis.
Lew

LEX: (English) Short form of Alexander.

LIAM: (*LYE-am*) (Irish) Variant of William.
Lyam

LINCOLN: (*LINK-en*) (English/Latin) "Lakeside colony." The name of an early Roman settlement in England.
Linc

LINDELL: (English) "From the linden tree dell."
Lendell, Lendall, Lin, Lindel, Linwood

LINUS: (*LYE-nus*) (Latin/Greek) "Net." Biblical; a Christian companion to Paul in Rome. Today, Linus has been made familiar by the child character in Schultz's cartoon *Peanuts*.

LIONEL: (English/French) "Young lion."
LEONEL (Spanish); Lionell, Lonell, Lonnell

LLEWELLYN: (*loo-ELL-an*) (Welsh) "Lionlike."
Lewellyn, Lew

LLOYD: (Welsh) "Gray." See also Floyd.
Loyd

LOCKE: (English) Surname referring to a lock or locksmith.

LOGAN: (Scottish) "Low meadow."
Logen

LONNIE: (English) An independent name and short form of Lionel and Alonzo.
Lonny, Lon, Lonne, Lonell, Lonnell

LONZO: (Spanish) "Ready, eager." Short form of Alonzo. See also Lanzo.
Lonza, Lonzell

LORCAN: (*LOR-ken*) (Irish) "Little fierce one."

LOREN: (English) Variant of Lorenzo and Lawrence.

Loran, Lorin, Lorren, Loryn

LORENZO: (Spanish/Italian) Variant of Lawrence. Notable name bearer: Lorenzo de' Medici, a Renaissance patron of Michaelangelo and Da Vinci. See also Lawrence and Renzo.

Lorenz (German); Larenzo

LORNE: (Scottish) Surname; also a variant form of Lawrence.

Lornell

LOUIS: (*LOO-iss*) (English) (*loo-WEE*) (French) (French/Teutonic) "Renowned fighter." A name used by 18 French Kings. See also Lewis and Luis.

Louie, Lou; Luigi (Italian)

LOVELL: (*la-VELL*) (English/French) "Young wolf."

Lowell (*LOW-el*)

LOYAL: (English/French) "Faithful, unswerving." See also Lyle.

LUCAS: (English/Latin) "Light, illumination." Variant of Luke. See also Luke.

Luc (French); Luciano, Lucio (Italian/Spanish/Portuguese); Lucian, Lucien (French); Lucius (English/Latin); Lucan

LUCKY: (English) "Fortunate." Lucky is also used as a nickname for Lucas and its variants.

LUIS: (*loo-EECE*) (Spanish) Variant of Louis. See also Lewis and Louis.

LUKE: (Latin/Greek) "Light giving." Biblical; a first-century Christian, called "the beloved physician," who wrote one of the four Gospel accounts of the life of Christ. See also Lucas.

Luka, Lukas (Dutch)

LUTHER: (German) "Renowned warrior."

Lothar

LYDELL: (*li-DELL*) (Scottish) Surname used as a given name.

LYLE: (French) "Islander." Lyell and Lyall are Scottish
surnames meaning "loyal." See also Loyal.
Lyell, Lyall

LYNDON: (English) "Place of linden trees." See Lindell.
Lyndale, Lyndall, Lyndell

LYSANDER: (*lye-SAN-der*) (Greek) "Liberator." Lysander
is one of the main characters in Shakespeare's *A Mid-
summer Night's Dream*.
Lisandro (Spanish)

M

MAC: (Gaelic) "Son of." Scottish and Irish surname prefix
used as a given name or nickname. Mack is an ancient
Scottish given name. See also Mc- names, Mackenzie
and Maxwell.
Mack, Mackey, Macklin

MACE: (English) Short form of names like Macy and Mason; also an English surname that may be a form of
Matthew. Literally, a mace was a medieval weapon used
by knights. See Martel.
Macerio (Spanish); Macey, Macy

MACKENZIE: (*ma-KEN-see*) (Scottish) "Son of Kenzie;
fair, favored one."

MADISON: (English) Surname derived from Matthew,
"gift of Jah," or Matilda, "strong fighter."

MAGNUS: (*MAG-ness*) (Latin) "Great, greatness." A
name favored by Scandinavian royalty.

MAJOR: (Latin) "Greater." Surname that is also a military
rank.

MAKANI: (*ma-KAH-nee*) (Hawaiian) "Wind."

MAKOTO: (*mah-KOH-toh*) (Japanese) "Good."

MALACHI: (*MAL-a-kye*) (Hebrew) "Messenger of God."
Biblical; a prophet and writer of the final book of the
Old Testament.

MALCOLM: (*MAL-cum*) (Scottish) "St. Columb's disciple."

Malcom

MALIK: (*MAL-lik, MAY-lik*) (Arabic) "Master."

MANFRED: (German) "Man of peace."

MANO: (*MAH-no*) (Hawaiian) "Shark." Figuratively, a passionate lover. Mano (Spanish) is a short form of Manuel.

MANUEL: (Spanish) "With us is God." Short form of Emmanuel.

Manolo, Manuelo, Manolito, Manny, Mannie

MANZO: (*MAHN-zoh*) (Japanese) "10,000-fold-strong third son."

MAR- names: (Contemporary) Blends based on Mark plus other names. See also Marquis and Mark.

Markaine, Markeith, Marquel, Marsean, Marshawn, Marshon

MARC: (French) See Mark.

MARCEL: (*mar-SELL*) (French) Variant of the Latin Marcellus, from Marcus. See also Marcus.

Marcell; Marcelo, Marcelino; Marcello, Marcellus, Marciano (Italian); Marceau (*mar-so*) (French)

MARCUS: (Latin) "Of Mars." Mythology: Mars, the Roman god of fertility, for whom the spring calendar month March was named, became identified with the Greek Ares, god of war. See also Marcel, Mark and Marquis.

MARCOS (Spanish/Portuguese); Marcas (Irish/Scottish); Markus, Markos (German/Dutch, Hungarian); Marcio (Italian)

MARDEN: (English) Surname used as a given name.

Mardel, Mardon

MAREO: (*mah-RAY-oh*) (Japanese) "Rare, uncommon."

MARIANO: (*mahr-ee-AHN-oh*) (Spanish) Masculine variant of Marie. Marion, the English form (Marian for girls), is very rarely used for American boys today.

MARINO: (*ma-REE-no*) (Latin) "Of the sea."

MARIO: (Latin) Masculine form of Mary. A number of male names have been created as variants of names attributed to the Virgin Mary. See also Mariano.

Marius

MARK: (English/Latin) "Of Mars, the god of war." Variant of Marcus. Biblical; the Roman surname of John Mark, missionary companion to Peter and Paul and writer of one of the four Gospel accounts of the life of Jesus. See also Marcel, Marcus, Martin and Marquis.

MARC (French); MARCO (Spanish/Portuguese); Marko, Markov (Russian); Marek (Czech); Markus (Scandinavian); Marquez (Spanish); Marques (Portuguese); Marx, Markel, Markell (German); Marq, Marque, Markey

MARLON: (English) Possibly a variant form of Merle. Marlin is occasionally used for girls.

Marlan, Marland, Marlin

MARLOW: (English) "Marshy meadow." Marlowe and Marley are occasionally used for girls.

Marlowe, Marley

MARO: (*MAH-roh*) (Japanese) "Myself."

MARQUIS: (*mar-KEECE, MAR-kuss*) (Contemporary) Phonetic variants indicate that parents favor *mar-KEECE*, probably using Marquis as a title name, ranking below a duke and above an earl. Marquis (*MAR-kuss*) is a variant of a Scottish surname.

Marquise (Italian); Marques (Portuguese); Marquez (Spanish); Markeese, Marqui, Markeece, Markese

MARSHALL: (English/French) "Caretaker of horses." In America "marshal" is a law-enforcement title similar to sheriff. In France, the title refers to a high military rank.

Marshal, Marsh, Marshawn, Marzell

MARSTON: (English) "Town near the marsh."
Marsten

MARTIN: (English/Latin) "Warrior of Mars."
Marten (Scandinavian); Martino, Martinus (Italian); Marty, Martyn (English); Marton (Hungarian); Marti (Swiss); Martell, Martel (German)

MARVIN: (English) Variant of Mervin.
Marvyn, Marven, Marwin

MASON: (English) "Worker in stone; stonemason."

MATTHEW: (Hebrew) "Gift of Jehovah." Biblical; the name of one of the 12 apostles, who wrote the first gospel account of the life of Jesus. The alternate spelling Mathew is an English surname variant spelling.
MATHEW, Matt, Matthias (*ma-THYE-us*) (English); Matias, Mateo (Spanish); Mathias (Scandinavian/ Welsh); Matteo (Italian); Mateus (Portuguese); Matthieu, Mathieu (French); Matheson (Scottish)

MAURICE: (*maw-REESE*) (English/French) "Dark-skinned; Moor." See also Merrick and Morris.
Mauricio, Maureo (Spanish/Portuguese); Mauro, Maurio (Italian); Maurin, Morino

MAVERICK: (*MAV-rick*) (Contemporary) A nineteenth-century American named Maverick refused to brand his calves as other ranchers did; his name entered the common language signifying an independent man who avoids conformity.
Mavrick

MAX: (Latin) "The greatest."
Maximo (Italian); Maxim (Russian); Maxime (*max-eem*) (French); Maximino, Maximiliano (Italian); Maximilian, Maximillian (English/German)

MAXFIELD: (English) "Field belonging to Mack."

MAXWELL: (English/Scottish) "Mack's well." See also Mac.

MAYER: (English/German) "Headman, mayor."

Meyer, Meir (Hebrew) "Shining"

MAYNARD: (French/German) "Powerful."

Maynor, Mayne

Mc- names: (Scottish/Irish) Surnames occasionally used as given names. See also Mac.

McArthur, McCain, McCarthy, McCaulay, McCormick, Magregor, McKade, McKay, McKinley, McClain

MEADE: (English/Irish) "Honey wine" or "meadow."

MELVIN: (English) Meaning uncertain; possibly "friend of Michael."

Melvon, Melvyn, Mel

MERCER: (English/French) "Merchant." Rare.

MERLE: (French) "Blackbird." Country-western singer Merle Haggard has made this name familiar today.

MERLIN: (Welsh) "Sea fortress." Mythology; Arthurian tales describe Merlin as the wizard who was King Arthur's mentor. See also Mervin.

Merlyn

MERRICK: (Welsh) Variant of Maurice.

Myrick

MERRILL: (English) "Shining sea."

Merril

MERRITT: (English) "Worthy."

MERVIN: (Welsh) Variant of Merlin. See also Marvin.

Mervyn, Merwyn

MICAH: (*MYE-cah*) (Hebrew) "Who is like Jah?" Biblical; a prophet and writer of the Book of Micah.

MICHAEL: (Hebrew) "Who is like God?" Michael the archangel (chief or principal angel) and Gabriel are the only two angels given personal names in the canonical Bible. Many saints, emperors and kings have borne the name, and there are many variants, male and female. In this century, Michael has been among the top 50 names for at least seven decades. Micheal, the Gaelic spelling, is frequently used. This may be intentional, or it may be

an accidental transposition of the "ae" vowels. See also
Mike, Mischa and Mitchell.

MIGUEL (Spanish/Portuguese); MICHEAL (Irish/
Scottish); Michel (French/Dutch); Mikael, Mikell,
Mikkel (Scandinavian); Mikhail, Michail (Russian);
Michal (Polish); Miko (Slavic); Mikel, Miquel (Basque/
French); Mychal, Mychael

MICHIO: (*mee-chee-OH*) (Japanese) "Man with strength
of three thousand."

MIKE: (English) Short form of Michael and Micah, often
used as an independent name. The nicknames Mick and
Mickey are considered to be particularly Irish. See also
Mischa.
Mickey, Mick

MIKI: (*MEE-kee*) (Japanese) "Tree." Mikio (*mee-kee-oh*)
"Three trees together."
Mikio

MILES: (English) "Merciful." See also Myles.
Milo, Mylo

MILLER: (English) "One who grinds grain." Occupational
surname.
Millard, Millen

MILTON: (English) "Mill town."

MINORU: (*mee-NOH-roo*) (Japanese) "Bear fruit."

MISCHA: (*MEE-sha*) (Russian) Nickname for Michael.
See also Mike.

MITCHELL: (English/Scottish/Irish) Variant of Michael.
Mitchel, Mitch

MODESTO: (*mo-DESS-toh*) (Latin) "Modesty, moderate."
A Spanish saint's name.

MOHAMMAD: (Arabic) "Praiseworthy, glorified." Name
of the founder of the Islamic religion. Listed here are
only a few of the dozens of names and name variants attributed to Mohammad. See also Ahmed and Hamid.

Mohammed, Mohamed, Mohamad, Muhammad, Muhammed, Mahmoud, Mohamet

MONROE: (Scottish) "From the river's mouth."

MONTAGUE: (*MON-tah-gew*) (French) "Steep mountain."

MONTANA: (*mon-TAN-nah*) (Latin) "Mountain." The name of the western state used as a given name.
Montaine (*mon-TAYNE*) (French)

MONTARO: (*mon-tah-ROH*) (Japanese) "Big boy."

MONTE: (*MON-tee, mon-TAY*) (Italian/Spanish) "Mountain." Short forms of Montague and Montgomery.
Monty, Montie (English); Montay, Montae, Montel, Montrell, Montrel, Montrelle, Montes, Montez (*mon-TEZ*)

MONTGOMERY: (English/French) "Mountain of the one who rules." A surname of English and Scottish earls.

MORELL: (*moh-REL*) (French) "Dark one; the Moor."

MORGAN: (Welsh) "Of the sea." Surname.
Morgen

MORIO: (*mor-ee-OH*) (Japanese) "Forest boy."

MORLAND: (English) "Marsh, wet land."

MORRIS: (*MOR-iss*) (English) "Dark." Variant of Maurice.
Morrey, Morrie, Morrison, Morse

MOSES: (*MOH-ziss*) (Hebrew) "Saved from the water." Biblical; name of the Hebrew child pulled out of the Nile river and adopted by the Egyptian Pharaoh's daughter. Moses lived one of the most eventful lives recorded in Scripture (see the Book of Exodus). Moss is an English medieval form of Moses.
MOISES (Spanish); Moshe (Hebrew); Moss, Mosiah

MURRAY: (*MUR-ee*) (Scottish) "From the sea." Surname of an ancient Scottish clan, occasionally used as a given name.

MYLES: (English) Variant form of Miles.

MYRON: (Aramaic/Arabic) "Myrrh, sweet oil."

N

NAMIR: (*nah-MEER*) (Israeli) "Leopard."

NAPOLEON: (*na-POH-lee-an*) (French/Italian) "Man from Naples."

NARDO: (Latin/German) "Strong, hardy." Short form of names like Bernardo and Leonardo.

NATHAN: (*NAY-than*) (Hebrew) "Given." Biblical; Nathan was God's prophet during the reigns of David and Solomon.
Nate, Nat

NATHANIEL: (*na-THAN-yel*) (Hebrew) "God has given." Biblical; one of the 12 apostles.
Nathanael (French); Nathanial

NAVARRO: (*na-VAR-oh*) (Spanish) "Plains." The name of a medieval kingdom in Spain.
Navarre (French)

NED: (English) Nickname for Edward.

NEHEMIAH: (*nee-ah-MYE-ah*) (Hebrew) "Jah comforts." Biblical; the prophet assigned to lead the Jews on their return to Jerusalem from exile in Babylon.

NEIL: (*neel*) (Gaelic/Scandinavian) "Champion." Scottish variant form of Niall. See also Nelson, Niall, Niles and Nyles.
NEAL (English); Neill, Neilan (Irish/Scottish); Neale, Neel

NELSON: (English/Gaelic) "Son of Neil."
Nels

NESTOR: (Greek) "Remembers." In legend, the learned Greek general who gave counsel during the Trojan War.

NEVADA: (*ne-VAH-dah*) (Spanish) "Snow-clad." The name of the western state used as a given name.

NEVILLE: (*NEV-il*) (English/French) "New village."

NIALL: (*NYE-al*) (English) (*NEE-al*) (Irish) "Champion." Historical; Niall of the Nine Hostages founded a dynasty of Irish kings. See also Neil, Nigel, Niles and Nyles.

NICHOLAS: (Greek) "Victorious; conquerer of the people." Biblical; one of seven "qualified men" in the first-century Christian congregation. St. Nicholas (fourth century) is known as the patron saint of Greece and Russia, children, scholars, sailors and pawnbrokers. Because Nicholas was such a popular name during the Middle Ages, many variant and short forms were created for men and women. Five popes and two emperors of Russia have borne the name. See also Cole, Colin and Nick.

NICOLAS (Spanish/French); NICKOLAS, Nicolai, Nicholai; Nikolas, Niklos (Slavic); Nikolaus, Nickolaus (German); Nikolai (Polish/Russian); Nicoli, Nicolo, Niccolo (Italian); Nicol (Scottish/English); Nikolos (Greek); Nicholaus, Nicolaus; Niklas, Nils, Niels, Nielsson, Neilson, Nilsen (Scandinavian)

NICK: (English) Short form of Nicholas. Mythology; the name Nicholas refers to Nike (*NYE-kee*), the Greek goddess of victory. Nikki and Nikko are also Japanese surnames with the potential meanings "two trees" and "daylight."

Nico, Nicky, Nikki, Nikko, Niko, Nikos, Nykko, Nickson, Nixon

NIGEL: (*NYE-jel*) (English/Scandinavian/Gaelic) Variant of Niall. The name traveled well. Niall in Ireland and Scotland became Njal in Scandinavia, was Latinized to Nigellus in Normandy, then finally became Nigel in England.

Niguel (*ni-GEL*) (Spanish), Nijel, Nygel

NILES: (English) Variant of Niall. See also Nyles.

NOAH: (Hebrew) "Rest, consolation." Biblical; the patriarch survivor of the great flood. According to the Biblical account, all the world's nations are descended from Noah's three sons.

NOE (Spanish)

NOEL: (*NOH-el*) (French) "Birth day." Commonly used in reference to Christ's birth, Noel is also an alternate name for Christmas.

NOLAN: (Irish) "Renowned, noble."
Nolen, Noland, Nolyn

NORBERT: (*NOR-bert*) (English/German) "Shining from the North."
Norberto

NORMAN: (English/German) "Man of the north."
Norman, Normand; Normando (Spanish)

NORRIS: (Scottish/English) "From the north."

NURI: (Israeli) "My fire."
Nuru (Swahili) "Born at night."

NYLES: (English) Variant of Niles, from Niall.

O

O'- names: (Irish) "Descendent of." Surnames occasionally used as given names.
O'Brian, O'Brien, Odell, O'Keefe, O'Shea, O'Shay

OCTAVIO: (*ahk-TAH-vee-oh*) (Latin) "Eighth."
Octavius, Octavian

OLAF: (*OH-loff*) (Scandinavian) "Ancestral heritage."
Olav

OLIVER: (English/French) "The olive tree." Biblical; the olive tree is a symbol of fruitfulness, beauty and dignity. Today "extending an olive branch" traditionally signifies an offer of peace.

OMAR: (*OH-mar*) (Arabic) "Long-lived." (Hebrew) "Speaker." Biblical; a sheik of Edom and son of Esau. Omar Khayyám (twelfth century) was a Persian poet, astronomer and mathematician. Caliph Omar II made Islam an imperial power.
Omarr, Omari (Swahili) "God the highest"

OREL: (Russian/Slavic) "Eagle."
Orrel, Oriel, Oral, Orell, Orry

OREN: (Hebrew) "Pine tree." See also Orrin.
   Orin, Oran (Gaelic) "Cold spring" or "green"
ORION: (*oh-RYE-on*) (Greek) "Rising in the sky; dawning." Greek mythology; Orion was a mighty hunter, the son of Poseidon. The Orion constellation contains three of the most conspicuous stars in the nighttime sky.
ORLANDO: (*or-LAHN-doh*) (Spanish/German) "Renowned in the land." Variant form of Roland.
   Orlan, Orland, Orlin, Orlondo
ORRIN: (English) The name of a river in England. See also Oren.
   Orran, Orren
ORSON: (Latin) "Little bear." Notable name bearer: actor/director Orson Welles.
   Orsino (Italian)
ORVILLE: (*OR-vul*) (French) "Gold town."
   Orvelle (*or-VELL*), Orvil
OSCAR: (English) "God's spear."
   Oskar (Scandinavian)
OSMAN: (English/Scandinavian) "Godly protection."
   Osmin, Osmond, Osmund, Oswin "God's friend."
OSWALD: (English) "God's power."
   Oswaldo (Spanish), Ozzie, Ozzy
OTTO: (German) "Wealthy."
   Otis
OWEN: (Welsh) "Wellborn." Variant of Ewan.
   Owynn

P

PALMER: (English/Latin) "Bearing a palm branch."
PANCHO: (*PAHN-cho*) (Spanish) Nickname for Francisco, Frank.
PARIS: (French) The name of the French capital used as a given name. Greek mythology; Paris was the Prince of

Troy whose love affair with Helen led to the Trojan War.

Parris, Parrish

PARKER: (English) "Keeper of the forest; forest ranger." A surname made familiar as a given name today by actor Parker Stevenson.

PARNEL: (English/Irish) Surname derived from a medieval given name. Use of Parnell may be in honor of Charles Parnell, nineteenth-century Irish Nationalist.

Parris, Parnell

PASCUAL: (*pahs-KWALL*) (Spanish/Hebrew) "Passover."

Pasqual; Pasquale (Italian); Pascal (French); Pascoe

PATRICK: (English/Irish/Latin) "Patrician, noble." The Romans once were divided socially and politically into plebeians (commoners) and patricians (aristocrats). Patrick, patron saint of Ireland, has given the name its Irish associations. See also Peyton.

Patricio (Spanish/Portuguese); Patric (French); Paden (Scottish); Padric, Padraic (Irish); Pat

PAUL: (English/French/Latin) "Little." Biblical; the apostle evangelist. Paul's letters to early Christians form the majority of the books of the New Testament.

PABLO (Spanish); Paolo (Italian); Paulo, Paulino (Portuguese); Poul, Pal (Scandinavian); Pauel (Dutch); Paulus (Latin); Pavel (Slavic); Pavlik, Pavlo (Russian); Paulson (English); Paulsen (Dutch/Scandinavian)

PERCY: (English/French) "Pierces."

Percival, Perceval

PERRY: (Latin) "Wanderer." (English) Surname and a short form of Peregrine. The peregrine falcon is the bird most favored in the ancient sport of falconry.

Peregrine (*PARE-a-green*)

PETER: (English/Greek) "A rock." Biblical; one of the 12 apostles, Peter the fisherman is remembered for his impulsive nature as well as for his rocklike faith. In

Catholic tradition, the first pope. There are dozens of variants of the name in many languages. See also Pierce.

PEDRO (Spanish/Portuguese); Pietro (Italian); Petros (Greek); Pierre (French); Piers (English/French); Per, Peer (German/Scandinavian); Pieter (Dutch); Petrov, Pyotr (Russian); Peadar (Gaelic); Pete, Peterson, Pernell (English)

PEYTON: (Irish) Variant of Patrick.
Payton

PHILLIP: (English/Greek) "Fond of horses." Biblical; one of the 12 apostles. See also Felipe.
PHILIP (English); Philippe (French); Phil

PHILO: (*FYE-loh*) (Greek) "Loves" or "loved."

PIERCE: (English/Irish) Variant of Piers, from Peter.
Pearce, Pearson, Pierson

PRENTICE: (English) "Apprentice, learner."
Prentiss

PRESCOTT: (*PRESS-kut*) (English) "Priest's cottage."

PRESTON: (English) "Priest's town."

PRINCE: (English/Latin) "Principal one; first." The rock musician Prince has made the royal title familiar as a given name today.
Princeton

Q

QUADE: (*kwayde*) (Gaelic) From McQuade, a Scottish clan name.

QUENTIN: (English/French) "Fifth." Related English/French surnames.
Quenton, Quinton, Quintrell, Quentrell, Quint, Quent

QUINCY: (*kwin-see*) (English/French) "Fifth," from a Roman clan name.
Quincey

QUINN: (*kwin*) (Gaelic) "Counsel." A Scottish and Irish

surname, used as a given name from very ancient times. Quin (*keen*) is a Spanish short form of Joaquin.
Quinlan, Quinnell, Quin

R

RADAMES: (*rah-da-mays*) The name given the Egyptian hero of Puccini's opera *Aida*.

RADFORD: (English) "From the reedy ford." Old English surname.
Redford

RAFAEL: (*rah-fah-EL*) (Spanish/Hebrew) "God has healed." See also Raphael.
Rafe

RAI: (*RYE-ee*) (Japanese) "Trust"; "lightning, thunder." Also a Spanish short form of Raimundo.

RAINER: (*RAY-ner*) (German/Scandinavian) "Strong counselor." Variant form of Raynor. Related surnames are occasionally used as given names. See also Raynor.
Rainier, Ranier (French); Rainor, Reiner

RAJAN: (*rah-JHAN*) (Sanskrit) "King." Raja is an Indian or Malay princely title; Raj means "rule."
Raj (*rahzh*), Raja, Rajah

RALEIGH: (*RAH-lee*) (English) "Deer's meadow."

RALPH: (English/Scandinavian) "Wolf counsel." Ralston, "Ralph's town," is an English surname. Rafe is used as a short form of Ralph and Raphael. See also Raul.
Rolf (German); Rafe, Rafer (Scandinavian); Ralston

RAM: (Sanskrit) "Pleasing." Mythology; as the seventh incarnation of Vishnu, Rama's story is told in the Hindu *Ramayana*.
Rama, Ramos

RAMI: (Arabic) "Loving."
Ramey, Ramy

RAMIRO: (*ra-MEER-oh*) (Spanish) "Wise, renowned."

RAMON: (*rah-MOHN*) (Spanish) Variant of Raymond.

Ramone, Rayman, Raymon

RAMSEY: (*RAM-zee*) (English/Scottish) "Ram's island."
Ramses (*ram-zees*) is an Egyptian name meaning "be-
gotten by Ra, the sun god."
Ramsay, Ramses, Rameses, Ramzi, Ramzey

RANDALL: (English) Randall and the other English sur-
name variants listed here are variants of Randolph.
Randal, Randell, Randel, Randale, Rand, Randon,
Rendall, Rendell

RANDOLPH: (Teutonic) "Wolf's shield." See also Randall.
Randolf, Ranolf, Ranulfo.

RANDY: (English) Short form of Randall and Randolph.
More frequently used than the longer forms.

RAPHAEL: (*rah-fah-EL*) (Hebrew) "God has healed." The
name of an archangel in the Apocryphal book of Tobit.
The renowned Italian Renaissance painter. Raphael is
also known today as the name of one of the four Teen-
age Mutant Ninja Turtles. See also Rafael.

RASHAD: (Arabic) "Thinker, counselor."
Rashaad, Rasheed, Rashid; Rashidi (Swahili)

RASHAUN: (Contemporary) Blend of Ray and Shawn. See
also Roshan.
Rayshawn, Rayshaun, Rashawn, Rashae, Rashane

RAUL: (*rah-OOL*) (Spanish) Variant of Ralph. See also
Ralph.
Raoul (French)

RAVI: (*RAH-vee*) (Sanskrit) "Sun." A name made familiar
by Ravi Shankar, renowned sitar player and composer.
Mythology; the Hindu god of the sun.

RAY: (English/French) "Counselor." A short form of
Raymond often used in contemporary blends. See also
Raynor.
Rayce, Rayder, Raylen, Raydon, Raynell, Rayford

RAYMOND: (French/German) "Guards wisely." See also Rainer, Ramon, Ray and Redmond.
Raimond, Ramond, Raymundo, Raimundo, Reymundo, Raymund, Reymond

RAYNOR: (English/Scandinavian) "Strong counselor." Variant of Ragnar, an ancient personal name. See also Rainer.
Rayner, Rayne, Rane, Ranell, Raynell, Raynord, Ragnar

REDMOND: (Irish/English) Surname: a variant of Raymond.

REECE: (Welsh/English) "Ardent, fiery." See also Rhys.
Reese; Reis (Israeli) "Giant"

REEVE: (English) Surname. The medieval reeve of a castle or landholding had oversight of all matters of feudal obligations. Reve is the French word "dream."
Reeves, Reve, Reeford

REGINALD: (English) "Counselor-ruler." Variant of Reynold.
Reggie, Reginaldo, Regino

REGIS: (Latin) (*REE-jis*) "Rules."

REI: (*RAY-ee*) (Japanese) "Law, rule; strive." Reizo can mean "cool, calm; well-groomed."
Reizo (*ray-ee-ZOH*)

REID: (English) "Redheaded." English and Scottish surname.
Reed, Reade, Redd

REMINGTON: (English) The character on the TV show *Remington Steele* may have influenced increased use of this English surname as a given name.
Remy, Remi, Remo

RENE: (*re-NAY*) (French/Latin) "To rise again."
Renny, Rennie, Renne; Renato (Spanish)

RENJIRO: (*ren-jee-ROH*) (Japanese) "Clean, upright, honest."

RENO: (*REE-noh*) (Spanish) Short form for names like

Moreno. May sometimes be used in reference to the city in Nevada.

RENZO: (Italian) Short form of Lorenzo. The Japanese name Renzo can mean "third link" or "third son."
Renzo

REUBEN: (*ROO-ben*) (Hebrew) "See, a son." Biblical; Reuben was the first born of Jacob's 12 sons.
RUBEN (Spanish/Scandinavian); Reuven (Israeli)

REX: (Latin) "Chieftain, ruler."
Rexford, Rexton

REYES: (*rays*) (Spanish) "Kings."
Rey

REYNARD: (French/German) "Strong counselor."
Reynardo (Spanish); Raynard, Renard, Renardo

REYNOLD: (*RENN-ald*) (English/German) "Counselor-ruler." See also Reginald and Ronald.
Reynaldo, Renaldo (Spanish); Reinaldo, Reynald, Raynaldo

RHETT: (Welsh) Variant of Rhys. Rhett is most familiar as the hero of Margaret Mitchell's *Gone With the Wind.*

RHYS: (*rees*) (Welsh) "Ardent, fiery." See also Reece.

RICHARD: (English/German/French) "Powerful; strong ruler." A Teutonic name that developed in several European countries during the Middle Ages, with many variants. England's King Richard Coeur de Lion gave the name lasting impressions of kingliness and the exploits of a crusading knight. See also Ricky and Ryker.
RICARDO (Spanish/Portuguese); Riccardo (Italian); Ricard, Richardo (French); Rickard (English)

RICKY: (English) Short form of Richard. See also Richard.
RICK, Rickey, Rickie; Ric, Ricco (Italian); Ritchie, Richie, Rico (Spanish); Rique (French); Rikke (Dutch); Rikki (Dutch)

RIGEL: (*RYE-jel*) (Arabic) "Foot." In the Orion constellation, Rigel is the blue star of the first magnitude that marks the hunter's left foot.

RILEY: (*RYE-lee*) (English/Irish) "Rye." Variant of Ryley.
Reilley, Reilly (Irish)

RINJI: (*RIN-jee*) (Japanese) "Peaceful forest."

RIO: (*REE-oh*) (Spanish) "River." An independent name and short form of names ending with "-rio." Rito is a male short form of Margaret.
Reilly, Rito

RIORDAN: (*REER-den*) (Gaelic) "King's minstrel."

ROALD: (*roh-ald*) (Scandinavian/Teutonic) "Renowned, powerful."

ROBERT: (English/French/German) "Famed; bright, shining." One of the all-time favorite names for boys since the Middle Ages. Specially favored by the Scots due to the fourteenth-century King Robert the Bruce (see Bruce) and to Robert Burns the poet. See also Robertson, Robin, Bobby and Rupert.
ROBERTO (Spanish/Italian/Portuguese); Robertson, Robby, Robbie, Rob, Robb

ROBIN: (English) Variant of Robert, in popular use as a boy's name since the medieval days of Robin Hood.
Robbin, Robinson

ROCKY: (English) Nickname for Rocco (Italian), the name of a fourteenth-century saint. Also used for the literal meaning "rock."
Roque (Portuguese/Spanish); Roel (French); Rocco (Italian); Rock, Rockford, Rockland, Rockwell

RODERICK: (English/German) "Famous ruler."
RODRIGO (Spanish/Portuguese); Roderic, Roderik; Rodrick, Rodric (Scottish); Roddric, Roddrick, Rod, Rodd, Roddy; Rodel, Rodell (French)

RODMAN: (English) "Guard wisely."

RODNEY: (English) "Island of reeds."

RODOLFO: (Spanish) Variant of Rudolph.

ROGER: (English/German) "Renowned spearman."
Rogelio (Spanish); Rutger (Dutch); Rojay

ROHAN: (Irish/Gaelic) "Red-haired; red." Also a Sanskrit name meaning "ascending."
Roane, Royan

ROKA: (*ROH-kah*) (Japanese) "White crest of the wave."

ROLAND: (English/French/German) "Renowned in the land." Roland is celebrated in French and Italian poetic sagas as a hero in the service of Charlemagne. See also Orlando.
ROLANDO, Rollan, Rolland, Rollo, Rollie, Rowland

ROMAN (*roe-MAHN*) (Latin) "Man of Rome."
Rome; Romain (French); Romeo, Romero, Romulo

RONALD: (English/Gaelic/Scandinavian) "Rules with counsel." Variant of Reynold.
RONNIE, Ronny, Ronal, Ronnell, Ronell, Ronn, Ron; Ronaldo (Spanish); Ranald (Scottish); Rondale

RORY: (Irish) "Red." Literary; tales of Rory O'More, sixteenth-century rebel chief, are celebrated in Irish poetry.
Rorey, Rorry; Rorric, Rorik (Scandinavian/Slavic)

ROSARIO: (*roe-ZAR-ee-oh*) (Spanish/Portuguese) "Rosary." The name refers to devotional prayers honoring Mary.

ROSCOE: (English/Scandinavian) "Heathland of the roe deer."
Rosco

ROSHAN: (*roh-shahn*) (Sanskrit) "Shining light." See also Rashawn.

ROSS: (Scottish/German) "Red."
Rossiter, Rosston, Roth

ROURKE: (Irish/Gaelic) An ancient given name of uncertain origin, adopted as an Irish clan name.

Roarke, Rorke

ROWDY: (English) "Boisterous." Western nickname.

ROY: (Scottish/Gaelic) "Red."

Royal, Royall; Roi (French) "king"

ROYCE: (English/German) "Famous."

RUDY: (English/German) Short form of Rudolph.

Rudelle, Rudolph, Rudolf, Rudolpho, Rudolfo

RUFUS: (*ROO-fuss*) (Latin) "Red-haired." See also Russell

Rufino

RUPERT: (*ROO-pert*) (English/German) Variant of Robert.

RUSSELL: (English/French) Variant of Rufus.

Russel, Russ, Rush

RUSTY: (English) Nickname for a red-haired person; also a short form or nickname for names like Russell and Ruston.

Rustin, Rusten, Rustan, Ruston, Rustyn

RYAN: (Irish) "Kingly."

Ryon, Ryen, Rian, Rion

RYDER: (English) "Horseman, rider."

Ryden, Rydell (Scandinavian)

RYKER: (*RYE-ker*) (Dutch) Surname form of Richard used as a given name, perhaps due to the character Commander Ryker on the TV show *Star Trek: The Next Generation.*

RYLEY: (*RYE-lee*) (English/Irish) "Island meadow." Also used for girls, though usually in variant forms like Rylee and Rylie. See also Riley.

Ryleigh, Rylan, Ryland, Rye

S

SABINO: (*sah-BEE-noh*) (Latin) "Of the Sabines." A saint's name in use at least since the second century.

Savino (Italian)

SACHIO: (*sah-chee-oh*) (Japanese) "Fortunately born."

SAGE: (English/French) "Wise one." The similar-sounding surnames Sagan (Slavic) and Sagar (English) are in rare use today as given names.
Sagan, Sagar

SALEM: (*SAY-lem*) (Hebrew) "Peace." Biblical; name of the ancient city that later was identified with Jerusalem.
Shalom

SALIM: (*sah-LEEM*) (Swahili/Arabic) "Peaceful."
Saleem

SALVADOR: (Spanish/Latin) "Savior."
Salvatore (Italian); Sal, Salvino

SAMSON: (Hebrew) "The sun." Biblical; a judge of ancient Israel, endowed by God with superhuman strength.
Sampson

SAMUEL: (Hebrew) "Name of God." Biblical; the prophet and judge who anointed Saul and David as kings of Israel.
Sam, Sammy, Sammie, Samuele; Sami (Arabic) "honored"

SANDY: (English/Scottish) Short form of Alexander.
Sandro (Italian); Sandor (Hungarian); Sandino

SANJIRO: (*sahn-jee-ROH*) (Japanese) "Praise; admirable."

SANTIAGO: (*sahn-tee-AH-go*) (Spanish) Variant of James, from "Saint Diego." James the Greater (of the two apostles by that name) is the patron saint of Spain.

SANTOS: (Latin) "Saints."
Santino (Italian) "Little saint"; Sancho (Spanish); Santee

SAUL: (Hebrew) "Asked; inquired of God." Biblical; the first king of Israel; also the Hebrew name of the Apostle Paul.

SAXON: (Teutonic) "Knife." English surname. Saxons were among the Germanic tribes that invaded and settled England in the fifth century. Saxton

SCHAEFFER: (*SHAY-fer*) (German) "Steward."
Schaffer

SCHUYLER: (*SKYE-ler*) (Dutch) "Scholar." See also
Skyler.
Schyler, Schylar

SCOTT: (English/Scottish) "From Scotland, a Gael."
Scotty, Scot, Scottie

SEAMUS: (*SHAY-mus*) (Irish/Gaelic) Variant of James.

SEAN: (*shonn*) (Irish) Variant of John, from the French
Jean. See also Shaun and Shane.

SEBASTIAN: (*se-BASS-tian*) (Latin/Greek) "Revered."
Shakespeare gave the name to the twin brother of Viola
in *Twelfth Night*. St. Sebastian was a third-century
martyred centurion who became a patron saint of
soldiers.
Sebastien (French); Sabastian

SEIJI: (*SAY-jee*) (Japanese) "Aright, lawful"; "manages affairs of state."

SERGIO: (Latin) "Protector; shepherd." A saint's name.
Serjio, Serge, Sergeo; Sergei (*sehr-GAY*) (Russian);
Sarkis (Armenian)

SETH: (Hebrew) "Appointed." Biblical; the third-named
son of Adam and Eve. Eve said Seth had been appointed to take the place of Abel, killed by Cain.

SEVERIN: (French/Latin) "Strict, restrained." Variant of
Severus, a saint's name. See also Soren.
Severo (Spanish); Severn, Severne (English); Sevrin

SEYMOUR: (*SEE-more*) (English) "St. Maurus, the
Moor."

SHAAN: (Hebrew) "Peaceful."

SHAD: (English) Short form of the Biblical Shadrach, the
Babylonian name of one of the three young Hebrew
men who were cast into a fiery furnace and miracu-
lously survived.

Shadd, Shadrach, Shadoe, Shadrick

SHAKA: (*SHAH-kah*) (African) The name of a Zulu tribal leader (sometimes compared to Attila the Hun) who shaped an amalgamation of tribes into the great Zulu nation in the early nineteenth century.

SHANE: (Irish) Variant of Shaun, from John. Shan is also a Gaelic name meaning "old, wise." See also Sean and Shawn.

Shayne, Shain, Shaine, Shan, Shann, Shandon, Shandy

SHANNON: (Irish) "Old, wise."

SHARIF: (*sha-REEF*) (Arabic) "Illustrious." A name of descendants of Mohammed.

Shareef, Shereef, Sherif

SHAW: (English) "Woods."

SHAWN: (Irish) Variant of John, from Sean. See also Sean and Shane.

SHAUN, Shaughn, Shawnn, Shonn, Shauden, Shaundre

SHEA: (*shay*) (Irish) "Courteous." Surname occasionally used as a given name or middle name.

Shay, Shaye, Shae, Shai, Shayan, Shaylon, Shey

SHELBY: (English/Scandinavian) "Willow farm." English surname used more for girls than for boys.

SHELDON: (English) "Deep valley."

Shelden, Shelton

SHEM: (Hebrew) "Name; renown." Biblical; first-named of the three sons of Noah.

SHERIDAN: (English/Gaelic) "Bright."

SHERMAN: (English) "Shireman" (German) "shear-man." In medieval times, a shireman served as governor-judge of an English shire or county; a shearman worked as a sheepshearer or finisher of cloth.

Shermann, Shermon, Sherwood "shire-wood"

SHILOH: (*SHYE-loh*) (Hebrew) "The one to whom it belongs." Biblical; a prophetic name for the Messiah.

Shiloh is also significant as the site of a crucial battle in the American Civil War.

Shilo

SHODA: (*SHOH-dah*) (Japanese) "Flat, level field."

SIDNEY: (English/French) "From St. Denis." Sidney is favored for boys; Sydney is almost entirely used for girls.

Sydney, Sid, Syd

SIGMUND: (German) "Victory, protection." A name made famous by the Austrian psychologist Sigmund Freud.

SILAS: (*SYE-las*) (English/Latin) Variant of Sylvanus, from a Greek name meaning "forest, woods." Biblical; Silas was a missionary companion to Paul and Timothy.

SILVANO: (Latin) Variant of Sylvanus, referring to the mythological Greek god of trees. A number of saints bore the name, and variants were formed in several language groups. See also Silas and Silvester.

Silverio (Spanish/Portuguese); Silvino (Spanish); Selwyn, Selvyn (English); Sylvanus

SILVESTER: (English/German) "Trees; sylvan." See also Sylvester and Silvano.

Silvestre (French)

SIMON: (English/Greek) Variant of a Hebrew name meaning "hear, listen." Biblical; Simon was the name of two of the apostles, including Simon Peter.

Simeon, Symon

SINCLAIR: (English/French) "St. Clair." Through long usage, some saints' names have been blurred into a single name. Sinjin is a blurred form of St. John. See also Seymour.

Sinclaire, Sinjin

SKYE: (English) Name used in reference to the Isle of Skye in Scotland, as a nickname for the Skyler variants or as a nature name referring to the sky. See also Schuyler and Skyler.

Sky

SKYLER: (English) Phonetic spelling of Schuyler. See also Schuyler and Skye.

Skylar, Skyelar, Skylor

SLADE: (English) "Valley."

SLOAN: (Scottish) "Fighter, warrior." Surname in rare use as a given name; Sloane is used as a feminine form.

SOLOMON: (Hebrew) "Peace." Variant form of Shalom. Biblical; Solomon, son of David and Bathsheba, succeeded his father as king of Israel. He wrote the Book of Proverbs, Ecclesiastes and the Song of Solomon.

Salomon (Spanish); Solomon, Sol

SONNY: (English) "Son." A nickname in steady use as a given name for boys.

Sonnie

SOREN: (Scandinavian) "Strict." Variant of Severin, a saint's name.

SPENCER: (English) "Dispenser, provider."

Spenser, Spence

STACY: (English) "Productive." Short form of Eustace.

Stacey

STANLEY: (English) "Stony meadow."

Stanford, Stanton, Stan

STEELE: (English) "Hard, durable."

STEPHEN: (English/Greek) "Crown, wreath." Biblical; Stephen was the first Christian martyr. See also Esteban, Etienne, Steve and Steven.

STEPHAN (French); STEFAN (German/Scandinavian/Slavic); Stefon, Stephon; Steffen, Steffan, Steffon (Welsh); Stephano, Stefano (Italian); Stephanos (Greek); Steaphan (Gaelic); Stephenson, Stefford

STERLING: (English/German) Variant of a name meaning "easterner" given to pre-medieval refiners of silver. Today Sterling means "of high quality, pure."

Sterlyn, Stirling

STEVE: (English) Short form of Steven and Stephen used as an independent name. Stevie is also used for girls. See also Steven and Stephen.

Stevie

STEVEN: (English) Variant form of Stephen. See also Stephen.

Stevan, Stevon, Stevyn, Stevenson

STEWART: (English/Scottish) "Steward." A medieval steward was charged with the care of castle and estate affairs. See also Stuart.

STONEY: (English) Nickname based on the word stone.

Stone, Stoner (English); Steiner (German)

STORM: (English/Teutonic) Surname with the literal meaning of a storm.

STUART: (Scottish) Stuart and Stewart are clan names of the royal house of Scotland; Stuart is the family name of many kings of England. See also Stewart.

SULLIVAN: (Irish) "Dark eyes."

SVEN: (Scandinavian) "Youth, boy."

SYDNEY: (English) See Sidney.

SYLVESTER: (English) See Silvester.

T

TABOR: (*TAY-bor*) (Hebrew) Biblical; Mt. Tabor, a landmark mountain near Nazareth.

Tab; Taber (Irish) "Well"

TAD: (English) Short form of Thaddeus.

Tadd; Tadeo (Spanish)

TADAO: (*tah-dah-oh*) (Japanese) "Complacent, satisfied."

TAJ: (*tahzh*) (Sanskrit) "Crown." Taji (*TAH-jee*) (Japanese) "Silver and yellow color."

Taji

TAKEO: (*tah-kay-oh*) (Japanese) "Strong like bamboo."

TAL: (English) "Tall, fierce." With related surnames. Tal is also an Israeli name meaning "dew."

Talbert, Talbot, Talbott, Talford, Talmadge, Tallon

TANJIRO: (*tahn-jee-ROH*) (Japanese) "High-valued second son."

TANNER: (English) "Worker in leather."

TARIQ: (*TAHR-eek*) (Arabic) "Morning star." Historical; the Islamic military leader (eighth century) who conquered Spain for the Moors.

Tarik, Tarek, Tarick, Tarique, Tareq

TARO: (*tah-ROH*) (Japanese) "Big boy."

TATE: (Scandinavian) "Cheerful." (Irish) "Measure of land." Rare.

Tait

TAU: (African) "Lion."

TAUREAN: (*TAH-ree-an*) (Latin) "Bull-like." From Taurinus, a saint's name. Taurus is a constellation picturing the forequarters of a bull and is the second sign of the astrological Zodiac.

Tauro, Taurino, Toro (Spanish); Taurus

TAVIS: (*TAV-iss*) (Scottish) Variant of Thomas. Tavio is a Spanish short form of Octavio. Tavin is a nickname for Gustav. Tavis and its variants may also have a connection with *teeve*, an Irish word meaning "hillside."

Taveon, Tavion, Tavon, Tavin, Tavio, Tevis, Tevin.

TAYLOR: (English) "Tailor." Surname used as a given name.

Tayler, Tayson, Taylan, Taylon

TEAGUE: (*teeg*) (Irish) "Handsome."

Tighe, Tag

TED: (English) Short form of Theodore. Tedrick is a variant of the old German name Theodoric, "ruler of the people." Tedman refers to St. Edmund.

Teddy, Tedd, Teddie, Tedman, Tedmund, Tedric, Tedrick

TEIJI: (*tay-EE-jee*) (Japanese) "Righteous, well governed."
Teijo (*TAY-joh*) "established," "regulated."
Teijo

TEMPLETON: (English) "Temple-town." This surname refers to the medieval priories and settlements of the Knights-Templars, a military religious order. Temple is in rare use today.
Temple

TEO: (*TAY-oh*) "God." Spanish short forms of names like Mateo and Teodor.
Teyo

TERRAN: (English) "Earthman." Variants are contemporary rhyming blends of Ter- plus Darin.
Terron, Terrin, Tarrin, Taron

TERRANCE: (English/Latin) Roman clan name. Terence is the older English and Irish form.
TERRENCE, Terence, Tarrence

TERRELL: (English/German) "Powerful." See also Tyrell.
Terrel, Terell, Terrelle, Terrall, Terrill

TERRY: (English) Short form of Terrance and Terrell. Terry is also an Anglicized phonetic form of the French given name Thierry, from an older Germanic name meaning "powerful; ruler of the people."

THADDEUS: (*thad-DAY-us, THAD-dee-us*) (Greek) Biblical; one of the 12 apostles. See also Tad.
Thadeus, Thaddius, Thad; Tadeo (Spanish)

THANE: (English/Scottish) Title of Anglo-Saxon and Scottish feudal lords. Shakespeare's *Macbeth* was Thane of Cawdor.

THEODORE: (Greek) "God given." See also Ted.
Teodoro (Italian/Portuguese); Theo, Theodor; Teodor (Spanish), Theodon, Theodric

THERON: (*THER-on*) (French/Greek) "Untamed."
Theon, Therron

THOMAS: (Aramaic) "Twin." Biblical; one of the 12 apostles. See also Tavis.

TOMMY; TOMAS (Spanish); Tom, Thompson, Thom

THOR: (Scandinavian) "Thunder." Mythology; Thor was the Norse god of thunder, one of the sons of Odin. Thursday was named for Thor.

Thorian, Thorin, Thorsson, Thurman, Thurstan

THORNTON: (English/Gaelic) "Town of thorns." Thorn variants are English surnames occasionally used as given names.

Thorn, Thorne

THURL: (Irish) "Strong fort."

Thurle

TIMOTHY: (English/Greek) "One who honors God." Biblical; Timothy was an energetic, well-trained young Christian to whom Paul wrote, "Let no man look down on your youth."

Timmy, Tim; Timoteo, Timo (Spanish); Timon

TITUS: (*TITE-us*) (Latin) Biblical; a Greek Christian missionary to whom Paul wrote the canonical letter *Titus*.

Tito

TOBY: (English) Short form of Tobiah, a Hebrew name meaning "Jah is good."

Tobiah; Tobias (Spanish); Tobey, Tobie, Tobin, Tobyn

TODD: (English) "Fox." Tod is a Scottish nickname meaning a clever or wily person.

Tod

TOMEO: (*toh-MAY-oh*) (Japanese) "Cautious man."

TONY: (English) Short form of Anthony and its variants, frequently used since medieval times as an independent name.

Tonio (Spanish)

TORIO: (*toh-ree-OH*) (Japanese) "Bird's tail." Torrio is a Spanish short form.

Torrio

TORRENCE: (Irish/Scottish) "From the craggy hills." Tor is a name for a craggy hilltop and also may refer to a watchtower. The Scandinavian Tor refers to Thor, god of thunder.

Torrance, Torence, Tor, Toran, Torin, Toren, Torran, Torean, Torion, Torrian

TORU: (*toh-roo*) (Japanese) "Sea."

TORY: (English/Irish/Scottish) Surname based on Tor, Torrence or Tower. Tory variants may also be short forms of Victor.

Torey, Torrey; Torre (Italian) "tower"; Torrie, Torry (Scottish)

TOSHIRO: (*toh-shee-ROH*) (Japanese) "Talented, intelligent."

TRACY: (English/French) "From Thracia." Surname dating from before the Norman conquest.

Trace

TRAVIS: (English/French) "Crossing, crossroads."

TREMAYNE: (*tre-MAYNE*) (English/Welsh) "From the big town."

Tremaine, Tramaine, Tremain

TRENT: (English) Refers to the river Trent in England.

TRENTON, Trenten, Trentin

TREVIN: (English/Welsh) "Fair town." Short form of Trevelyan. Variants probably are influenced by Devon and Davion.

Travon, Trevon, Trevonn (*tre-VON*), Trevan, Treven, Trevyn, Travion, Traveon, Trevian, Trevion

TREVIS: (English/Welsh) Variant of Treves, French surname and place-name. Contemporary usage is probably due to its sounding like Travis.

TREVOR: (Welsh) "Goodly town."

TREY: (*tray*) (English) "Three." May also be a variant of *traigh* (Irish) "Strand."

TRISTAN: (*TRISS-tan*) (English/French) "Tumult, outcry." From Tristan, a Celtic name. In Arthurian legend, Tristan was a Knight of the Round Table and the tragic hero of the medieval tale *Tristram and Isolde*.
Tristin, Tristen, Tristian; Trystan, Tristyn (Welsh)

TROY: (English) As a given name, Troy may derive from the ancient Greek city of Troy or from an Irish surname meaning "soldier."
Troi, Troye

TUCKER: (English) "Clothmaker."

TY: (English) Short form for names beginning with "Ty-."
Tye

TYLER: (English) "Tile layer" or a variant of Taylor. An English surname frequently used as a given name.
Tylor

TYRELL: (*tye-RELL, TER-ell*) (English/Irish/Teutonic) Derivative of Tyr, the name of the Scandinavian god of battle. Tuesday was named for Tyr. See also Terrill.
Tyrel, Tyrelle, Tyrrell; Tyree (Scottish), Tyreece

TYRONE: (*TY-rone, te-RONE*) (Irish) "From Owen's territory." County Tyrone in Ireland has been made familiar as a boy's given name primarily due to the late actor Tyrone Power.
Tyronne

TYRUS: (Contemporary) Blend of Tyrone and Cyrus, or a reference to the ancient Phoenician city of Tyre.

TYSON: (English/French) "Fiery."
Tyce, Tyeson

U

ULYSSES: (*you-LISS-ees*) (Latin) Variant of the Greek name Odysseus. Mythology; Ulysses was the clever and resourceful hero of Homer's epic tale *The Odyssey*.
Ulises (Spanish)

URIEL: (*OOR-ee-el*) (Heb) "Angel of light." In the Apocrypha, Uriel is one of seven archangels. In Muslim tradition, he is the angel of music who will sound the trumpet on Judgment day.

V

VALENTINE: (English/Latin) "Strong." Variant of Valentinus, the name of more than 50 saints and three Roman emperors.

Val; Valentin (Spanish); Valentino (Italian); Valente (Italian/Portuguese); Valen, Vallen

VAN: (Dutch) "Of." Equivalent of "de" in French names. Van was sometimes converted from a surname prefix to a given name by early immigrants to America.

VANCE: (English) "Marshland."

VAUGHN: (*von*) (Welsh) "Little." Von is the German equivalent of Van.

Vaughan, Von, Vonn, Vontell

VERDELL: (*ver-DELL*) (French/Latin) "Green, flourishing."

Vernell

VERNON: (English/French) "Alder tree grove." Aristocratic surname brought to England at the time of the Norman conquest. Vern and Verne are related English/French surnames frequently used as short forms of Vernon or Lavern.

Vern, Verne, Vernard

VICTOR: (Latin) "Conqueror." A very popular saint's name. At one time more than 200 were listed in the *Catholic Dictionary of Saints.*

Vittorio (Italian); Viktor (Czech); Vic; Victoriano, Victorino, Victorio (Spanish)

VIDAL: (*vee-DAL*) (Latin) "Life." Several language groups (French, English, Spanish and Portuguese) use Vidal as a surname or given name. See also Vito.

Videl

VINCENT: (Latin) "Conquering."
   VICENTE (Spanish/Portuguese); Vincenzo (Italian);
   Vince, Vinson, Vinnie
VIRGIL: (*VER-jil*) (English/Latin) "Flourishing." The writ-
   ings of Virgil, the Roman poet-philosopher, have pro-
   vided classic texts for the study of Roman history and
   the Latin language for the past 2000 years.
VITO: (*VEE-toh*) (Latin) "Life." See also Vidal.
   Vitale (Italian)

W

WADE: (English/Scandinavian) Medieval given name
   taken from Scandinavian mythology. Also an English
   surname referring to a water crossing.
   Wayde, Waydell
WALDO: (English/German) "Powerful." Short form of
   Oswald.
   Walden, Waldron
WALKER: (English) "Worker in cloth."
WALLACE: (English/Scottish) "Welshman, stranger."
WALTER: (German) "Rules, conquers."
   Walt, Walton, Wally
WARD: (English) "Protector."
   Warde, Wardell
WARNER: (English/German) "Defender."
WARREN: (English/German) "Defender."
WAYLON: (English/Scandinavian) Variant of Wayland.
   Mythology; the Scandinavian Wayland was a blacksmith
   with supernatural powers, corresponding to the Roman
   Vulcan. A notable name bearer today is singer Waylon
   Jennings.
   Wayland, Waylan, Waylin
WAYNE: (English) "Wagon driver."
WEBSTER: (English) "Weaver." (Note: the "-ster" ending
   on English occupational surnames like Webster and

Brewster is an indication that the work was originally a female occupation. When the occupations were taken over by males, the names were adopted as well.)

WENDELL: (English/German) "Traveler, wanderer."
Wendall, Wendale, Windell

WESLEY: (English) "West meadow." Variant of the English surname Westley.
Wes, Westley, Wessley

WESTON: (English) "West town."
Westin, Westen, West

WILBERT: (English/German) "Willful, bright."
Wilber, Wilbur, Wilburn, Wilburt

WILEY: (*WYE-lee*) (English) "Well-watered meadow."
Wylie

WILFRED: (English/German) "Desires peace."
Wilfredo, Wilfrid, Wilford

WILLARD: (English/German) "Bold, resolute."

WILLIAM: (English/German) "Resolute protector." For a long time after the Norman conquest in A.D. 1066, three out of four English boys were given some form of the conqueror's name, William. Short forms and variants came into being with a common basic meaning of "will," "determined" or "resolute." The firstborn son of the current Prince of Wales is named William. See also Guillermo, Liam, Willard, Willie, Wilmer and Wilson.
Williams, Willis; Wilhelm (German); Willem (Dutch)

WILLIE: (English) Short form of names beginning with "Wil-."
Willy, Will, Wil

WILMER: (English/German) "Resolute, famous."

WILSON: (English) "Son of Will."

WINSTON: (English) "Stone marker of friendship."
Winslow, Winfield, Win, Winn

WOODROW: (English) "From the cottages in the wood."
Woody

WYATT: (English) "Lively." Variant of Guy.

WYNN: (English) "Friend." Variants are English surnames in rare use as given names.
Wynton, Wyndell

X

XAVIER: (*ecks-ZAY-vee-er*) (Spanish/Arabic) "Bright, splendid." See also Javier.

XIOMAR: (*zhoh-MAR*) "Famous in battle." Variant of Geomar.

Y

YALE: (Welsh) "Heights, upland."
Yael (Israeli) "God's strength."

YORK: (English) Place-name and surname.

YURI: (Russian) Variant of George.

YVES: (*eeve*) (French) Variant of the Germanic name Ivo, meaning "archer's bow." See also Ivar.

Z

ZACCHAEUS: (*za-KAY-us*) (Hebrew) "Clean, pure." Biblical; a tax collector who became one of the disciples of Jesus.

ZACHARIAH: (*zak-a-RYE-ah*) (Hebrew) "Jehovah has remembered." Variant of Zechariah. Biblical; the name of 31 persons including the prophet who wrote the Book of Zechariah. See also Zachary.
Zacharias, Zackariah; Zacharia (German); Zacarias (Spanish/Portuguese); Zechariah

ZACHARY: (*ZAK-a-ree*) (English) Variant of Zachariah. Zachary is one of several names from the Bible that have enjoyed a revival of favor in modern times. See Jacob, Jared and Joshua.
ZACHERY, ZACKARY, Zackery, Zakary, Zack, Zach, Zak, Zakari

ZADOK: (*ZAY-dok*) (Israeli) "Just."

ZANDER: (Contemporary) Short form of Alexander. Also a German Yiddish name.

ZANE: (English) Possibly a variant of John. Notable name bearer: western writer Zane Grey.

　　Zain, Zaine, Zayne

ZAREK: (Slavic) "God protects."

ZEKE: (English/Hebrew) Short form of Ezekiel.

FOR YOU AND YOUR TODDLER

—————◆—————

__GOOD-BYE DIAPERS *Batya Swift Yasgur*
0-425-14185-3/$4.50

The parents' guide to successful, stress-free toilet training. *Good-bye Diapers* presents a variety of new techniques, enabling you to specifically design your child a complete toilet training program. Includes chapters on toilet training an older child, a one-day intensive program, and defining and preventing bedwetting.

__TIME-OUT FOR TODDLERS
Dr. James W. Varni and Donna G. Corwin
0-425-12943-8/$8.00

This guide illustrates the revolutionary TIME-OUT method that benefits both child and parent, showing parents how to cope with common childhood behaviors—such as temper tantrums, sibling rivalry, whining, and selfishness—in a positive and effective manner.

__FOODS FOR HEALTHY KIDS
Dr. Lendon Smith 0-425-09276-3/$4.99

Dr. Lendon Smith, America's leading authority on nutrition for children, tells how to prevent and alleviate health problems such as asthma, allergies, depression, constipation, hyperactivity, sleep problems and tension—not with medicine, but with good, nourishing food. He gives you his total nutrition program, complete with more than 100 recipes.